Large-Dimensional Panel Data Econometrics

Testing, Estimation and
Structural Changes

Large-Dimensional Panel Data Econometrics
Testing, Estimation and Structural Changes

QU FENG
Nanyang Technological University, Singapore

CHIHWA KAO
University of Connecticut, USA

 **World Scientific**

NEW JERSEY · LONDON · SINGAPORE · BEIJING · SHANGHAI · HONG KONG · TAIPEI · CHENNAI · TOKYO

Published by

World Scientific Publishing Co. Pte. Ltd.

5 Toh Tuck Link, Singapore 596224

USA office: 27 Warren Street, Suite 401-402, Hackensack, NJ 07601

UK office: 57 Shelton Street, Covent Garden, London WC2H 9HE

Library of Congress Cataloging-in-Publication Data

Names: Feng, Qu, author. | Kao, Chihwa, author.

Title: Large-dimensional panel data econometrics : testing, estimation and structural changes /
Qu Feng, Nanyang Technological University, Singapore,
Chihwa Kao, University of Connecticut, USA.

Description: USA : World Scientific, 2020. | Includes bibliographical references and index.

Identifiers: LCCN 2020026843 | ISBN 9789811220777 (hardcover) |
ISBN 9789811220784 (ebook) | ISBN 9789811220791 (ebook other)

Subjects: LCSH: Econometrics. | Panel analysis.

Classification: LCC HB139 .F46 2020 | DDC 330.01/5195--dc23

LC record available at https://lccn.loc.gov/2020026843

British Library Cataloguing-in-Publication Data

A catalogue record for this book is available from the British Library.

For any available supplementary material, please visit
https://www.worldscientific.com/worldscibooks/10.1142/11842#t=suppl

Desk Editors: Balamurugan Rajendran/Karimah Samsudin

Typeset by Stallion Press
Email: enquiries@stallionpress.com

Printed in Singapore

Preface

With the availability of Big Data, one may have more information to identify the underlying causality of economic relationship or forecast important macroeconomic variables or indicators. However, when large volume of data is involved, large dimension could be an issue in the statistical inference of traditional regression models. This book is motivated by the recent development in panel data models with large individuals/countries (n) and large amount of observations over time (T). It introduces testing for cross-sectional dependence and structural breaks in large panels. This book also summarizes important advancement in estimating factor-augmented panel data models and group patterns in panels in recent literature.

This book can be considered complementary to popular panel data econometrics textbooks such as Baltagi (2013), Hsiao (2014) and Pesaran (2015). It is designed for high-level graduate courses in econometrics and statistics. It can be used as a reference for researchers. In specific, Chapters 2 and 4 drew heavily from our published works with Badi H. Baltagi. Chapters 3 and 5 summarize important methods from the recent literature.

We would like to thank Badi H. Baltagi for his collaborative work that stimulated our interest in writing this book. We would also like to thank Kunpeng Li for sharing his code, which is used to produce empirical results in Chapter 3. Wei Wang and Mengying Yuan are also acknowledged for helping read the drafts and research assistance. We also wish to thank World Scientific Publishing for giving us the opportunity to undertake this work.

As a personal note, the authors would like to thank their family members. Chihwa thanks his wife Ivy Liu who convinced him of the need for writing this book. Qu wishes to thank his loving wife and parents. The completion of this book would not have been possible without their support.

About the Authors

 Chihwa Kao is a professor of economics and the department head at the University of Connecticut, USA. He received his Ph.D. from SUNY, Stony Brook in 1983. He held a faculty position at Syracuse University from 1985 to 2016. Chihwa's research focuses primarily on large dimensional econometrics, such as testing and estimation arising in cross-sectional dependence, panel change points, large factor models, and asset pricing. His work has been published in top economics and statistics journals, including *Econometrica, Journal of the American Statistical Association, Journal of Econometrics, Journal of Business and Economic Statistics, Review of Economics and Statistics, Journal of Business, Econometrics Journal*, and *Econometric Reviews*.

 Qu Feng is an associate professor and the head of economics, School of Social Sciences at Nanyang Technological University (NTU), Singapore. Qu joined NTU after he received his Ph.D. from Syracuse University in 2009. His research fields include econometrics, Chinese economy, and financial markets. His papers have been published in top economics journals, including *Journal of Econometrics*,

Journal of Applied Econometrics, and *Econometrics Journal*. He was honored at the NTU Convocation Ceremony in 2013 for inspirational teaching and mentorship, and was nominated by the department for the Nanyang Award for Research Excellence, NTU, 2012.

Contents

Chapter 1

Introduction

This book is motivated by the recent development in high-dimensional panel data models with large amount of individuals/countries (n) and observations over time (T). Specifically, it introduces four important research topics in large panels, including testing for cross-sectional dependence, estimation of factor-augmented panel data models, structural changes and group patterns in panels in the following four chapters. To address these issues, we examine the properties of traditional tests and estimators in large-dimensional setup. In addition, we also take advantage of some techniques in *Random Matrix Theory* and *Machine Learning*.

Chapter 2 covers testing for cross-sectional dependence in panel data regression models with large n and large T. Cross-sectional dependence, described as the interaction between cross-sectional units (e.g., households, firms and states, etc.), has been well discussed in the spatial econometrics literature. Intuitively, dependence across "space" can be regarded as the counterpart of serial correlation in time series. It could arise from the behavioral interaction between individuals, e.g., imitation and learning among consumers in a community, or firms in the same industry. This has been widely studied in game theory and industrial organization. It could also be due to unobservable common factors or common shocks popular in macroeconomics.

In recent literature, cross-sectional dependence among individuals is a concern when n is large. As serial correlation in time-series analysis, the

1

cross-sectional of dependence/correlation leads to efficiency loss for least squares and invalidates conventional t-tests and F-tests which use standard variance–covariance estimators. In some cases, it could potentially result in inconsistent estimators (Lee, 2002; Andrews, 2005). Several estimators have been proposed to deal with cross-sectional dependence, including the popular spatial methods (Anselin, 1988; Anselin and Bera, 1998; Kelejian and Prucha, 1999; Kapoor, Kelejian and Prucha, 2007; Lee, 2007; Lee and Yu, 2010), and factor models in panel data (Pesaran, 2006, Kapetanios, Pesaran and Yamagata, 2011; Bai, 2009). However, before imposing any structure on the disturbances of our model, it may be wise to test the existence of cross-sectional dependence.

There has been a lot of work on testing for cross-sectional dependence in the spatial econometrics literature, see Anselin and Bera (1998) for cross-sectional data and Baltagi, Song and Koh (2003) for panel data, to mention a few. The latter derives a joint Lagrange multiplier (LM) test for the existence of spatial error correlation as well as random region effects in a panel data regression model. Panel data provide richer information on the covariance matrix of the errors than cross-sectional data. This is especially relevant for the off-diagonal elements which are of particular importance in determining cross-sectional dependence. With panel data one can test for cross-sectional dependence without imposing *ad hoc* specifications on the error structure generating the covariance matrix, e.g., the spatial autoregressive model in the spatial literature, or the single or multiple factor structures imposed on the errors in the macro literature. Ng (2006) and Pesaran (2004) propose two test procedures based on the sample covariance matrix in panel data. Ng (2006) develops a test tool using spacing method in a panel model. Pesaran (2004) proposes a cross-sectional dependence (CD) test using the pairwise average of the off-diagonal sample correlation coefficients in a seemingly unrelated regressions model. The CD test is closely related to the R_{AVE} test statistic advanced by Frees (1995). Unlike the traditional Breusch-Pagan (1980) LM test, the CD test is applicable for a large number of cross–sectional units (n) observed over T time periods. In Pesaran (2015), the CD test is interpreted as a test for weak cross-sectional dependence. Sarafidis, Yamagata and Robertson (2009) develop a test for cross-sectional dependence based on Sargan's difference test in a linear dynamic panel data model, in which the error cross-sectional dependence is modeled by a multifactor structure. Hsiao, Pesaran and Pick (2012) propose a LM-type test for nonlinear panel data models. For a recent survey of some cross-sectional dependence tests in panels, see Moscone and Tosetti (2009). Baltagi, Feng and Kao (2011) propose a test for sphericity following John (1972) and Ledoit and Wolf (2002) in the statistics literature. Sphericity means that the variance–covariance matrix is proportional to the identity matrix. The rejection of the null could be due to cross-sectional dependence or heteroskedasticity or both.

Based on Baltagi, Feng and Kao (2012), Chapter 2 discusses testing procedures in the fixed effects panel data models, including static and dynamic cases. It is well known that the standard Breusch and Pagan (1980) LM test for cross-equation correlation in a SUR model is not appropriate for testing cross-sectional dependence in panel data models when n is large and T is small. We derive the asymptotic bias of this scaled version of the LM test in the context of a fixed effects panel data model. This asymptotic bias is found to be a constant related to n and T, which suggests a simple bias corrected LM test for the null hypothesis.

There are two ways of modeling cross-sectional dependence: spatial models and factor models. In Chapter 3, we introduce three leading approaches of estimating large panel data regression models with an error factor structure: the common correlated effects (CCE) approach proposed by Pesaran (2006), Bai's (2009) iterated principal components (IPC) approach and the maximum likelihood estimation (MLE) method proposed by Bai and Li (2014). The use of these approaches is illustrated by an empirical example in the context of the productivity of infrastructure investment in China.

Chapter 4 examines the issue of structural changes in large panel data regression models. In the literature on panel data models with large time dimension, e.g., Kao (1999), Phillips and Moon (1999), Hahn and Kuersteiner (2002), Alvarez and Arellano (2003), Phillips and Sul (2007), Pesaran and Yamagata (2008), Hayakawa (2009), to name a few, the implicit assumption is that the slope coefficients are constant over time. However, due to policy implementation or technological shocks, structural breaks are possible especially for panels with a long time span. Consequently, ignoring structural breaks may lead to inconsistent estimation and invalid inference.

Based on Baltagi, Feng and Kao (2016, 2019), Chapter 4 extends Pesaran's (2006) work on CCE estimators for large heterogeneous panels with a general multifactor error structure by allowing for unknown common structural breaks in slopes and unobserved factor structure. We propose a general framework that includes heterogeneous panel data models and structural break models as special cases. The least squares method proposed by Bai (1997a, 2010) is applied to estimate the common change points, and the consistency of the estimated change points is established. We find that the CCE estimators have the same asymptotic distribution as if the true change points were known. Additionally, Monte Carlo simulations are used to verify the main findings.

By considering both cross-sectional dependence and structural breaks in a general panel data model, this chapter also contributes to the change point literature in several ways. First, it extends Bai's (1997a) time-series regression model to heterogeneous panels, showing that the consistency of estimated change points can be achieved with the information along the cross-sectional dimension. This result confirms the findings of Bai (2010) and Kim (2011). Second, it also enriches the analysis of common breaks of Bai (2010) and Kim (2011) in a panel mean-shift model and a panel deterministic time trend model by extending them to a regression model using panel data. This makes it possible to allow for structural breaks and cross-sectional dependence in empirical work using panel regressions. In particular, our methods can be applied to regression models using large stationary panel data, such as country-level panels and state/provincial-level panels.

Regarding estimating common breaks in panels, Feng, Kao and Lazarova (2009) and Baltagi, Kao and Liu (2012) also show the consistency of the estimated change point in a simple panel regression model. Hsu and Lin (2012) examine the consistency properties of the change point estimators for nonstationary panels. More recently, Qian and Su (2016) and Li, Qian and Su (2016) study the estimation and inference of common breaks in panel data models with and without interactive fixed effects using Lasso-type methods. Westerlund (2019) establishes the consistency of least squares estimator of break point in a mean-shift model with fixed T, using the CCE approach to deal with unobserved error factors. In terms of detecting structural breaks in panels, some recent literature includes Horváth and Hušková (2012) in a panel mean-shift model with and without cross-sectional dependence, De Wachter and Tzavalis (2012) in dynamic panels, and Pauwels, Chan and Mancini-Griffoli (2012) in heterogeneous panels, Oka and Perron (2018) in multiple equation systems, to name a few.

Chapter 5 studies heterogeneity and grouping issues in large dimensional panel data models. When a large number of individuals/countries are involved in the regression, it is costly to allow for individual unobserved heterogeneity, for example, fixed effects, which may lead to incidental parameter problem in the regression. One way to balance between modeling heterogeneity and incidental parameters is grouping. With within-group homogeneity and cross-group difference, we can still allow for a certain degree of heterogeneity and avoid incidental parameter problem.

Chapter 2

Tests for Cross-Sectional Dependence in Fixed Effects Panel Data Models

In recent literature, cross-sectional dependence among individuals is a concern when n is large. As serial correlation in time-series analysis, the cross-sectional of dependence/correlation could invalidate inference. In some cases, it could even render inconsistent estimation. This chapter discusses testing procedures in the fixed effects panel data models, including static and dynamic cases.

In the fixed n case and as $T \to \infty$, the Breusch and Pagan's (1980) LM test can be applied to test for the cross-sectional dependence in panels. Under the null hypothesis of cross-sectional independence in errors, the test statistic is asymptotically Chi-square distributed with $n(n-1)/2$ degrees of freedom. However, this test is not applicable when $n \to \infty$. Therefore, Pesaran (2004) proposes a scaled version of this LM test, denoted by CD_{lm} which has a $N(0,1)$ distribution as $T \to \infty$ first, followed by $n \to \infty$. As pointed out by Pesaran (2004), the CD_{lm} test is not correctly centered at zero for finite T and is likely to exhibit large size distortions as n increases. To solve this problem, Pesaran (2004) proposes a diagnostic test based on the average of the sample correlations, which he denotes by the CD test, and this is valid for large n. Additionally, Pesaran, Ullah and Yamagata (2008) develop a bias-adjusted LM test using finite sample approximations in the context of a heterogeneous panel model.

Based on Baltagi, Feng and Kao (2012), this chapter introduces tests for cross-sectional dependence in panel data models. In specific, we derive the asymptotic bias of this scaled version of the LM test in the context of a fixed effects homogeneous panel data model. Because it is based on the fixed effects residuals, we denote it by LM_P to distinguish it from CD_{lm}. The asymptotic bias of LM_P is found to be a constant related to n and T, suggesting a simple bias corrected LM test for the null hypothesis. This chapter differs from the bias-adjusted LM test of Pesaran, Ullah and Yamagata (2008) in that the latter assumes a *heterogeneous* panel data model, whereas this chapter assumes a fixed effects *homogeneous* panel data model. Also, the bias correction derived in this chapter is based on asymptotic results as $(n, T) \to \infty$, while the bias adjustment in Pesaran, Ullah and Yamagata (2008) is obtained using finite sample approximation. Phillips and Moon (1999) provide regression limit theory for panels with $(n, T) \to \infty$. Here, we adopt the asymptotics used in the statistics literature for high-dimensional inference, see Ledoit and Wolf (2002) and Schott (2005), to mention a few. This literature usually deals with multivariate normal distributed variables where the number of variables (in our case n) is comparably as large as the sample size (T). We find that under this joint asymptotics framework with $(n, T) \to \infty$ simultaneously, the limiting distribution of the LM_P statistic is not standard normal under the assumption of a fixed effects model. Consequently, it can suffer from large size distortions.

The organization of this chapter is as follows. Section 2.1 reviews several LM tests for cross-sectional dependence in the literature. Section 2.2 derives the limiting distribution of the LM_P test in the raw data case. Section 2.3 derives a bias-corrected LM test in the context of a fixed effects model. In Section 2.4, we show that the proposed bias-corrected LM test can be extended to the dynamic panel data model. Section 2.5 reports the size and power of the tests for cross-sectional dependence using Monte Carlo experiments. Section 2.6 reviews the recent development in this topic. The technical details are included in Section 2.7.

2.1. LM Tests for Cross-Sectional Dependence

Consider the heterogeneous panel data model:

$$y_{it} = x'_{it}\beta_i + u_{it}, \quad \text{for } i = 1, \ldots, n; \ t = 1, \ldots, T, \qquad (2.1)$$

where i indexes the cross-sectional units and t the time-series observations. y_{it} is the dependent variable and x_{it} denotes the exogenous regressors of dimension $k \times 1$ with slope parameters β_i that are allowed to vary across i. u_{it} is allowed to be cross-sectionally dependent but is uncorrelated with

x_{it}. Let $U_t = (u_{1t}, \ldots, u_{nt})'$. The $n \times 1$ vectors $U_1, U_2, \ldots, U_T$ are assumed i.i.d. $N(0, \Sigma_u)$ over time. Let σ_{ij} be the (i, j)th element of the $n \times n$ matrix Σ_u. The errors u_{it} are cross-sectionally dependent if Σ_u is nondiagonal, i.e., $\sigma_{ij} \neq 0$ for $i \neq j$. The null hypothesis of cross-sectional independence can be written as

$$H_0 : \sigma_{ij} = 0 \quad \text{for } i \neq j,$$

or equivalently as

$$H_0 : \rho_{ij} = 0 \quad \text{for } i \neq j, \tag{2.2}$$

where ρ_{ij} is the correlation coefficient of the errors with $\rho_{ij} = \frac{\sigma_{ij}}{\sqrt{\sigma_i^2 \sigma_j^2}}$. Under the alternative hypothesis, there is at least one nonzero correlation coefficient ρ_{ij}, i.e., $H_a : \rho_{ij} \neq 0$ for some $i \neq j$.

The OLS estimator of y_{it} on x_{it} for each i, denoted by $\hat{\beta}_i$, is consistent. The corresponding OLS residuals $\hat{u}_{it}$ defined by $\hat{u}_{it} = y_{it} - x_{it}'\hat{\beta}_i$ are used to compute the sample correlation $\breve{\rho}_{ij}$ as follows:

$$\breve{\rho}_{ij} = \left(\sum_{t=1}^{T} \hat{u}_{it}^2\right)^{-1/2} \left(\sum_{t=1}^{T} \hat{u}_{jt}^2\right)^{-1/2} \sum_{t=1}^{T} \hat{u}_{it}\hat{u}_{jt}. \tag{2.3}$$

In the fixed n case and as $T \to \infty$, the Breusch and Pagan's (1980) LM test can be applied to test for the cross-sectional dependence in heterogeneous panels. In this case, it is given by

$$\text{LM}_{\text{BP}} = T \sum_{i=1}^{n-1} \sum_{j=i+1}^{n} \breve{\rho}_{ij}^2.$$

This is asymptotically distributed under the null as a χ^2 with $n(n-1)/2$ degrees of freedom. However, this Breusch–Pagan LM test statistic is not applicable when $n \to \infty$. In this case, Pesaran (2004) proposes a scaled version of the LM_{BP} test given by

$$\text{CD}_{\text{lm}} = \sqrt{\frac{1}{n(n-1)}} \sum_{i=1}^{n-1} \sum_{j=i+1}^{n} \left(T\breve{\rho}_{ij}^2 - 1\right). \tag{2.4}$$

Pesaran (2004) shows that CD_{lm} is asymptotically distributed as $N(0, 1)$, under the null, with $T \to \infty$ first, and then $n \to \infty$. However, as pointed out by Pesaran (2004), for finite T, $E[T\breve{\rho}_{ij}^2 - 1]$ is not correctly centered at zero, and with large n, the incorrect centering of the CD_{lm} statistic is likely to be accentuated. Thus, the standard normal distribution may be a bad approximation of the null distribution of the CD_{lm} statistic in finite samples, and using the critical values of a standard normal may lead to big size distortion. Using finite sample approximation, Pesaran, Ullah and Yamagata (2008) rescale and recenter the CD_{lm} test. The new LM test, denoted as PUY's LM test, is given by

$$
\text{PUY's LM} = \sqrt{\frac{2}{n(n-1)}} \sum_{i=1}^{n-1} \sum_{j=i+1}^{n} \frac{(T-k)\breve{\rho}_{ij}^2 - \mu_{Tij}}{\sigma_{Tij}}, \qquad (2.5)
$$

where

$$
\mu_{Tij} = \frac{1}{T-k} \text{tr}[E(M_i M_j)]
$$

is the exact mean of $(T-k)\breve{\rho}_{ij}^2$ and

$$
\sigma_{Tij}^2 = \{\text{tr}[E(M_i M_j)]\}^2 a_{1T} + 2\,\text{tr}\{E[(M_i M_j)^2]\} a_{2T}
$$

is its exact variance. Here

$$
a_{1T} = a_{2T} - \frac{1}{(T-k)^2},
$$

$$
a_{2T} = 3\left[\frac{(T-k-8)(T-k+2)+24}{(T-k+2)(T-k-2)(T-k-4)}\right]^2,
$$

and $M_i = I - X_i(X_i'X_i)^{-1}X_i'$, where $X_i = (x_{i1}, \ldots, x_{iT})'$ contains T observations on the k regressors for the ith individual regression. PUY's LM is asymptotically distributed as $N(0,1)$, under the null, with $T \to \infty$ first, and then $n \to \infty$.

This chapter considers the fixed effects homogeneous panel data model

$$
y_{it} = \alpha + x_{it}'\beta + \mu_i + v_{it}, \quad \text{for } i = 1, \ldots, n;\ t = 1, \ldots, T, \qquad (2.6)
$$

where μ_i denotes the time-invariant individual effect. The $k \times 1$ regressors x_{it} could be correlated with μ_i, but are uncorrelated with the idiosyncratic error v_{it}. This is a standard model in the applied panel data literature and differs from (2.1) in that the β_i''s are the same, and heterogeneity is introduced through the μ_i''s. The intercept α appears explicitly so that the regressor vector x_{it} includes only time-variant variables. Throughout our derivations for the fixed effects model, we require the following assumptions.

Assumption 2.1. $\frac{n}{T} \to c \in (0, \infty)$ as $(n, T) \to \infty$.

c is a nonzero bounded constant. This assumption approximates the case where the dimension n is comparably as large as T.

For a static panel data model, we assume the following.

Assumption 2.2. (i) The $n \times 1$ vectors of idiosyncratic disturbances $V_t = (v_{1t}, \ldots, v_{nT})'$, $t = 1, \ldots, T$, are i.i.d. $N(0, \Sigma_v)$ over time; (ii) $E[v_{it}|x_{i1}, \ldots, x_{iT}] = 0$ and $E[v_{it}|x_{j1}, \ldots, x_{jT}] = 0$, $i = 1, \ldots, n$, $t = 1, \ldots, T$; (iii) For the demeaned regressors $\tilde{x}_{it} = x_{it} - \frac{1}{T}\sum_{s=1}^{T} x_{is}$, $\frac{1}{T}\sum_{t=1}^{T} \tilde{x}_{it}$, $\frac{1}{T}\sum_{t=1}^{T} \tilde{x}_{it}\tilde{x}'_{jt}$ are stochastic bounded for all $i = 1, \ldots, n$ and $j = 1, \ldots, n$, and $\lim_{(n,T)\to\infty} \frac{1}{nT}\sum_{i=1}^{n}\sum_{t=1}^{T} \tilde{x}_{it}\tilde{x}'_{it}$ exists and is nonsingular.

The normality assumption (Assumption 2.2(i)) may be strict but it is a standard assumption in the statistical literature and is also assumed by Pesaran, Ullah and Yamagata (2008). Other distributions will be examined for robustness checks in the Monte Carlo experiments. Assumption 2.2(ii) is standard. Assumption 2.2(iii) excludes nonstationary or trending regressors. Under these assumptions, the within estimator $\tilde{\beta}$ is $\sqrt{nT}$-consistent. This estimator is obtained by regressing $\tilde{y}_{it} = y_{it} - \frac{1}{T}\sum_{s=1}^{T} y_{is}$ on $\tilde{x}_{it}$. The corresponding within residuals given by $\hat{v}_{it} = \tilde{y}_{it} - \tilde{x}'_{it}\tilde{\beta}$ are used to compute the sample correlation $\hat{\rho}_{ij}$ as follows:

$$\hat{\rho}_{ij} = \left(\sum_{t=1}^{T} \hat{v}_{it}^2\right)^{-1/2} \left(\sum_{t=1}^{T} \hat{v}_{jt}^2\right)^{-1/2} \sum_{t=1}^{T} \hat{v}_{it}\hat{v}_{jt}. \tag{2.7}$$

For a dynamic panel data model with the lagged-dependent variable as a regressor, more assumptions are needed. We will discuss this case in Section 2.4.

The scaled version of the LM$_{\text{BP}}$ test suggested by Pesaran (2004) but now applied to the fixed effects model is given by

$$\text{LM}_{\text{P}} = \sqrt{\frac{1}{n(n-1)}} \sum_{i=1}^{n-1}\sum_{j=i+1}^{n} \left(T\hat{\rho}_{ij}^2 - 1\right). \tag{2.8}$$

This replaces $\breve{\rho}_{ij}$ with $\hat{\rho}_{ij}$ and it now tests the null given in (2.2) only applied to the remainder disturbance v_{it}. In order to see this, let $u_{it} = \mu_i + v_{it}$ denote the disturbances in (2.6). The fixed effects estimator wipes out the individual effects, and that is why it does not matter whether the μ'_i's are correlated with the regressors or not. The test for no cross-sectional dependence of the disturbances given in (2.2) becomes a test for no cross-sectional dependence of the v_{it}. This LM$_{\text{P}}$ test, for the fixed effects model (2.8), suffers from the same problems discussed by Pesaran (2004) for the corresponding CD_{lm} statistic (2.4) for the heterogeneous panel model. We show that it will exhibit substantial size distortions due to incorrect centering when n is large. Unlike the finite sample adjustment in Pesaran, Ullah and Yamagata (2008), this chapter derives the asymptotic distribution of the LM_P statistic under the null as $(n, T) \to \infty$, and proposes a bias corrected LM test. The asymptotics are done using the high-dimensional inference in the statistics literature, see Ledoit and Wolf (2002) and Schott (2005), to mention a few. Our derivation begins with the raw data case and then extends it to a fixed effects regression model. We find that in a fixed effects panel data model, after subtracting a constant that is a function of n and T, the LM_P test is asymptotically distributed, under the null, as a standard normal. Therefore, a bias-corrected LM test is proposed.

2.2. LM$_P$ Test in the Raw Data Case

In the raw data case, the $n \times 1$ vectors $Z_1, Z_2, \ldots, Z_T$ are a random sample drawn from $N(0, \Sigma_z)$. The tth observation Z_t has n components, $Z_t = (z_{1t}, \ldots, z_{nt})'$. The null hypothesis of independence among these n components is the same as (2.2) but now pertaining to Σ_z rather than Σ_u. For fixed n, and as $T \to \infty$, the traditional LM test statistic is $T \sum_{i=1}^{n-1} \sum_{j=i+1}^{n} r_{ij}^2$, which converges in distribution to $\chi^2_{n(n-1)/2}$ under the null of independence. The sample correlation r_{ij} is defined as

$$r_{ij} = \left(\sum_{t=1}^{T} z_{it}^2 \right)^{-1/2} \left(\sum_{t=1}^{T} z_{jt}^2 \right)^{-1/2} \sum_{t=1}^{T} z_{it} z_{jt}. \qquad (2.9)$$

However, as the dimension n becomes as comparably large as T, this traditional LM test becomes invalid. A scaled LM test statistic

$$LM_z = \sqrt{\frac{1}{n(n-1)}} \sum_{i=1}^{n-1} \sum_{j=i+1}^{n} \left(Tr_{ij}^2 - 1 \right) \qquad (2.10)$$

is thus considered. This LM_z statistic (2.10) is closely related to the test statistic proposed by Schott (2005)

$$\sum_{i=1}^{n-1} \sum_{j=i+1}^{n} r_{ij}^2 - \frac{n(n-1)}{2T}.$$

For high-dimensional data, as $n/T \to c \in (0, \infty)$, Schott (Theorem 1, 2005) shows that under the null of independence, ·

$$\sum_{i=1}^{n-1} \sum_{j=i+1}^{n} r_{ij}^2 - \frac{n(n-1)}{2T} \xrightarrow{d} N\left(0, \lim_{(n,T)\to\infty} \frac{n(n-1)(T-1)}{T^2(T+2)}\right) \qquad (2.11)$$

or, equivalently, that

$$\sqrt{\frac{T^2(T+2)}{n(n-1)(T-1)}} \left[\sum_{i=1}^{n-1} \sum_{j=i+1}^{n} r_{ij}^2 - \frac{n(n-1)}{2T}\right] \xrightarrow{d} N(0,1).$$

Using Schott's (2005) result and the fact that

$$\sqrt{\frac{T^2(T+2)}{n(n-1)(T-1)}} \left[\sum_{i=1}^{n-1} \sum_{j=i+1}^{n} r_{ij}^2 - \frac{n(n-1)}{2T}\right] = \sqrt{\frac{T+2}{T-1}}\mathrm{LM}_z,$$

it is straightforward to infer that the limiting distribution of LM_z is $N(0,1)$ under the null. Srivastava (2005, Theorem 5.1) also derives the null limiting distribution of the LM_z statistic given in (2.10) using $T \to \infty$ and focusing on the case where $T = O(n^\delta)$ where $0 < \delta \le 1$.

2.3. A Bias-Corrected LM Test in a Fixed Effects Panel Data Model

This section derives the limiting distribution of the $\mathrm{LM_P}$ test defined in (2.8). This tests the null of no cross-sectional dependence in the fixed effects regression model given in (2.6). The null hypothesis of no cross-sectional dependence is the same as (2.2) but now pertaining to Σ_ν rather than Σ_u.

Theorem 2.1. *Under Assumptions* 2.1, 2.2 *and the null hypothesis of no cross-sectional dependence*

$$\mathrm{LM_P} - \frac{n}{2(T-1)} \xrightarrow{d} N(0,1).$$

The key step of proof of Theorem 2.1 is provided in Section 2.7. The asymptotics are derived under the joint asymptotics of $(n,T) \to \infty$ with $n/T \to c \in (0, \infty)$.

Based on this result, this chapter proposes a bias-corrected LM test statistic given by

$$\text{LM}_{\text{BC}} = \text{LM}_{\text{P}} - \frac{n}{2(T-1)}$$

$$= \sqrt{\frac{1}{n(n-1)} \sum_{i=1}^{n-1} \sum_{j=i+1}^{n} (T\hat{\rho}_{ij}^2 - 1)} - \frac{n}{2(T-1)}. \tag{2.12}$$

Theorem 2.1 shows that, under the null, the limiting distribution of the bias-corrected LM test is standard normal.

Comparing LM_{P} in the fixed effects model versus the corresponding LM_z in the raw data case, it is clear that LM_{P} exhibits an asymptotic bias, while LM_z does not. The asymptotic bias in the fixed effect model results from the incidental parameter problem. Due to the presence of unobserved heterogeneity μ_i, the idiosyncratic error v_{it} cannot be estimated accurately by the within residuals $\hat{v}_{it} = \tilde{y}_{it} - \tilde{x}'_{it}\hat{\beta} = v_{it} - \frac{1}{T}\sum_{s=1}^{T} v_{is} - \tilde{x}'_{it}(\hat{\beta} - \beta)$. The second term $\frac{1}{T}\sum_{s=1}^{T} v_{is}$, created by the within transformation to wipe out the unobserved heterogeneity μ_i, is $O_p(\frac{1}{T})$. Hence, the accuracy of the within residuals depends on T. For small T, the within residuals are inaccurate, and so are the sample correlations $\hat{\rho}_{ij}$'s computed using the within residuals. For large T, the terms involved with odd power of $\frac{1}{T}\sum_{s=1}^{T} v_{is}$ vanish due to the law of large numbers. However, the sum of a large number of squared terms of $\frac{1}{T}\sum_{s=1}^{T} v_{is}$ cannot be ignored. The inaccuracy due to the within transformation accumulates in the sum of squared terms of the statistic with comparably large n and $n/T \to c \in (0, \infty)$, consequently, resulting in asymptotic bias.

2.4. Dynamic Panel Data Models

In a dynamic panel data model

$$y_{it} = \alpha + \xi y_{i,t-1} + x'_{it}\beta + \mu_i + v_{it}, \quad \text{for } i = 1, \ldots, n; \ t = 1, \ldots, T, \tag{2.13}$$

where $y_{i,t-1}$ is the lagged-dependent variable. As documented by Nickell (1981), the within estimator is inconsistent for finite T as $n \to \infty$. Various consistent estimators have been proposed in the literature, including Anderson and Hsiao (1981), Arellano and Bond (1991), Kiviet (1995), Bun and Carree (2005), Phillips and Sul (2007) etc., to name a few. For a detailed discussion, see Baltagi (2008). Recently, Hahn and Kuersteiner (2002) studied the asymptotic properties of the within estimator in a dynamic panel model with fixed effects when n and T grow at the same rate. They show, after a bias-correction, the within estimator is $\sqrt{nT}$-consistent.

For the dynamic panel data model in (2.13), let us denote $\theta = (\xi, \beta')'$. Based on the bias-corrected estimator $\widehat{\widehat{\theta}}$ proposed by Hahn and Kuersteiner (2002), we can compute the within residuals $\widehat{v}_{it} = \tilde{y}_{it} - (\tilde{y}_{i,t-1}, \tilde{x}'_{it})\widehat{\widehat{\theta}}$ with $\tilde{y}_{i,t-1} = y_{i,t-1} - \frac{1}{T}\sum_{s=1}^{T} y_{i,s-1}$, and the corresponding sample correlations $\hat{\rho}_{ij}$ and the bias-corrected LM test statistic (LM$_{BC}$). Theorem 1 of Hahn and Kuersteiner (2002) shows that the limiting distribution of $\sqrt{nT}(\tilde{\theta}-\theta)$, where $\tilde{\theta}$ denotes the within estimator, is not centered at zero when both n and T are large. Due to this noncentrality, we find in Monte Carlo experiments that the proposed bias-corrected LM test using the within estimator is oversized in micro panels when n is much larger than T. This is why we use the bias-corrected estimator $\widehat{\widehat{\theta}}$ proposed by Hahn and Kuersteiner (2002). We show that as long as $\widehat{\widehat{\theta}}$ is $\sqrt{nT}$-consistent, the proposed LM$_{BC}$ test in the dynamic panel data model still has standard normal limiting distribution under the null. However, stronger assumptions are needed than the static panel data model.

Assumption 2.3. (i) $\sqrt{nT}(\widehat{\widehat{\theta}} - \theta) = O_p(1)$; (ii) $|\xi| < 1$; (iii) $\frac{1}{n}\sum_{i=1}^{n} y_{i,0}^2 = O_p(1)$ and $\frac{1}{n}\sum_{i=1}^{n} \mu_i^2 = O_p(1)$; (iv) $\frac{1}{T}\sum_{s=1}^{T}\sum_{\tau=1}^{s-1}\xi^{\tau-1}x_{i,s-\tau} = O_p(1)$ and $\frac{1}{T}\sum_{s=1}^{T}\sum_{\tau=1}^{s-1}\xi^{\tau-1}v_{i,s-\tau} = O_p(T^{-1/2})$.

Assumption 2.3(iii) is the same as condition 4(iv) in Hahn and Kuersteiner (2002). It implies $y_{i,0} = O_p(1)$ and $\mu_i = O_p(1)$. Under Assumptions 2.3(iii) and (iv), the dependent variable y_{it} and its time average $\frac{1}{T}\sum_{t=1}^{T} y_{i,t}$ are stochastically bounded.

Theorem 2.2. *Under Assumptions 2.1–2.3 and the null hypothesis of no cross-section dependence*

$$\text{LM}_{\text{BC}} \xrightarrow{d} N(0,1).$$

Under Assumption 2.3(iii), the proof follows along the same lines as that of Theorem 2.1.

2.5. Monte Carlo Simulations

This section employs Monte Carlo simulations to examine the empirical size and power of our bias-corrected LM test defined in (2.12) in a static panel data model. We compare its performance with that of Pesaran's (2004) CD test given by

$$\text{Pesaran's CD} = \sqrt{\frac{2T}{n(n-1)}} \sum_{i=1}^{n-1} \sum_{j=i+1}^{n} \breve{\rho}_{ij},$$

and PUY's LM test given in (2.5). The sample correlations $\breve{\rho}_{ij}$ are computed using OLS residuals, see (2.3).

2.5.1. *Experiment design*

The experiments use the following data generating process:

$$y_{it} = \alpha + \beta x_{it} + \mu_i + v_{it}, \quad i = 1, \ldots, n; \ t = 1, \ldots, T, \qquad (2.14)$$

$$x_{it} = \zeta x_{i,t-1} + \mu_i + \eta_{it}. \qquad (2.15)$$

Following Im, Ahn, Schmidt and Wooldridge (1999) x_{it} in (2.15) is correlated with the μ_i, but not with v_{it}.

To calculate the power of the tests considered, two different models of the cross-sectional dependence are used: a factor model and a spatial model. In the former, it is assumed that

$$v_{it} = \gamma_i f_t + \varepsilon_{it}, \qquad (2.16)$$

where f_t ($t = 1, \ldots, T$) are the factors and γ_i ($i = 1, \ldots, n$) are the loadings. In a spatial model, we consider a first-order spatial autocorrelation (SAR(1) in (2.17)) and a spatial moving average (SMA(1) in (2.18)) model as follows:

$$v_{it} = \delta(0.5 v_{i-1,t} + 0.5 v_{i+1,t}) + \varepsilon_{it}, \qquad (2.17)$$

$$v_{it} = \delta(0.5 \varepsilon_{i-1,t} + 0.5 \varepsilon_{i+1,t}) + \varepsilon_{it}. \qquad (2.18)$$

Cross-sectional dependence can also be modeled by including a spatially lagged-dependent variable, denoted as the mixed regressive, spatial autoregressive (MRSAR) model:

$$y_{it} = \alpha + \delta(0.5 y_{i-1,t} + 0.5 y_{i+1,t}) + \beta x_{it} + \mu_i + v_{it}, \qquad (2.19)$$

where, similar to the SAR(1) model in (2.17), the term $\delta(0.5 y_{i-1,t} + 0.5 y_{i+1,t})$ represents the spatial interaction in the dependent variable.

The null can be regarded as a special case of $\gamma_i = 0$ in the factor model (2.16) and $\delta = 0$ in the spatial models (2.17)–(2.19).

v_{it} (under the null) and ε_{it} (under the alternative) are from i.i.d. $N(0, \sigma_i^2)$. To model the heteroskedasticity, we follow Baltagi, Song and Kwon (2009) and Roy (2002) and assume that

$$\sigma_i^2 = \sigma^2 (1 + \theta \bar{x}_i)^2, \tag{2.20}$$

where $\bar{x}_i$ is the individual mean of x_{it}. Here θ is assigned values 0, 0.5 with $\theta = 0$ denoting the homoskedastic case. For nonzero θ, we fix the average value of σ_i^2 across i as 0.5 in our experiments. We obtain the value of $\sigma^2 = 0.5 / \left[\frac{1}{n} \sum_{i=1}^n (1 + \theta \bar{x}_i)^2\right]$ using (2.20) and subsequently the value of σ_i^2. For the case of $\theta = 0$, $\sigma_i^2 = \sigma^2$ is fixed at 0.5.

The parameters α and β are set arbitrarily to 1 and 2, respectively. μ_i is drawn from i.i.d. $N(\phi_\mu, \sigma_\mu^2)$ with $\phi_\mu = 0$ and $\sigma_\mu^2 = 0.25$ for $i = 1, \ldots, n$. For the regressor in (2.15), $\zeta = 0.7$ and $\eta_{it} \sim$ i.i.d. $N(\phi_\eta, \sigma_\eta^2)$ with $\phi_\eta = 0$ and $\sigma_\eta^2 = 1$. For the factor model in (2.16), $f_t \sim$ i.i.d. $N(0, 1)$ and two sets of experiments are conducted for $\gamma_i \sim$ i.i.d. $U(-0.5, 0.55)$ and $\gamma_i \sim$ i.i.d. $U(0.1, 0.3)$. For the spatial model, $\delta = 0.4$ in (2.17)–(2.19).

The Monte Carlo experiments are conducted for $n = 5, 10, 20, 30, 50, 100, 200$ and $T = 10, 20, 30, 50$. For each replication, we compute the bias-corrected LM test, Pesaran's CD and PUY's LM test. A total of 2000 replications are performed. To obtain the empirical size, the proposed bias-corrected LM test and PUY's LM test are conducted at the positive one-sided 5% nominal significance level, while Pesaran's CD test is implemented at the two-sided 5% nominal significance level.

2.5.2. *Results*

Table 2.1 presents the empirical size of these tests under the null of cross-sectional independence with heteroskedasticity ($\theta = 0.5$). The size of the bias-corrected LM test is close to 5%, even for micro panels with small T and large n. For example, the size of the bias-corrected LM test is 5.1% for $n = 200$ and $T = 10$. The simulation results are consistent with the asymptotic theory given in Theorem 2.1 in Section 2.4. As discussed in Pesaran, Ullah and Yamagata (2008), for large T there is no bias issue, so PUY's LM test has the correct size for large T. For large n and small T, it is slightly oversized. For example, the size of PUY's LM test is 9.2% for $T = 10$, $n = 200$. Pesaran's CD test has the correct size for all combinations of n and T.

Table 2.1.　Size of tests under heteroskedasticity ($\theta = 0.5$).

Size	$T\backslash n$	5	10	20	30	50	100	200
Bias-corrected LM	10	5.4	5.5	5.8	5.4	6.2	5.9	5.1
	20	5.6	6.3	5.0	4.8	6.2	5.5	5.4
	30	6.5	5.5	5.0	6.1	6.0	6.1	5.3
	50	5.8	6.0	5.4	5.9	5.1	5.7	4.3
PUY's LM	10	6.7	6.9	5.9	6.1	6.5	7.3	9.2
	20	6.4	6.3	5.6	6.0	7.2	5.2	6.7
	30	7.0	6.0	4.8	6.0	5.5	5.8	5.7
	50	6.7	6.5	5.8	5.5	4.7	5.3	4.5
Pesaran's CD	10	4.9	5.9	5.0	4.9	5.9	5.3	5.4
	20	4.9	5.5	5.3	5.8	4.5	4.7	4.9
	30	5.5	5.1	5.0	6.2	5.1	5.3	4.8
	50	5.0	5.3	5.1	4.8	4.4	4.2	5.4

Table 2.2 shows the size-adjusted power of these tests under the alternative specified by a factor model. The bias-corrected LM test has bigger size-adjusted power than PUY's LM test for small T. However, both tests have size-adjusted power that is almost 1 when n and T are larger than 20. By contrast, the power of Pesaran's CD test is much smaller than those of the two LM tests. While the power of the LM tests becomes one for large n and T, the power of the CD test reaches a maximum of 36.5% for $n = 200$ and $T = 50$ when γ_i is drawn from $U(-0.5, 0.55)$. This is expected under the current design. As pointed out by Pesaran, Ullah and Yamagata (2008), in the factor model above in (2.16), $\text{Cov}(v_{it}, v_{jt}) = E[\gamma_i]E[\gamma_j]$, implying that the value of Pesaran's CD test statistic is close to zero if the mean of γ_i is zero. This explains the low power of Pesaran's CD test when γ_i is drawn from $U(-0.5, 0.55)$. However, this is not the case for the proposed LM and PUY's LM tests which involve the squared terms of sample correlation coefficients. For the case of γ_i drawn from $U(0.1, 0.3)$, the power of Pesaran's CD test increases to 1 with n or T.

Tables 2.3 and 2.4 give the size-adjusted power of these tests under the alternative specifications of SAR(1) and SMA(1), respectively. In these cases, the size-adjusted power of Pesaran's CD test performs much better than in the case of a factor model, increasing to 1 with T.

Table 2.5 provides the results of robustness check on the size of the tests with some nonnormal or asymmetric distributions on the errors. We ran experiments with uniform distribution $U[1, 2]$, Chi-square distribution with 1 degree of freedom, χ_1^2, and t-distribution with 5 degrees of freedom,

Table 2.2. Size-adjusted power of tests: Factor model.

Size-adjusted power	$T\backslash n$	5	10	20	30	50	100	200
				$\gamma_i \sim$ i.i.d. $U(-0.5, 0.55)$				
Bias-corrected LM	10	23.8	50.4	82.1	92.9	99.2	99.9	100.0
	20	50.4	82.9	98.5	100.0	100.0	100.0	100.0
	30	61.9	93.2	99.7	100.0	100.0	100.0	100.0
	50	79.1	98.1	100.0	100.0	100.0	100.0	100.0
PUY's LM	10	21.6	44.8	77.9	88.9	98.0	99.7	100.0
	20	49.0	81.7	98.2	99.8	100.0	100.0	100.0
	30	60.5	93.0	99.7	100.0	100.0	100.0	100.0
	50	78.2	97.3	100.0	100.0	100.0	100.0	100.0
Pesaran's CD	10	7.6	7.8	8.0	8.7	9.2	10.6	13.8
	20	16.4	14.2	13.7	12.6	13.3	17.7	21.5
	30	18.0	17.8	17.9	18.4	18.9	22.1	27.2
	50	26.4	25.8	27.1	29.1	29.3	32.8	36.5
				$\gamma_i \sim$ i.i.d. $U(0.1, 0.3)$				
Bias-corrected LM	10	15.3	35.5	64.8	83.3	95.0	99.2	100.0
	20	33.6	68.8	95.6	98.9	100.0	100.0	100.0
	30	46.5	83.4	98.9	100.0	100.0	100.0	100.0
	50	66.7	93.2	99.9	100.0	100.0	100.0	100.0
PUY's LM	10	14.7	29.2	59.6	76.2	91.9	98.0	100.0
	20	33.5	68.7	94.1	98.8	99.9	100.0	100.0
	30	46.3	83.6	98.7	100.0	100.0	100.0	100.0
	50	65.3	92.8	99.9	100.0	100.0	100.0	100.0
Pesaran's CD	10	20.8	51.4	86.5	96.6	99.7	100.0	100.0
	20	42.6	83.3	99.1	99.9	100.0	100.0	100.0
	30	52.8	93.2	100.0	100.0	100.0	100.0	100.0
	50	72.3	98.6	100.0	100.0	100.0	100.0	100.0

$t(5)$, and we compare these results with those of Gaussian case $N(0, 0.5)$. For large T, these experiments show that the size of the bias-corrected LM, PUY's LM and Pesaran's CD tests are not that sensitive to the normality assumption on the errors. The same results obtain although the magnitude are different. PUY's LM test is still oversized around 8% for large $n = 100$, small $T = 10$ no matter what distribution is used. The bias-corrected LM test has size close to 5% for the uniform and t distributions and is a little oversized for $T \geq 10$ when using the χ_1^2 distribution.

Dynamic panel data models. To examine the finite sample properties of the proposed bias-corrected LM test in a dynamic panel data model,

Table 2.3.   Size-adjusted power of tests: SAR (1) model.

Size-adjusted power	$T\backslash n$	5	10	20	30	50	100	200
Bias-corrected LM	10	62.4	66.0	65.8	68.3	68.2	69.9	73.6
	20	96.0	98.1	99.4	99.9	99.8	99.9	100.0
	30	99.5	100.0	100.0	100.0	100.0	100.0	100.0
	50	100.0	100.0	100.0	100.0	100.0	100.0	100.0
PUY's LM	10	57.5	54.9	55.8	53.4	54.3	54.6	45.6
	20	95.4	97.5	98.8	99.4	99.1	99.7	100.0
	30	99.3	100.0	100.0	100.0	100.0	100.0	100.0
	50	100.0	100.0	100.0	100.0	100.0	100.0	100.0
Pesaran's CD	10	70.5	59.4	55.6	53.7	52.6	53.9	52.9
	20	94.5	88.6	84.2	83.7	84.2	86.0	83.4
	30	98.5	97.0	95.9	94.4	95.6	95.5	96.1
	50	100.0	100.0	99.8	99.6	99.8	99.7	99.8

Table 2.4.   Size-adjusted power of tests: SMA (1) model.

Size-adjusted power	$T\backslash n$	5	10	20	30	50	100	200
Bias-corrected LM	10	50.3	52.3	53.0	53.0	50.8	52.3	57.4
	20	92.3	95.2	97.7	97.8	97.7	99.0	99.0
	30	99.2	99.9	100.0	100.0	100.0	100.0	100.0
	50	100.0	100.0	100.0	100.0	100.0	100.0	100.0
PUY's LM	10	45.1	40.1	45.4	41.8	40.9	40.6	33.6
	20	90.0	93.2	96.0	95.9	95.8	97.0	95.9
	30	98.4	99.8	100.0	100.0	100.0	100.0	100.0
	50	100.0	100.0	100.0	100.0	100.0	100.0	100.0
Pesaran's CD	10	46.8	40.7	38.2	37.3	35.6	36.9	37.3
	20	80.5	70.9	66.7	63.1	65.9	69.1	66.4
	30	90.8	87.6	84.2	81.8	80.9	78.4	80.2
	50	99.5	98.1	97.3	97.0	96.1	97.3	96.8

Table 2.5.   Size of tests: Robustness to nonnormal errors.

Size	$T\backslash n$	$N(0, 0.5)$			$U[1, 2]$			χ_1^2			$t(5)$		
		20	50	100	20	50	100	20	50	100	20	50	100
Bias-corrected LM	10	5.8	6.2	5.9	5.6	6.2	6.0	6.5	7.4	6.8	6.1	5.7	5.8
	30	5.0	6.0	6.1	5.3	5.4	5.6	7.8	7.5	8.7	6.1	6.0	5.6
PUY's LM	10	5.9	6.5	7.3	5.9	6.9	8.3	7.1	7.4	7.9	6.4	8.0	7.6
	30	4.8	5.5	5.8	6.2	5.6	5.5	8.3	7.1	8.0	5.9	5.9	6.2
Pesaran's CD	10	5.0	5.9	5.3	4.7	5.7	5.5	5.5	5.2	4.8	4.9	4.5	5.7
	30	5.0	5.1	5.3	4.8	4.7	4.4	4.7	4.4	4.6	5.3	5.0	4.0

we follow the same design as that of Hahn and Kuersteiner (2002):

$$y_{it} = \alpha + \xi y_{i,t-1} + \mu_i + v_{it}, \quad i = 1, \ldots, n;$$

$t = -50, -49, \ldots, 0, 1, \ldots, T$, where v_{it} is assumed $N(0,1)$ independent across i and t, $\mu_i \sim N(0,1)$, $y_{i0}|\mu_i \sim N\left(\frac{\mu_i}{1-\xi}, \frac{Var(v_{it})}{1-\xi^2}\right)$ and $\xi = \{0.3, 0.6, 0.9\}$. For this model, Hahn and Kuersteiner (2002) propose a bias-corrected estimator $\widehat{\xi} = \frac{T+1}{T}\widehat{\xi} + \frac{1}{T}$, where $\widehat{\xi}$ is the within estimator of ξ. Hahn and Kuersteiner (2002) show that $\sqrt{nT}(\widehat{\xi} - \xi) \xrightarrow{d} N(0, 1 - \xi^2)$. In our Monte Carlo experiments, heteroskedasticity of v_{it} is allowed. In fact, $v_{it} \sim N(0, \sigma_i^2)$ where $\sigma_i^2 \sim \chi^2(2)/2$ as in the dynamic setup of Pesaran, Ullah and Yamagata (2008). The first 50 observations are discarded to lessen the effects of the initial values of y_{i0} on the results.

Table 2.6 reports the size of the tests for the dynamic panel data model. It shows that the proposed bias-corrected LM test has the correct size, close to the 5% nominal significance level, e.g., 5.1% and 5.4% for $n = 100$, $T = 10$ and $n = 200$, $T = 10$ in the case of $\xi = 0.3$. For the cases of $\xi = 0.3, 0.6$, it is slightly oversized for $n = 200$, $T = 10$. The PUY's LM test tends to over-reject in micro panels with large n and small T, and this fact is also observed in Table 6 of Pesaran, Ullah and Yamagata (2008). Pesaran's CD has correct size as in Pesaran (2004) and Pesaran, Ullah and Yamagata (2008).

2.6. Recent Development

Halunga, Orme and Yamagata (2017) propose a heteroskedasticity-robust Breusch–Pagan test in heterogeneous dynamic panel data models. The key idea is to replace the sample correlation coefficient $\breve{\rho}_{ij} = \left(\sum_{t=1}^{T} \hat{u}_{it}^2\right)^{-1/2}\left(\sum_{t=1}^{T} \hat{u}_{jt}^2\right)^{-1/2}\sum_{t=1}^{T} \hat{u}_{it}\hat{u}_{jt}$ in equation (2.3) with

$$\hat{\gamma}_{ij} = \left(\sum_{t=1}^{T} \hat{u}_{it}^2 \hat{u}_{jt}^2\right)^{-1/2} \sum_{t=1}^{T} \hat{u}_{it}\hat{u}_{jt}$$

in the statistics $\mathrm{LM_{BP}}$ and $\mathrm{CD_{lm}}$ in the fixed n and large n cases. Using $\hat{\gamma}_{ij}$ instead of $\breve{\rho}_{ij}$ allows for heteroskedasticity across both the cross-section and time dimension. Heteroskedasticity across time dimension emerges in a one-break-in-volatility model or a trending volatility model.

Table 2.6. Size of tests: A dynamic panel data model.

Size	$T\backslash n$	5	10	20	30	50	100	200
				$\xi = 0.3$				
Bias-corrected LM	10	5.3	5.8	5.5	4.5	5.6	5.1	5.4
	20	6.5	4.9	5.1	5.5	5.5	4.8	5.0
	30	6.2	6.2	5.6	4.8	5.7	4.8	4.5
	50	6.1	6.1	5.0	5.1	5.1	5.6	5.2
PUY's LM	10	7.2	7.6	9.0	9.9	15.9	29.5	65.5
	20	6.4	5.7	7.2	6.9	7.9	11.1	17.8
	30	7.5	6.1	5.9	6.2	7.4	7.9	8.8
	50	6.0	6.3	6.2	5.4	6.3	6.9	7.0
Pesaran's CD	10	6.5	5.9	5.5	6.2	5.0	6.1	4.5
	20	5.1	5.4	4.5	5.1	5.3	5.1	5.7
	30	5.1	4.6	5.7	5.6	5.1	5.5	5.7
	50	5.2	5.0	4.0	5.0	4.5	4.9	5.4
				$\xi = 0.6$				
Bias-corrected LM	10	4.1	5.2	5.1	4.4	5.2	5.5	6.3
	20	4.9	5.3	4.2	4.7	5.7	5.4	4.9
	30	4.9	4.9	4.6	5.1	5.0	5.2	5.1
	50	6.4	5.1	5.3	5.7	4.8	5.3	5.9
PUY's LM	10	7.4	9.1	11.5	12.4	22.0	42.8	84.6
	20	6.0	6.9	6.0	7.9	9.6	17.9	36.3
	30	6.3	5.8	6.7	7.4	8.2	11.0	17.8
	50	6.7	6.0	6.5	6.9	5.7	7.4	7.8
Pesaran's CD	10	6.2	6.0	5.5	4.6	5.1	5.2	5.7
	20	5.9	5.7	7.1	5.5	6.0	6.4	5.0
	30	6.3	5.3	5.2	4.7	4.9	4.5	5.5
	50	4.6	5.7	5.5	5.5	4.5	5.1	4.5

In their Theorem 1, Halunga, Orme and Yamagata (2017) show that under some conditions, for all $i \neq j$, as $T \to \infty$

$$\sqrt{T}\hat{\gamma}_{ij} \xrightarrow{d} N(0,1).$$

Based on this result, they proposed two robust versions of Breusch–Pagan tests using $\hat{\gamma}_{ij}$. However, the proposed tests are only valid when n is fixed or much smaller than T. For the case of comparably large n and T, wild bootstrap procedures based on these two robust tests are proposed and illustrated to work well in finite samples.

In Table 2.4 above, we find that under the alternative of an SMA(1) model, the power of LM_{BC} increases with T, but not substantially with n. For example, when n increases from 100 to 200 with $T = 10$, the power of LM_{BC} increases from 52.3% to 57.4%. This means that the LM_{BC} test is likely to be not powerful enough to reject the null in some cases. Recently, Fan, Liao and Yao (2015) find that in the high-dimensional setup, the quadratic tests, like LM_{BC} and PUY's LM, lack power to detect the sparse alternatives with only a few nonzero off-diagonal elements.

To deal with this issue, they propose a power enhanced version of LM_{BC} test by adding a power enhancement component J_0 (≥ 0 almost surely),

$$J = \text{LM}_{\text{BC}} + J_0,$$

where J_0 converges in probability to zero under H_0, and diverges in probability under sparse alternatives. An example of J_0 is a screening statistic,

$$J_0 = \sqrt{n(n-1)/2} \sum_{(i,j)\in\hat{S}} \hat{\rho}_{ij}^2 \hat{v}_{ij}^{-1},$$

$$\hat{S} = \{(i,j) : \hat{\rho}_{ij}\hat{v}_{ij}^{-1/2} > \delta_{N,T}, i < j \leq n\},$$

where $\hat{v}_{ij} = (1 - \hat{\rho}_{ij}^2)^2/T$ is the estimated asymptotic variance of $\hat{\rho}_{ij}$, and $\delta_{n,T} = \log(\log T)\sqrt{\log(n(n-1)/2)}$. Using a threshold $\delta_{n,T}$, the set $\hat{S}$ screens out most of the estimation error and determines a few nonzero off-diagonal entries with an overwhelming probability.

Recently, Mao (2016) extends Pesaran's (2004) CD test and PUY's bias-adjusted LM test in a static heterogeneous panel data model based on pairwise-augmented regressions. Demetrescu and Homm (2016) derive tests for cross-sectional correlation in large panels based on White's (1982) information matrix equality test principle. This approach is considered as a specification test. Instead of looking at the diagonality of error variance matrix directly, the proposed tests examine the difference of variance estimators of slope parameters in the cases with and without cross-sectional correction.

2.7. Technical Details

The section provides some technical details needed to prove Theorem 2.1. In the fixed effects model $y_{it} = \alpha + x'_{it}\beta + \mu_i + v_{it}$, $\tilde{\beta}$ is the within estimator and the within residuals are given by $\hat{v}_{it} = \tilde{y}_{it} - \tilde{x}'_{it}\tilde{\beta}$, where $\tilde{y}_{it} = y_{it} - \bar{y}_i$.

and $\tilde{x}_{it} = x_{it} - \bar{x}_{i\cdot}$, with $\bar{y}_{i\cdot} = \frac{1}{T}\sum_{s=1}^{T} y_{is}$, and $\bar{x}_{i\cdot}$ similarly defined. Define $\tilde{v}_{it} = v_{it} - \bar{v}_{i\cdot}$ with $\bar{v}_{i\cdot} = \frac{1}{T}\sum_{s=1}^{T} v_{is}$. The within residuals can be written as $\hat{v}_{it} = \tilde{v}_{it} - \tilde{x}'_{it}(\hat{\beta} - \beta)$. Let $V_i = (v_{i1}, \ldots, v_{iT})'$, $\hat{V}_i = (\hat{v}_{i1}, \ldots, \hat{v}_{iT})'$, $\bar{V}_i = (\bar{v}_{i\cdot}, \ldots, \bar{v}_{i\cdot})'$, $X_i = (x_{i1}, \ldots, x_{iT})'$, $\tilde{X}_i = (\tilde{x}_{i1}, \ldots, \tilde{x}_{iT})'$, $Y_i = (y_{i1}, \ldots, y_{iT})'$, $\tilde{Y}_i = (\tilde{y}_{i1}, \ldots, \tilde{y}_{iT})'$ for $i = 1, \ldots, n$. In vector form,

$$\hat{V}_i = V_i - \bar{V}_i - \tilde{X}_i(\hat{\beta} - \beta). \tag{2.21}$$

Using this notation, the sample correlation r_{ij} in the raw data case can be written as

$$r_{ij} = \frac{V_i' V_j}{(V_i' V_i)^{1/2}(V_j' V_j)^{1/2}} \tag{2.22}$$

and its sample counterpart using within residuals in the fixed effects model is given by

$$\hat{\rho}_{ij} = \frac{\hat{V}_i' \hat{V}_j}{(\hat{V}_i' \hat{V}_i)^{1/2}(\hat{V}_j' \hat{V}_j)^{1/2}}. \tag{2.23}$$

Dividing $\hat{v}_{it}$ by σ_i, we obtain

$$\frac{\hat{v}_{it}}{\sigma_i} = \frac{v_{it}}{\sigma_i} - \frac{1}{T}\sum_{s=1}^{T} \frac{v_{is}}{\sigma_i} - \left(\frac{\tilde{x}_{it}}{\sigma_i}\right)'(\hat{\beta} - \beta).$$

As shown below, the terms involving $(\frac{\tilde{x}_{it}}{\sigma_i})'(\hat{\beta} - \beta)$ have no effect on the test statistic asymptotically. Without loss of generality, σ_i is assumed to be 1 in the derivations below. Under Assumption 2.2, $\frac{1}{T}\tilde{X}_i'\tilde{X}_i = O_p(1)$, $\frac{1}{T}\tilde{X}_i'\tilde{X}_j = O_p(1)$ and $(\hat{\beta} - \beta) = O_p((nT)^{-1/2})$. In addition, we need the following lemma in the proofs below.

Lemma 2.1. *Under Assumptions* 2.1, 2.2 *and the null,*

(1) $\frac{1}{T}V_i'V_i = 1 + O_p(T^{-1/2})$;

(2) $\frac{1}{T}V_i'V_j = O_p(T^{-1/2})$ *for* $i \neq j$;

(3) $\frac{1}{T}\bar{V}_i'\bar{V}_i = \frac{1}{T}V_i'\bar{V}_i = O_p(T^{-1})$;

(4) $\frac{1}{T}\bar{v}_{i\cdot}\bar{v}_{j\cdot} = O_p(T^{-2})$;

(5) $\frac{1}{T}\tilde{X}_i'V_i = O_p(T^{-1/2})$;

(6) $\frac{1}{T}\tilde{X}_i'\bar{V}_i = O_p(T^{-1/2})$;

(7) $\frac{1}{T}\tilde{X}_j'V_i = O_p(T^{-1/2})$;

(8) $\frac{1}{T}\tilde{X}_j'\bar{V}_i = O_p(T^{-1/2})$.

Lemma 2.2. *Under Assumptions 2.1, 2.2 and the null,*

(1) $\hat{V}_i'\hat{V}_i = V_i'V_i - \bar{V}_i'\bar{V}_i + E_i$, *where* $E_i = -2(\tilde{\beta}-\beta)'\tilde{X}_i'V_i + 2(\tilde{\beta}-\beta)'\tilde{X}_i'\bar{V}_i + (\tilde{\beta}-\beta)'\tilde{X}_i'\tilde{X}_i(\tilde{\beta}-\beta) = O_p(n^{-1/2})$;

(2) $\hat{V}_i'\hat{V}_j = V_i'V_j - \bar{V}_i'\bar{V}_j + F$, *where* $F = -(\tilde{\beta}-\beta)'\tilde{X}_j'V_i + (\tilde{\beta}-\beta)'\tilde{X}_j'\bar{V}_i - (\tilde{\beta}-\beta)'\tilde{X}_i'V_j + (\tilde{\beta}-\beta)'\tilde{X}_i'\bar{V}_j + (\tilde{\beta}-\beta)'\tilde{X}_i'\tilde{X}_j(\tilde{\beta}-\beta) = O_p(n^{-1/2})$.

Lemma 2.3. *Under Assumptions 2.1, 2.2 and the null,*

(1) $(\hat{V}_i'\hat{V}_j)^2 - (\hat{V}_i'\hat{V}_i)(\hat{V}_j'\hat{V}_j)(V_i'V_j)^2/[(V_i'V_i)(V_j'V_j)] = G + H$, *where*

$$G = (\bar{V}_i'\bar{V}_j)^2 - 2(V_i'V_j)(\bar{V}_i'\bar{V}_j) + (\bar{V}_j'\bar{V}_j)(V_i'V_j)^2/(V_j'V_j)$$
$$+ (\bar{V}_i'\bar{V}_i)(V_i'V_j)^2/(V_i'V_i) - (\bar{V}_i'\bar{V}_i)(\bar{V}_j'\bar{V}_j)(V_i'V_j)^2/[(V_i'V_i)(V_j'V_j)]$$
$$+ 2(V_i'V_j)F = O_p(1) + O_p\left(\sqrt{\frac{T}{n}}\right)$$

and

$$H = F^2 - 2(\bar{V}_i'\bar{V}_j)F - [(V_i'V_i)E_j - (\bar{V}_i'\bar{V}_i)E_j + (V_j'V_j)E_i$$
$$- (\bar{V}_j'\bar{V}_j)E_i + E_iE_j](V_i'V_j)^2/[(V_i'V_i)(V_j'V_j)] = O_p(n^{-1/2});$$

(2) $(\frac{\hat{V}_i'\hat{V}_i}{T})(\frac{\hat{V}_j'\hat{V}_j}{T}) = (1 - \frac{1}{T})^2 + O_p(T^{-1/2})$.

Lemma 2.4. *Under Assumptions 2.1, 2.2 and the null,*

(1) $$\sqrt{\frac{1}{n(n-1)}} \sum_{i=1}^{n-1} \sum_{j=i+1}^{n} \frac{1}{T}(V_i'V_j)(\bar{V}_i'\bar{V}_j)$$
$$= \sqrt{\frac{1}{n(n-1)}} \left[\frac{n(n-1)}{2T} + O_p\left(\frac{n\sqrt{n}}{T}\right) + O_p\left(\frac{n}{\sqrt{T}}\right)\right];$$

(2) $$\sqrt{\frac{1}{n(n-1)}} \sum_{i=1}^{n-1} \sum_{j=i+1}^{n} \frac{1}{T}(\bar{V}_i'\bar{V}_j)^2$$
$$= \sqrt{\frac{1}{n(n-1)}} \left[\frac{n(n-1)}{2T} + O_p\left(\frac{n\sqrt{n}}{T}\right)\right];$$

(3) $\sqrt{\dfrac{1}{n(n-1)}} \sum\limits_{i=1}^{n-1} \sum\limits_{j=i+1}^{n} \dfrac{1}{T}(\bar{V}_j'\bar{V}_j)(V_i'V_j)^2/(V_j'V_j)$

$= \sqrt{\dfrac{1}{n(n-1)}} \left[\dfrac{n(n-1)(T+2)}{2T^2} + O_p\left(\dfrac{n\sqrt{n}}{T}\right) \right];$

(4) $\sqrt{\dfrac{1}{n(n-1)}} \sum\limits_{i=1}^{n-1} \sum\limits_{j=i+1}^{n} \dfrac{1}{T}(\bar{V}_i'\bar{V}_i)(V_i'V_j)^2/(V_i'V_i)$

$= \sqrt{\dfrac{1}{n(n-1)}} \left[\dfrac{n(n-1)(T+2)}{2T^2} + O_p\left(\dfrac{n\sqrt{n}}{T}\right) \right];$

(5) $\sqrt{\dfrac{1}{n(n-1)}} \sum\limits_{i=1}^{n-1} \sum\limits_{j=i+1}^{n} \dfrac{1}{T}(\bar{V}_i'\bar{V}_i)(\bar{V}_j'\bar{V}_j)(V_i'V_j)^2/[(V_i'V_i)(V_j'V_j)]$

$= \sqrt{\dfrac{1}{n(n-1)}} \left[\dfrac{n(n-1)(T^2+20T+60)}{2T^4} + O_p\left(\dfrac{n\sqrt{n}}{T^2\sqrt{T}}\right) \right];$

(6) $\sqrt{\dfrac{1}{n(n-1)}} \sum\limits_{i=1}^{n-1} \sum\limits_{j=i+1}^{n} \dfrac{1}{T}(V_i'V_j)F$

$= \sqrt{\dfrac{1}{n(n-1)}} \left[O_p\left(\dfrac{n}{T}\right) + O_p\left(\sqrt{\dfrac{n}{T}}\right) \right].$

Now we are in good position to prove Theorem 2.1.

Proof of Theorem 2.1. It is equivalent to show that for large n and T,

$$\text{LM}(\hat{\rho}_{it}) - \text{LM}(r_{it}) - \dfrac{n}{2(T-1)} = o_p(1).$$

By (2.22), (2.23) and Lemma 2.3,

$\text{LM}(\hat{\rho}_{ij}) - \text{LM}(r_{it})$

$= \sqrt{\dfrac{1}{n(n-1)}} \sum\limits_{i=1}^{n-1} \sum\limits_{j=i+1}^{n} (T\hat{\rho}_{ij}^2 - 1) - \sqrt{\dfrac{1}{n(n-1)}} \sum\limits_{i=1}^{n-1} \sum\limits_{j=i+1}^{n} (Tr_{ij}^2 - 1)$

$= \sqrt{\dfrac{1}{n(n-1)}} \sum\limits_{i=1}^{n-1} \sum\limits_{j=i+1}^{n} T\dfrac{(\hat{V}_i'\hat{V}_j)^2 - (\hat{V}_i'\hat{V}_i)(\hat{V}_j'\hat{V}_j)(V_i'V_j)^2/[(V_i'V_i)(V_j'V_j)]}{(\hat{V}_i'\hat{V}_i)(\hat{V}_j'\hat{V}_j)}$

$$= \frac{1}{(1-\frac{1}{T})^2} \sqrt{\frac{1}{n(n-1)}} \sum_{i=1}^{n-1} \sum_{j=i+1}^{n} \frac{\frac{1}{T}(G+H)}{(\hat{V}_i'\hat{V}_i/T)(\hat{V}_j'\hat{V}_j/T)/(1-\frac{1}{T})^2}$$

$$= \frac{1}{(1-\frac{1}{T})^2} \sqrt{\frac{1}{n(n-1)}} \sum_{i=1}^{n-1} \sum_{j=i+1}^{n} \frac{G}{T}$$

$$+ \frac{1}{(1-\frac{1}{T})^2} \sqrt{\frac{1}{n(n-1)}} \sum_{i=1}^{n-1} \sum_{j=i+1}^{n} \frac{H}{T}$$

$$+ \frac{1}{(1-\frac{1}{T})^2} \sqrt{\frac{1}{n(n-1)}} \sum_{i=1}^{n-1} \sum_{j=i+1}^{n} \left[\frac{1}{(\hat{V}_i'\hat{V}_i/T)(\hat{V}_j'\hat{V}_j/T)/(1-\frac{1}{T})^2} - 1 \right]$$

$$\times \frac{1}{T}(G+H).$$

Using $H = O_p(n^{-1/2})$, the second term above can be written as follows:

$$\frac{1}{(1-\frac{1}{T})^2} \sqrt{\frac{1}{n(n-1)}} \sum_{i=1}^{n-1} \sum_{j=i+1}^{n} \frac{H}{T}$$

$$= \frac{1}{(1-\frac{1}{T})^2} \frac{1}{T} \sqrt{\frac{1}{n(n-1)}} \sum_{i=1}^{n-1} \sum_{j=i+1}^{n} O_p(n^{-1/2}) = O_p\left(\frac{\sqrt{n}}{T} \right).$$

By Lemma 2.3, $(\frac{1}{T}\hat{V}_i'\hat{V}_i)(\frac{1}{T}\hat{V}_j'\hat{V}_j) = (1-\frac{1}{T})^2 + O_p(T^{-1/2})$, it follows that $\frac{1}{(\hat{V}_i'\hat{V}_i/T)(\hat{V}_j'\hat{V}_j/T)/(1-\frac{1}{T})^2} - 1 = O_p(T^{-1/2})$. Thus, it is straightforward to calculate the order of magnitude of the third term,

$$\frac{1}{(1-\frac{1}{T})^2} \sqrt{\frac{1}{n(n-1)}} \sum_{i=1}^{n-1} \sum_{j=i+1}^{n} \left[\frac{1}{(\hat{V}_i'\hat{V}_i/T)(\hat{V}_j'\hat{V}_j/T)/(1-\frac{1}{T})^2} - 1 \right] \frac{G+H}{T}$$

$$= \frac{1}{(1-\frac{1}{T})^2} \frac{1}{T} \sqrt{\frac{1}{n(n-1)}} \sum_{i=1}^{n-1} \sum_{j=i+1}^{n} O_p(T^{-1/2})$$

$$\times \left[O_p(1) + O_p\left(\sqrt{\frac{T}{n}} \right) + O_p(n^{-1/2}) \right]$$

$$= O_p\left(\frac{n}{T\sqrt{T}} \right) + O_p\left(\frac{\sqrt{n}}{T} \right).$$

Now we consider the first term,

$$\frac{1}{(1-\frac{1}{T})^2}\sqrt{\frac{1}{n(n-1)}}\sum_{i=1}^{n-1}\sum_{j=i+1}^{n}\frac{G}{T}$$

$$=\frac{1}{(1-\frac{1}{T})^2}\sqrt{\frac{1}{n(n-1)}}\sum_{i=1}^{n-1}\sum_{j=i+1}^{n}\frac{1}{T}[(\bar{V}_i'\bar{V}_j)^2 - 2(V_i'V_j)(\bar{V}_i'\bar{V}_j)$$

$$+(\bar{V}_j'\bar{V}_j)(V_i'V_j)^2/(V_j'V_j) + (\bar{V}_i'\bar{V}_i)(V_i'V_j)^2/(V_i'V_i)$$

$$-(\bar{V}_i'\bar{V}_i)(\bar{V}_j'\bar{V}_j)(V_i'V_j)^2/[(V_i'V_i)(V_j'V_j)] + 2(V_i'V_j)F].$$

By Lemma 2.4,

$$\frac{1}{(1-\frac{1}{T})^2}\sqrt{\frac{1}{n(n-1)}}\sum_{i=1}^{n-1}\sum_{j=i+1}^{n}\frac{G}{T}$$

$$=\frac{1}{(1-\frac{1}{T})^2}\sqrt{\frac{1}{n(n-1)}}\left[-2\frac{n(n-1)}{2T} + O_p\left(\frac{n\sqrt{n}}{T}\right) + O_p\left(\frac{n}{\sqrt{T}}\right)\right.$$

$$+\frac{n(n-1)}{2T} + O_p\left(\frac{n\sqrt{n}}{T}\right)$$

$$+\frac{n(n-1)(T+2)}{2T^2} + O_p\left(\frac{n\sqrt{n}}{T}\right)$$

$$+\frac{n(n-1)(T+2)}{2T^2} + O_p\left(\frac{n\sqrt{n}}{T}\right)$$

$$-\frac{n(n-1)(T^2+20T+60)}{2T^4} + O_p\left(\frac{n\sqrt{n}}{T^2\sqrt{T}}\right)$$

$$\left.+O_p\left(\frac{n}{T}\right) + O_p\left(\sqrt{\frac{n}{T}}\right)\right]. \tag{2.24}$$

For large n and T, the expression above (2.24) can be approximated by

$$\frac{1}{(1-\frac{1}{T})^2}\left(-2\frac{n}{2T} + \frac{n}{2T} + \frac{n}{2T} + \frac{n}{2T} - \frac{n}{2T^2}\right)$$

$$+O_p\left(\frac{n}{T^2}\right) + O_p\left(\frac{\sqrt{n}}{T}\right) + O_p\left(\frac{1}{\sqrt{T}}\right)$$

$$=\frac{n}{2(T-1)} + O_p\left(\frac{n}{T^2}\right) + O_p\left(\frac{\sqrt{n}}{T}\right) + O_p\left(\frac{1}{\sqrt{T}}\right).$$

Combining these three terms, we obtain

$$\text{LM}(\hat{\rho}_{it}) - \text{LM}(r_{it})$$

$$= \left[\frac{n}{2(T-1)} + O_p\left(\frac{n}{T^2}\right) + O_p\left(\frac{\sqrt{n}}{T}\right) + O_p\left(\frac{1}{\sqrt{T}}\right) \right]$$

$$+ O_p\left(\frac{\sqrt{n}}{T}\right) + \left[O_p\left(\frac{n}{T\sqrt{T}}\right) + O_p\left(\frac{\sqrt{n}}{T}\right) \right]$$

$$= \frac{n}{2(T-1)} + O_p\left(\frac{n}{T^2}\right) + O_p\left(\frac{\sqrt{n}}{T}\right) + O_p\left(\frac{1}{\sqrt{T}}\right).$$

Therefore, as $(n, T) \to \infty$ with $n/T \to c \in (0, \infty)$,

$$\text{LM}(\hat{\rho}_{ij}) - \text{LM}(r_{it}) - \frac{n}{2(T-1)} \overset{p}{\to} 0. \qquad \square$$

2.8. Exercises

(1) Under Assumptions 2.1, 2.2 and the null, show:

  (a) $\frac{1}{T}\sum_{t=1}^{T} v_{it}v_{jt} = O_p(T^{-1/2})$ for $i \neq j$;

  (b) $\frac{1}{T^2}\sum_{i=1}^{n-1}\sum_{j=i+1}^{n}\sum_{t=1}^{T} v_{it}^2 v_{jt}^2 = \frac{n(n-1)}{2T} + O_p\left(\frac{n\sqrt{n}}{T\sqrt{T}}\right)$;

  (c) $\frac{1}{T^2}\sum_{i=1}^{n-1}\sum_{j=i+1}^{n}\sum_{t=1}^{T}\sum_{\tau \neq t} v_{it}^2 v_{jt}v_{j\tau} = O_p\left(\frac{n\sqrt{n}}{T}\right)$;

  (d) $\sqrt{\frac{1}{n(n-1)}} \sum_{i=1}^{n-1}\sum_{j=i+1}^{n} \frac{1}{T}(V_i'V_j)(\bar{V}_i'\bar{V}_j) = \sqrt{\frac{1}{n(n-1)}} \left[\frac{n(n-1)}{2T} + O_p\left(\frac{n\sqrt{n}}{T}\right) + O_p\left(\frac{n}{\sqrt{T}}\right) \right]$.

(2) (Baltagi, Feng, Kao, 2011, Proposition 4.1) In the fixed effects model, for $i = 1, \ldots, n;\ t = 1, \ldots, T$

$$y_{it} = \alpha + x_{it}'\beta + \mu_i + v_{it},$$

let $v_t = (v_{1t}, \ldots, v_{nT})'$. The $n \times 1$ vectors $v_1, v_2, \ldots, v_T$ are assumed to be i.i.d. $N(0, \Sigma_n)$. Denote the $n \times n$ sample covariance matrix by $S = \frac{1}{T}\sum_{t=1}^{T} v_t v_t'$. For the within residuals $\hat{v}_{it}$, the residual-based sample covariance matrix can be obtained as $\hat{S} = \frac{1}{T}\sum_{t=1}^{T} \hat{v}_t \hat{v}_t'$ where $\hat{v}_t = (\hat{v}_{1t}, \ldots, \hat{v}_{nt})'$ for $t = 1, \ldots, T$. Under the null hypothesis $H_0 : \Sigma_n = \sigma_v^2 I_n$, show

$$\frac{1}{n}\operatorname{tr}\hat{S} - \frac{1}{n}\operatorname{tr} S = O_p\left(\frac{1}{T}\right).$$

(3) [Breusch and Pagan, 1980]

$$\text{LM}_{\text{BP}} = T \sum_{i=1}^{n-1} \sum_{j=i+1}^{n} \breve{\rho}_{ij}^2 \overset{d}{\to} \chi_{n(n-1)/2}^2$$

under the null of diagonality or cross-sectional uncorrelation.

(4) [Halunga, Orme and Yamagata (2017), Theorem 1] Under certain conditions, for fixed n, as $T \to \infty$, show

(a) $\sqrt{T}\gamma_{ij} = \dfrac{\frac{1}{\sqrt{T}} \sum_{t=1}^{T} u_{it} u_{jt}}{\sqrt{\frac{1}{T} \sum_{t=1}^{T} u_{it}^2 u_{jt}^2}} \overset{d}{\to} N(0,1)$.

(b) $\hat{\gamma}_{ij} - \gamma_{ij} = \dfrac{\frac{1}{\sqrt{T}} \sum_{t=1}^{T} \hat{u}_{it} \hat{u}_{jt}}{\sqrt{\frac{1}{T} \sum_{t=1}^{T} \hat{u}_{it}^2 \hat{u}_{jt}^2}} - \dfrac{\frac{1}{\sqrt{T}} \sum_{t=1}^{T} u_{it} u_{jt}}{\sqrt{\frac{1}{T} \sum_{t=1}^{T} u_{it}^2 u_{jt}^2}} = o_p(1)$.

(5) [Pesaran (2015), Theorem 2] Under the null, as n and T go to infinity,

$$\text{CD} \overset{d}{\to} N(0,1).$$

(6) Prove (2.11).

(7) [Ledoit and Wolf, 2002] Let x_i, $i = 1, \ldots, n+1$, be i.i.d. as a p-dimensional random vector such that

$$x_i \sim N(\mu, \Sigma).$$

Let

$$S = \frac{1}{n} \sum_{i=1}^{n+1} (x_i - \bar{x})(x_i - \bar{x})'$$

with

$$\bar{x} = \frac{1}{n+1} \sum_{i=1}^{n+1} x_i.$$

Show that as $\frac{p}{n} \to c$

$$\frac{1}{p} \text{tr}(S) \overset{p}{\to} \alpha,$$

$$\frac{1}{p} \text{tr}\left(S^2\right) \overset{p}{\to} (1+c)\alpha^2 + \delta^2,$$

and

$$n \begin{bmatrix} \dfrac{1}{p}\operatorname{tr}(s) - \alpha \\ \dfrac{1}{p}\operatorname{tr}\left(S^2\right) - \dfrac{n+p+1}{n}\alpha^2 \end{bmatrix}$$

$$\xrightarrow{d} N\left(\begin{bmatrix} 0 \\ 0 \end{bmatrix}, \begin{bmatrix} \dfrac{2\alpha^2}{c} & 4\left(1+\dfrac{1}{c}\right)\alpha^3 \\ 4\left(1+\dfrac{1}{c}\right)\alpha^3 & 4\left(\dfrac{2}{c}+5+2c\right)\alpha^4 \end{bmatrix} \right)$$

with

$$\alpha = \frac{1}{p}\sum_{j=1}^{p}\lambda_j$$

and

$$\delta^2 = \frac{1}{p}\sum_{j=1}^{p}(\lambda_j - \alpha)^2$$

where $\lambda_1, \ldots, \lambda_p$ are the eigenvalues of Σ.

(8) [Jiang (2004)] Let $x_n = (x_{ij})$ be $n \times p$, where the n rows are observations from a multivariate normal distribution and each of p columns has n observations. Let

$$\rho_{ij} = \frac{\sum_{k=1}^{n}\left(x_{ki} - \overline{x}_i\right)\left(x_{kj} - \overline{x}_j\right)}{\sqrt{\sum_{k=1}^{n}\left(x_{ki} - \overline{x}_i\right)^2 \sum_{k=1}^{n}\left(x_{kj} - \overline{x}_j\right)^2}},$$

where

$$\overline{x}_i = \frac{1}{n}\sum_{k=1}^{n}x_{ki}.$$

Then $R = (\rho_{ij})$ is a $p \times p$ sample correlation matrix. Define

$$L_n = \max_{1 \le i \le j \le p} |\rho_{ij}|.$$

Show that if $\frac{n}{p} \to \gamma \in (0, \infty)$

$$\lim_{n \to \infty} \sqrt{\frac{n}{\log n}} L_n = 2$$

almost surely and

$$P\left(nL_n^2 - 4\log n + \log(\log n) \le y\right) \to e^{-ke^{-y/2}}$$

with

$$k = \frac{1}{\gamma^2 \sqrt{8\pi}}.$$

(9) (Jiang and Yang, 2013) Let $p \times 1$ vector $x_i \overset{\text{i.i.d.}}{\sim} N(\mu, \Sigma)$, $i = 1, \dots, n$. Consider the spherical test

$$H_0 : \Sigma = \lambda I_p$$

versus

$$H_a : \Sigma \neq \lambda I_p$$

for a λ. Define

$$\bar{x} = \frac{1}{n} \sum_{i=1}^{n} x_i$$

and

$$S = \frac{1}{n} \sum_{i=1}^{n} (x_i - \bar{x})(x_i - \bar{x})'.$$

Let

$$V_n = |S| \left(\frac{\text{tr}(S)}{p} \right)^{-p}.$$

(a) Show that under the null

$$-(n-1)\rho \log V_n \overset{d}{\to} \chi_f^2$$

as $n \to \infty$ with p fixed where

$$\rho = 1 - \frac{2p^2 + p + 2}{6(n-1)p}$$

and

$$f = \frac{1}{2}(p-1)(p+2).$$

(b) Show that

$$\frac{\log V_n - \mu_n}{\sigma_n} \overset{d}{\to} N(0, 1)$$

as $\frac{p}{n} \to y \in (0,1]$ where

$$\mu_n = -p - \left(n - p - \frac{3}{2}\right) \log\left(1 - \frac{p}{n-1}\right)$$

and

$$\sigma_n^2 = -2\left[\frac{p}{n-1} + \log\left(1 - \frac{p}{n-1}\right)\right].$$

(10) (Chen and Jiang, 2018) Define

$$\Lambda_n = \left(\frac{e}{n-1}\right)^{\frac{(n-1)p}{2}} e^{-\frac{\mathrm{tr}(S)}{2}} |S|^{\frac{n-1}{2}}.$$

Show that as $(n, p) \to \infty$

$$\frac{\log \Lambda_n - \mu_n}{n\sigma_n} \xrightarrow{d} N(0,1)$$

with

$$\mu_n = -\frac{1}{4}(n-1)(2n - 2p - 3)\log\left(1 - \frac{p}{n-1}\right) + \frac{1}{2}.$$

(11) Let

$$\Sigma = \left(\rho^{|j-i|}\right)_{p \times p}$$

for $\rho \in (-1,1)$. Show that

$$\mathrm{tr}(\Sigma^2) = \frac{p}{1-p^2} + \frac{\rho^2 (\rho^{2p} - 1)}{(1-\rho^2)^2} = O(p),$$

$$\mathrm{tr}(\Sigma^4) = 2\sum_{k=1}^{p-1}(p-k)(k+1)^2 \rho^{2k}$$

$$+ p\frac{(1 + \rho^2 + 7\rho^4 - \rho^6)}{(1-\rho^2)^3} + O(1),$$

$$\mathrm{tr}(\Sigma^4) = O(p),$$

and

$$\mathrm{tr}(\Sigma^4) = o\{\mathrm{tr}^2(\Sigma^2)\}.$$

(12) (Chen *et al.*, 2010) Let $x_i \overset{\text{i.i.d.}}{\sim} N(\mu, \Sigma)$, $i = 1, \ldots, n$, where x_i is $p \times 1$. Let

$$y_{1n} = \frac{1}{n} \sum_{i=1}^{n} x_i' x_i,$$

$$y_{2n} = \frac{1}{P_n^2} \sum_{i \neq j} \left(x_i' x_j \right)^2,$$

$$y_{3n} = \frac{1}{P_n^2} \sum_{i \neq j} x_i' x_j,$$

$$y_{4n} = \frac{1}{P_n^3} \sum_i \sum_j \sum_k x_i' x_j x_j' x_k,$$

and

$$y_{5n} = \frac{1}{P_n^4} \sum_i \sum_j \sum_k \sum_l x_i' x_j x_k' x_l$$

with

$$P_n^r = \frac{n!}{(n-r)!}.$$

Define

$$T_{1n} = y_{1n} - y_{3n},$$

$$T_{2n} = y_{2n} - 2y_{4n} + y_{5n},$$

and

$$U_n = p \left(\frac{T_{2n}}{T_{1n}^2} \right) - 1.$$

Show that as $\text{tr}(\Sigma^2) \to \infty$ and $\frac{\text{tr}(\Sigma^4)}{\text{tr}^2(\Sigma^2)} \to 0$

$$\frac{1}{\sigma_{1n}} \left[\left(\frac{U_n + 1}{p} \right) \left(\frac{\text{tr}^2(\Sigma)}{\text{tr}(\Sigma^2)} \right) - 1 \right] \overset{d}{\to} N(0, 1)$$

with

$$\sigma_{1n}^2 = \frac{4}{n^2} + \frac{8}{n} \text{tr} \left[\left(\frac{\Sigma^2}{\text{tr}(\Sigma^2)} - \frac{\Sigma}{\text{tr}(\Sigma)} \right)^2 \right]$$

$$+ \frac{4\Delta}{n} \text{tr} \left[\left(\frac{A^2}{\text{tr}(\Sigma^2)} - \frac{A}{\text{tr}(\Sigma)} \right) \circ \left(\frac{A^2}{\text{tr}(\Sigma^2)} - \frac{A}{\text{tr}(\Sigma)} \right) \right],$$

where for two matrices $C = (c_{ij})$ and $B = (b_{ij})$, $C \circ B = (c_{ij} b_{ij})$.

Chapter 3

Factor-Augmented Panel Data Regression Models

3.1. Motivation

In the past decades, factor-augmented panel data regression models have received tremendous attention in econometrics literature and empirical studies. Adding an interactive form of unobserved factors could include the traditional linear panel data regression models as special cases. In addition, the factor structure could be used to model heterogeneous impacts of unobserved common shocks and cross-sectional dependence. Recently, Hsiao (2018) provides a very detailed and insightful review on the main modeling and estimation approaches in the literature. In this chapter, three main approaches are introduced, including Pesaran's (2006) common correlated effect (CCE) approach and Bai's (2009) iterated principal component (IPC) approach and the likelihood approach proposed by Bai and Li (2014) and advocated by Hsiao (2018).

Pesaran (2006) develops CCE estimators for large heterogeneous panels with a general multifactor error structure. The idea of CCE approach is to use cross-sectional averages of dependent and independent variables to proxy for the unobserved factors, thus the slope parameters can be estimated by least squares using augmented data when the cross-section dimension is large. Kapetanios, Pesaran and Yamagata (2011) show that the CCE estimator can be extended to the case of nonstationary unobserved common factors. Additionally, the CCE approach is also shown to be applicable to situations of spatial and other forms of weak cross-sectional dependent errors (Pesaran and Tosetti, 2011; Chudik, Pesaran and Tosetti, 2011), and heterogeneous dynamic panel data models with weakly exogenous regressors (Chudik and Pesaran, 2015). Baltagi, Feng and Kao (2016, 2019) generalize Pesaran's (2006) heterogeneous panels by allowing for unknown common structural breaks in slopes and factor loadings due to global technological or financial shocks in the cases of exogenous and endogenous regressors.

Bai (2009) takes a different perspective and treats the unobservable factor structure as interactive fixed effects in a homogeneous panel data model. In this model, factors and loadings are treated as parameters to be estimated, so the correlations between regressors and factors and loadings are allowed. An IPC estimator is developed to consistently estimate slopes and factor structure.

Since the advancement of Pesaran's (2006) CCE approach and Bai's (2009) IPC method, a multifactor error structure has been widely employed in empirical studies to model cross-sectional dependence and heterogeneous effects of unobserved macro shocks. For example, in the applications of the CCE approach, common factors are used to account for spillover in a study of private returns to R&D (Eberhardt, Helmers and Strauss, 2013), and to control for unobserved heterogeneity when examining the relationship between public debt and long-run growth (Eberhardt and Presbitero, 2015). In Boneva and Linton's (2017) research on the issuing of a corporate bond, unobserved common shocks such as the global financial crisis are modeled by interactive fixed effects in a discrete-choice model in heterogeneous panels. In addition, heterogeneous responses to aggregate shocks are allowed for by common factors in examining the effect of financial aid on macro outcomes by Temple and Van de Sijpe (2017), also, the reaction in a given US state to capital tax changes in other states by Chirinko and Wilson (2017).

In the applications of the IPC approach, Kim and Oka (2014) examine the effects of unilateral divorce laws on divorce rates in the US. They control for endogeneity due to the correlation between the unobserved heterogeneity and regressors to deal with bias in the resulting estimates of the treatment effects. Similarly, Gobillon and Magnac (2016) use Bai's (2009) IPC approach to evaluate the effect of an enterprise zone program. Totty (2017), on the other hand, estimates the effect of minimal wage increase on employment in the US with a factor structure to address concerns related to unobserved heterogeneity.

In this chapter, we introduce these three main approaches in the factor-augmented panel data regression models. In particular, in Section 3.2, Pesaran's (2006) CCE approach is discussed in detail. Section 3.3 presents Bai's (2009) IPC approach. A likelihood approach is introduced in

Section 3.4, and other studies are briefly discussed in Section 3.5. Finally, an empirical example is used to illustrate these approaches.

3.2. CCE Approach

Pesaran's (2006) CCE approach is originally developed in a static heterogeneous panel data model with large n and large T. It can be applied to the cases of homogeneous panels, dynamic and fixed T, etc. Here, we start with a simplified version and then extend to the general model considered by Pesaran (2006). In a heterogeneous panel data model:

$$y_{it} = x'_{it}\beta_i + e_{it}, \quad i = 1,\ldots,n;\ t = 1,\ldots,T, \tag{3.1}$$

x_{it} is a $p \times 1$ vector of explanatory variables, and the errors are cross-sectionally correlated, modeled by a multifactor structure

$$e_{it} = \gamma'_i f_t + \varepsilon_{it}, \tag{3.2}$$

where f_t is an $m \times 1$ vector of unobserved factors and γ_i is the corresponding loading vector. Here ε_{it} is the idiosyncratic error independent of x_{it}. However, x_{it} could be affected by the unobservable common effects f_t. Projecting x_{it} on f_t, we obtain

$$x_{it} = \Gamma'_i f_t + v_{it}, \quad i = 1,\ldots,n;\ t = 1,\ldots,T, \tag{3.3}$$

where Γ_i is an $m \times p$ factor loading matrix, and v_{it} is a $p \times 1$ vector of disturbances. Due to the correlation between x_{it} and e_{it}, the ordinary least squares (OLS) for each individual regression could be inconsistent.

To deal with the endogeneity due to the unobserved factors, Pesaran (2006) proposes an innovative idea of using the cross-sectional averages of y_{it} and x_{it} as proxies for f_t. Plugging (3.2) and (3.3) into (3.1) gives

$$\begin{aligned}
y_{it} &= x'_{it}\beta_i + \gamma'_i f_t + \varepsilon_{it} \\
&= (\Gamma'_i f_t + v_{it})'\beta_i + \gamma'_i f_t + \varepsilon_{it} \\
&= (\beta'_i \Gamma_i + \gamma'_i)f_t + (\beta'_i v_{it} + \varepsilon_{it}). \tag{3.4}
\end{aligned}$$

Combining (3.4) and (3.3) yields

$$\begin{aligned}
\underset{(p+1)\times 1}{w_{it}} &= \begin{pmatrix} y_{it} \\ x_{it} \end{pmatrix} = \begin{pmatrix} (\beta'_i \Gamma_i + \gamma'_i)f_t + (\beta'_i v_{it} + \varepsilon_{it}) \\ \Gamma'_i f_t + v_{it} \end{pmatrix} \\
&= \underset{(p+1)\times m}{C'_i}\ \underset{m\times 1}{f_t}\ +\ \underset{(p+1)\times 1}{u_{it}}, \tag{3.5}
\end{aligned}$$

where

$$\underset{m \times (p+1)}{C_i} = (\gamma_i, \Gamma_i) \begin{pmatrix} 1 & 0 \\ \beta_i & I_p \end{pmatrix},$$

$$u_{it} = \begin{pmatrix} \beta_i' v_{it} + \varepsilon_{it} \\ v_{it} \end{pmatrix}.$$

Let $\bar{w}_t = \sum_{i=1}^n \theta_i w_{it}$ be the cross-sectional averages of w_{it} using weights θ_i, $i = 1, \ldots, n$. They satisfy conditions: $\theta_i = O(\frac{1}{n})$, $\sum_{i=1}^n \theta_i = 1$ and $\sum_{i=1}^n |\theta_i| < \infty$. A simple example is the equal weights, i.e., $\theta_i = 1/n$. In particular,

$$\bar{w}_t = \bar{C}' f_t + \bar{u}_t, \tag{3.6}$$

where $\bar{C} = \sum_{i=1}^n \theta_i C_i$ and

$$\bar{u}_t = \sum_{i=1}^n \theta_i u_{it} = \begin{pmatrix} \bar{\varepsilon}_t + \sum_{i=1}^n \theta_i \beta_i' v_{it} \\ \bar{v}_t \end{pmatrix} \tag{3.7}$$

with $\bar{\varepsilon}_t = \sum_{i=1}^n \theta_i \varepsilon_{it}$ and $\bar{v}_t = \sum_{i=1}^n \theta_i v_{it}$.

When $\bar{C}$ is of full rank, $\bar{C}\bar{C}'$ is invertible. From (3.6), f_t can be written as follows:

$$f_t = [\bar{C}\bar{C}']^{-1} \bar{C}(\bar{w}_t - \bar{u}_t).$$

Intuitively, in the case of equal weights $\theta_i = 1/n$, $i = 1, \ldots, n$, $\bar{u}_t$ is the combination of averaged errors. By the Law of Large Numbers and the assumption of independence between β_i and x_{it} (or v_{it}), $\bar{u}_t \to 0$ as $n \to \infty$, yielding

$$f_t - [\bar{C}\bar{C}']^{-1} \bar{C}\bar{w}_t \xrightarrow{p} 0. \tag{3.8}$$

This implies that it is asymptotically valid to consider f_t as a linear function of $\bar{w}_t$. Pesaran (2006) suggests augmenting the original regression (3.1) by adding $\bar{w}_t$, the cross-sectional averages of dependent and independent variables, as additional regressors to control for the effects of f_t. That is, the regression becomes

$$y_{it} = x_{it}' \beta_i + \varphi_i' \bar{w}_t + \epsilon_{it}.$$

From this perspective, this CCE approach is regarded as a way to predict the unobserved f_t using observables. It is also similar to IV estimation in the sense that the CCE approach uses predicted value to solve the endogeneity issue.

The matrix form of (3.4) is

$$Y_i = X_i\beta_i + F\gamma_i + \varepsilon_i. \tag{3.9}$$

If F were treated as observable regressors, then the OLS estimator of β_i can be estimated by partitioned regression. However, equation (3.8) suggests that f_t can be proxied by $\bar{w}_t$. Or F can be wiped out asymptotically by a projection matrix based on $\bar{w}_t$. Let $\bar{W} = (\bar{w}_1, \bar{w}_2, \dots, \bar{w}_T)'$ denote the $T \times (p+1)$ matrix of cross-sectional averages of dependent and independent variables. Denote the $T \times T$ matrix M_w by $M_w = I_T - \bar{W}(\bar{W}'\bar{W})^{-1}\bar{W}'$. Premultiplying both sides of (3.9) by M_w, we obtain

$$M_w Y_i = M_w X_i\beta_i + M_w F\gamma_i + M_w\varepsilon_i. \tag{3.10}$$

It is expected that the terms involving $M_w F$ are ignorable asymptotically as $n \to \infty$, and that there is no endogeneity due to unobserved factors in equation (3.10). Thus, the CCE estimator of β_i is defined as the least squares of transformed data

$$\hat{\beta}_{i,\text{CCE}} = (X_i' M_w X_i)^{-1} X_i' M_w Y_i.$$

When a common slope β, instead of individual slope β_i, is the parameter of interest in empirical studies, under the random coefficient assumption, it can be obtained by the CCE mean group (CCEMG) estimator

$$\hat{\beta}_{\text{CCEMG}} = \frac{1}{n}\sum_{i=1}^{n}\hat{\beta}_{i,\text{CCE}},$$

or CCE-pooled (CCEP) estimator

$$\hat{\beta}_{\text{CCEP}} = \left(\sum_{i=1}^{n}\tilde{\theta}_i X_i' M_w X_i\right)^{-1}\sum_{i=1}^{n}\tilde{\theta}_i X_i' M_w Y_i,$$

where $\tilde{\theta}_i$ is a different set of weights. Under some conditions,

$$\sqrt{n}(\hat{\beta}_{\text{CCEMG}} - \beta) \xrightarrow{d} N(0, \Sigma_{\text{MG}}),$$

where Σ_{MG} can be consistently estimated by

$$\frac{1}{n-1}\sum_{i=1}^{n}(\hat{\beta}_{i,\text{CCE}} - \hat{\beta}_{\text{CCEMG}})(\hat{\beta}_{i,\text{CCE}} - \hat{\beta}_{\text{CCEMG}})'.$$

The general case considered by Pesaran (2006) includes observed factors, e.g., season dummies denoted by d_t:

$$y_{it} = \alpha_i' d_t + x_{it}'\beta_i + e_{it}, \quad i = 1, \dots, n; \ t = 1, \dots, T.$$

Thus, equation (3.9) becomes

$$Y_i = D\alpha_i + X_i\beta_i + F\gamma_i + \varepsilon_i,$$

where $D = (d_1, d_2, \ldots, d_T)'$. Different from unobserved factors F, the observed factors D can be partialled out directly. In this case, the projection matrix M_w (3.10) can be replaced by $M_h = I_T - H(H'H)^{-1}H'$, where $H = (D, \bar{W})$.

3.3. IPC Approach

Another popular approach of estimating factor-augmented panel regression model is IPC proposed by Bai (2009) in a homogeneous panel data model:

$$y_{it} = x_{it}'\beta + u_{it} = x_{it}'\beta + \lambda_i'f_t + \varepsilon_{it}, \quad i = 1, \ldots, n; \ t = 1, \ldots, T. \quad (3.11)$$

In this model, the factor structure $\lambda_i'f_t$ is considered as a generalized version of fixed effects with an interaction form, instead of an additive form $\lambda_i + f_t$ in a two-way error component panel data model. Different from the model above using CCE approach, here γ_i could be correlated with regressors x_{it}, as in the traditional fixed effects model. Thus, there is an additional source of endogeneity. Therefore, the CCEMG or CCEP could be inconsistent in the model (3.11) under this assumption.

To obtain a consistent estimator of β in equation (3.11), Bai (2009) proposes an iteration method based on the principal components method. Different from Pesaran's (2006) approach, in which the unobserved factors are partialled out, the IPC approach treats factors and loadings as parameters and estimates them directly. The matrix form of (3.11) is

$$Y_i = X_i\beta + F\lambda_i + \varepsilon_i. \quad (3.12)$$

Define $n \times r$ matrix $\Lambda = (\lambda_1, \ldots, \lambda_n)'$. The parameters of interest here include β, F and Λ. The least squares estimator is defined as the solution to minimizing the sum of squared residuals

$$\min \text{SSR}(\beta, F, \Lambda) = \sum_{i=1}^{n}(Y_i - X_i\beta - F\lambda_i)'(Y_i - X_i\beta - F\lambda_i). \quad (3.13)$$

Stacking observations through all n individuals, we write equation (3.12) as

$$Y = X\beta + F\Lambda' + \varepsilon,$$

where $Y = (Y_1, \ldots, Y_n)$, $X = (X_1, \ldots, X_n)$ and $\varepsilon = (\varepsilon_1, \ldots, \varepsilon_n)$. Since F and Λ are not identifiable, additional restrictions are imposed on the factor structure: $F'F/T = I_r$ and $\Lambda'\Lambda = diagonal$.

With these additional restrictions, an iterated estimation procedure is proposed. First, for each given F, OLS of β is obtained in (3.13)

$$\hat{\beta}(F) = \left(\sum_{i=1}^{n} X_i' M_F X_i \right)^{-1} \sum_{i=1}^{n} X_i' M_F Y_i,$$

where $M_F = I_T - F(F'F)^{-1}F' = I_T - FF'/T$. Second, for a given β, $Y_i - X_i\beta = F\lambda_i + \varepsilon_i$ has a pure factor structure. The least squares estimator of F is equal to the first r eigenvectors (multiplied by $\sqrt{T}$) associated with the r largest eigenvalues of the matrix $\sum_{i=1}^{n}(Y_i - X_i\beta)(Y_i - X_i\beta)'$. Once the estimated factor $\hat{F}$ is obtained in the second step, the slope estimator $\hat{\beta}(F)$ in the first step can be updated. Thus, the final least squares estimator $(\hat{\beta}, \hat{F})$, referred to as the IPC estimator, is the solution of following iteration:

$$\hat{\beta} = \left(\sum_{i=1}^{n} X_i' M_{\hat{F}} X_i \right)^{-1} \sum_{i=1}^{n} X_i' M_{\hat{F}} Y_i, \tag{3.14}$$

$$\left[\frac{1}{nT} \sum_{i=1}^{n} (Y_i - X_i\beta)(Y_i - X_i\beta)' \right] \hat{F} = \hat{F} V_{nT}, \tag{3.15}$$

where V_{nT} is a diagonal matrix that consists of the r largest eigenvalues of $\frac{1}{nT} \sum_{i=1}^{n} (Y_i - X_i\beta)(Y_i - X_i\beta)'$, arranged in descending order. The loading estimator is

$$\hat{\Lambda}' = \hat{F}'(Y - X\hat{\beta})/T.$$

In practice, Bai (2009) proposes a more robust iteration procedure: given F, Λ, slope estimate can be computed by

$$\hat{\beta}(F, \Lambda) = \left(\sum_{i=1}^{n} X_i' X_i \right)^{-1} \sum_{i=1}^{n} X_i'(Y_i - F\lambda_i), \tag{3.16}$$

and given $\hat{\beta}$ above, F and Λ can be computed from the pure factor structure $Y_i - X_i\hat{\beta} = F\lambda_i + e_i$, $i = 1, \ldots, n$. This new iteration scheme calculates a matrix inverse $(\sum_{i=1}^{n} X_i' X_i)^{-1}$ in (3.16) and avoids updating matrix inverse in each iteration in (3.14).

In the absence of correlations and heteroskedasticity, the IPC estimator $\hat{\beta}$ defined above is $\sqrt{nT}$ consistent without a bias. However, in a general case, $\hat{\beta}$ is asymptotically biased. Thus, Bai (2009) proposes a bias-corrected version of IPC estimator of β.

Compared to the CCE estimator proposed by Pesaran (2006), the IPC approach has the advantage of allowing for the correlation between factor loadings and regressors. In addition, no rank condition is required.

3.4. Likelihood Approach

Bai's (2009) IPC approach treats both factors and loadings as parameters, and controls the interactive fixed effects through estimating them. The benefit of this approach is allowing for arbitrary correlations between regressors and factors and loadings. However, there are too many parameters to estimate and a bias due to incidental parameters may arise. To address this concern, Bai and Li (2014) propose a likelihood approach to estimate the sample covariance matrix of factors (or loadings), instead of factors (or loadings) themselves, thus eliminating the incidental parameters problem in the time dimension (or cross-sectional dimension).

The model considered in Bai and Li (2014) is

$$y_{it} = x'_{it}\beta + \lambda'_i f_t + \varepsilon_{it}, \quad i = 1, \ldots, n; t = 1, \ldots, T. \tag{3.17}$$

To estimate β, Hsiao (2018) considers a quasi-likelihood approach for (3.17) using the following objective function:

$$-\frac{T}{2} \ln |\Sigma_\varepsilon| - \frac{1}{2} \sum_{i=1}^n (Y_i - X_i\beta - F\lambda_i)' \Sigma_\varepsilon^{-1} (Y_i - X_i\beta - F\lambda_i),$$

in a special case of homoskedasticity, i.e., $\Sigma_\varepsilon = E(\varepsilon_i \varepsilon'_i) = \sigma_\varepsilon^2 I_T$. Bai and Li (2014) take a different approach. Similar to Pesaran's (2006) model, the relationship between x_{it} and factor structure is specified in an additional equation:

$$x_{it} = \gamma'_i f_t + v_{it}. \tag{3.18}$$

Different from Pesaran (2006), this model allows for the correlation between x_{it} and λ_i through the correlation between γ_i and λ_i. Bai and Li (2014) treat loadings λ_i, γ_i as parameters and estimate them jointly with β by forming (3.17) and (3.18) in a simultaneous equation system. Let $\Gamma_i = (\lambda_i, \gamma_i)$, $z_{it} = (y_{it}, x'_{it})'$ and $u_{it} = (\varepsilon_{it}, v'_{it})'$. The model consisting of (3.17) and (3.18) can be written as

$$\begin{bmatrix} 1 & -\beta' \\ 0 & I_p \end{bmatrix} z_{it} = \Gamma'_i f_t + u_{it}.$$

Let $B = \begin{bmatrix} 1 & -\beta' \\ 0 & I_p \end{bmatrix}$, $z_t = (z'_{1t}, \ldots, z'_{nt})'$ and $\Gamma = (\Gamma_1, \ldots, \Gamma_n)'$, $u_t = (u'_{1t}, \ldots, u'_{nt})'$. Stacking observations across i, we obtain

$$(I_N \otimes B)z_t = \Gamma f_t + u_t, \quad t = 1, \ldots, T. \tag{3.19}$$

Thus, the model (3.19) becomes a high-dimensional factor model considered in Bai and Li (2012) except the term $(I_n \otimes B)$ in front of the observable z_t. As in the estimation of system of equations, the objective function of maximum likelihood estimation considered in Bai and Li (2014) is

$$\ln L = -\frac{1}{2n} \ln |\Sigma_{zz}| - \frac{1}{2n} \text{tr}[(I_n \otimes B) M_{zz} (I_n \otimes B') \Sigma_{zz}^{-1}] \qquad (3.20)$$

where $\Sigma_{zz} = \Gamma M_{ff} \Gamma' + \Sigma_u$, $M_{zz} = \frac{1}{T} \sum_{t=1}^{T} (z_t - \bar{z})(z_t - \bar{z})'$ is the data matrix and $\bar{z} = \frac{1}{T} \sum_{t=1}^{T} z_t$. The parameters to be estimated here are $(\beta, \Gamma, M_{ff}, \Sigma_u)$. Here $N(p+1) \times r$ matrix Γ contains all factor loadings λ_i, γ_i in equations of y_{it} and x_{it}, $i = 1, \ldots, n$, and $r \times r$ matrix $M_{ff} = \frac{1}{T} \sum_{t=1}^{T} (f_t - \bar{f})(f_t - \bar{f})'$ has $r \times (r+1)/2$ distinct elements, $\bar{f} = \frac{1}{T} \sum_{t=1}^{T} f_t$. Different from Bai (2009), here only matrix M_{ff}, instead of $r \times T$ parameters $f_t, t = 1, \ldots, T$, is to be estimated. Thus, the incidental parameters problem in time dimension is avoided. Moreover, $n(p+1) \times n(p+1)$ matrix $\Sigma_u = E(u_t u_t') = \text{diag}(\Sigma_{11}, \ldots, \Sigma_{nn})$ is a block diagonal matrix due to the uncorrelation of u_{it} across i.

The maximum likelihood estimator (MLE) of $(\beta, \Gamma, M_{ff}, \Sigma_u)$ is defined to maximize $\ln L$ in equation (3.20). The identification conditions required are as follows: $M_{ff} = I_r$, $\frac{1}{T} \sum_{t=1}^{T} f_t = 0$, and $\frac{1}{n} \Gamma' \Sigma_u^{-1} \Gamma$ is a diagonal matrix with its diagonal elements distinct and arranged in descending order. Under these conditions, parameters to be estimated reduce to $(\beta, \Gamma, \Sigma_u)$.

Bai and Li (2014) show that under some conditions and $\sqrt{n}/T \to 0$, the MLE of β is $\sqrt{nT}$ consistent, efficient and has no asymptotic bias, which is different from Bai's (2009) IPC estimator. To implement the maximum likelihood method, Bai and Li (2014) adapt the ECM (expectation and conditional maximization) procedures.

In equation (3.19), an individual specific intercept term can be introduced to accommodate an intercept in equation (3.17) and nonzero means in equation (3.18). As shown in (3.20), only the second moments are involved, so including an intercept term does not affect the MLE.

Bai (2013) extends the likelihood approach to a dynamic panel data model with a factor error structure. With a proper treatment of the initial observation, the proposed MLE is consistent, efficient and asymptotically unbiased in cases of fixed T and large T.

3.5. Other Studies

Other important approaches to deal with the unobserved factor structure in static panel data models include the quasi-difference method by Ahn *et al.* (2013), instrumental variable approach by Sarafidis and Robertson

(2015), etc. In a dynamic model, Moon and Weidner (2017) propose a bias-corrected least squares estimator. Hsiao (2018) reviews the existing factor-augmented panel data regression models in the literature and categorizes them into four groups by treating λ_i and f_t as random or fixed effects. In terms of the potential correlations between λ_i and x_{it}, and between f_t and x_{it}, Pesaran's (2006) model and CCE approach introduced in Section 3.2 can be considered as the case of treating λ_i as random and f_t as fixed. Since in Bai's (2009) model, both λ_i and f_t are allowed to be correlated with x_{it}, the IPC approach is considered as the case of treating both λ_i and f_t as fixed.

Hsiao (2018) suggests a quasi-likelihood approach as a common framework for four different combinations of random and fixed λ_i and f_t. In a dynamic model,

$$y_{it} = \beta_1 y_{it-1} + x'_{it}\beta_2 + \lambda'_i f_t + \varepsilon_{it}, \quad i = 1, \dots, n; t = 1, \dots, T,$$

when T is fixed, it is reasonable to treat λ_i as random and f_t as fixed. In Hsiao's (2018) Monte Carlo experiments, both CCE and IPC approaches are invalid for the case of the dynamic model when T is fixed. In this case, a quasi-maximum likelihood estimator introduced by Hsiao (2018) is consistent and asymptotically unbiased as $n \to \infty$.

3.6. An Empirical Example

In this section, CCE, IPC and likelihood approaches introduced above are illustrated by using a panel data set for China's provincial infrastructure investments over the period of 1996–2015. This data set is employed by Feng and Wu (2018) to investigate the productivity effect of infrastructure by estimating the output elasticity with respect to public infrastructure in an aggregate production function.

We start with a homogeneous panel data model based on an aggregate production function:

$$g_{it} = \beta_0 + \beta_b b_{it} + \beta_k k_{it} + \mu_i + \lambda_t + \epsilon_{it}, \tag{3.21}$$

where g_{it} is the logarithm of GDP per labor in province i in year t, and b_{it} is the logarithm of public infrastructure stock per labor, and k_{it} is the logarithm of noninfrastructure capital stock per labor. In this equation, β_b and β_k are, respectively, the output elasticities of public infrastructure and noninfrastructure capital, and μ_i denotes province specific factors, such as location, weather, endowments of raw materials. Time effects

λ_t are used to control for national-level macro shocks, and ε_{it} denotes the idiosyncratic error. To estimate the parameter of interest β_b, the following first-differenced equation form is used to deal with the nonstationarity of macroeconomic variables g_{it}, b_{it}, k_{it}:

$$\Delta g_{it} = \beta_b \Delta b_{it} + \beta_k \Delta k_{it} + \Delta \lambda_t + \Delta \epsilon_{it}. \tag{3.22}$$

Summary statistics of the variables used in the regressions and detailed information of the data construction and variables can be found in Feng and Wu (2018).

Table 3.1 gives the first-differenced (FD) estimates assuming that the regressors Δb_{it} and Δk_{it} are exogenous. Besides the full sample estimates in column (1), estimates using subsamples of noneastern and eastern provinces are reported in columns (2) and (3) to highlight cross-region heterogeneity. Similarly, to allow for structural changes in elasticities, subsample estimates using the periods of 1997–2007 and 2008–2015 are presented in columns (4) and (5). Substantial differences in the magnitude of the estimated β_b are observed, indicating that cross-region heterogeneity and structural changes should be accommodated in an empirically more flexible model.

Table 3.1 also reports Bai's (2009) IPC estimates in column (6), Bai and Li's (2014) MLE in column (7) and Pesaran's (2006) CCE mean group (CCEMG) estimates in column (8). In column (6), the IPC estimates of β_b and β_k are 0.197 and 0.349, respectively.[1] Compared with column (1), the IPC estimate of β_k varies little after controlling for interactive fixed effects, while the IPC estimate of β_b increases from 0.127 to 0.197. MLE results proposed by Bai and Li (2014) are included in column (7). In the case of two factors, the MLE of β_b and β_k are 0.233 and 0.517, slightly bigger than those of IPC. When there is one unobserved factor in errors, the MLE results are very close to IPC estimates.

Column (8) estimates a heterogeneous model to allow for different elasticities across provinces:

$$\Delta g_{it} = \beta_{b,i} \Delta b_{it} + \beta_{k,i} \Delta k_{it} + \Delta \lambda_t + \Delta \epsilon_{it}. \tag{3.23}$$

Column (8) assumes a factor structure in the error $\Delta \epsilon_{it} = \gamma_i' f_t + \varepsilon_{it}$ in equation (3.23) to capture the heterogeneous impact of unobserved macro shocks f_t, and the fact that regressors Δb_{it}, Δk_{it} can be affected by the

---

[1] A Stata ado file *regife* developed by Gomez (2015) is used to calculate Bai's (2009) IPC estimates. Here, two factors are assumed. The estimates are quantitatively similar to those with three factors in the errors.

Table 3.1. Output elasticities estimates.

Dependent variable: Output per labor

Independent variables	FD					IPC	MLE	CCEMG
	(1)	(2)	(3)	(4)	(5)	(6)	(7)	(8)
Infrastructure per labor	0.127***	0.166***	0.107***	0.144***	0.088**	0.197***	0.233	0.194***
	(0.025)	(0.025)	(0.026)	(0.031)	(0.036)	(0.017)		(0.023)
Noninfrastructure per labor	0.324***	0.346***	0.321***	0.340***	0.315***	0.349***	0.517	0.407***
	(0.027)	(0.024)	(0.025)	(0.040)	(0.024)	(0.018)		(0.037)
Regions	All	Noneastern	Eastern	All	All	All	All	All
Periods	All	All	All	1997–2007	2008–2015	All	All	All
Year effects	Yes	Yes	Yes	Yes	Yes	Yes	Yes	Yes
No. of observations	569	360	209	329	240	569	569	569
Overall R^2	0.727	0.762	0.758	0.755	0.670			0.72

Notes: Standard errors are reported in parentheses. The stars, *, **, and *** indicate the significance level at 10%, 5% and 1%, respectively.

unobserved common factors f_t. For this model, Pesaran's (2006) CCEMG can be applied directly. Compared with the usual first-difference estimates in column (1), CCEMG in column (8) accommodates two empirical features: slope heterogeneity and cross-sectional dependence. The CCEMG estimates of β_b and β_k are 0.194 and 0.407, respectively, very close to the corresponding IPC estimates in column (6) and both are slightly different from the FD estimates in column (1).

3.7. Exercises

(1) (Doz, Giannone, and Reichlin, 2012) Consider

$$y_t = \Lambda f_t + e_t,$$

where $f_t = (f_{1t}, \ldots, f_{rt})'$ is an $r \times 1$, Λ is an $n \times r$ factor loading matrix, and $e_t = (e_{1t}, \ldots, e_{nt})'$ is an $n \times 1$ idiosyncratic components with $e_t \overset{\text{i.i.d.}}{\sim} N(0, \Sigma)$ where Σ is a diagonal matrix. Assume

$$A(L)f_t = u_t$$

with

$$A(L) = I - A_1 L - \cdots - A_p L^p$$

an $r \times r$ filter of finite length p with roots outside the unit circle, and u_t an r-dimensional Gaussian white noise, $u_t \overset{\text{i.i.d.}}{\sim} N(0, I_r)$. Let $\widehat{\theta}$ be the quasi maximum likelihood estimator (QMLE) of parameters θ. Define

$$\widehat{F}_{\widehat{\theta}} = E_{\widehat{\theta}}[F|Y]$$

with $F = (f_1, \ldots, f_T)'$ and $Y = (y_1, \ldots, y_T)'$ where $\widehat{F}_{\widehat{\theta}} = (\widehat{f}_{\widehat{\theta}1}, \ldots, \widehat{f}_{\widehat{\theta}T})'$. Show that

$$\text{trace}\left(\frac{1}{T}(F - \widehat{F}_{\widehat{\theta}}\widehat{H})'(F - \widehat{F}_{\widehat{\theta}}\widehat{H})\right) = O_p\left(\frac{1}{\Delta_{nT}}\right)$$

as $(n, T) \to \infty$ where $\widehat{H} = (\widehat{F}_{\widehat{\theta}}'\widehat{F}_{\widehat{\theta}})^{-1}\widehat{F}_{\widehat{\theta}}'F$ and $\Delta_{nT} = \min\{\sqrt{T}, \frac{n}{\log n}\}$.

(2) (*Continued*) Assume

$$f_t \overset{\text{i.i.d.}}{\sim} N(0, I_r)$$

and

$$e_t \overset{\text{i.i.d.}}{\sim} N(0, \sigma^2 I_r).$$

Show that:

(a) the log-likelihood function is

$$\log L(Y; \theta) = -\frac{nT}{2} \log 2\pi - \frac{T}{2} \log |\Lambda\Lambda' + \sigma^2 I_n| - \frac{T}{2} \operatorname{trace}(\Lambda\Lambda' + \sigma^2 I_n);$$

(b) the QMLE are

$$\widehat{\Lambda} = V(D - \widehat{\sigma}^2 I_r)^{1/2}$$

and

$$\widehat{\sigma}^2 = \frac{1}{n} \operatorname{trace}(S - \widehat{\Lambda}\widehat{\Lambda}'),$$

where D is an $r \times r$ diagonal matrix containing the r largest eigenvalues of the sample covariance matrix

$$S = \frac{1}{T} Y'Y,$$

and V is the $n \times r$ matrix whose columns are the corresponding normalized eigenvectors such that $V'V = I_r$ and $SV = VD$;

(c) $$\widehat{F}_{\widehat{\theta}} = YV(D - \widehat{\sigma}^2 I_r)^{1/2} D^{-1}.$$

(3) (Barigozzi and Cho, 2019) Consider

$$y_{it} = \chi_{it} + e_{it}$$

with

$$\chi_{it} = \lambda_i' f_t.$$

Let

$$\widehat{\chi}_{it}^{pc} = \sum_{j=1}^{r} \widehat{w}_{ij} \widehat{w}_j y_t,$$

where $\widehat{w}_j = (\widehat{w}_{1j}, \ldots, \widehat{w}_{nj})$ is the normalized eigenvector corresponding to the jth largest eigenvalue of the sample covariance matrix of y_t. Show that

$$\max_i \max_t |\widehat{\chi}_{it}^{pc} - \chi_{it}| = O_p \left(\max \left(\sqrt{\frac{\log n}{T}}, \frac{1}{\sqrt{n}} \right) \log T \right).$$

(4) (Bai and Liao, 2013) Consider

$$y_{it} = \lambda_i' f_t + u_{it}$$

where f_t is an $r \times 1$ vector of common factors, λ_i is a vector of factor loadings, and u_{it} is the idiosyncratic component.

Let $y_t = (y_{it}, \ldots, y_{nt})'$, $\Lambda = (\lambda_1, \ldots, \lambda_n)'$ and $u_t = (u_{1t}, \ldots, u_{nt})'$. In vector form,

$$y_t = \Lambda f_t + u_t.$$

Define

$$(\widehat{\Lambda}, \widehat{f_t}) = \arg\min_{\Lambda, f_t} \sum_{t=1}^{T} (y_t - \Lambda f_t)' W_T (y_t - \Lambda f_t)$$

subject to $\frac{1}{T} \sum_{t=1}^{T} \widehat{f_t} \widehat{f_t}' = I_r$ and $\widehat{\Lambda}' W_T \widehat{\Lambda}$ is diagonal, where W_T is an $n \times n$ weight matrix. Let Y be the $n \times T$ matrix of y_{it}. Show that $\widehat{\lambda}_i$ and $\widehat{f_t}$ are both $r \times 1$ vectors such that the columns of the $T \times r$ matrix $\frac{1}{\sqrt{T}} \widehat{F} = \frac{1}{\sqrt{T}} (\widehat{f_1}, \ldots, \widehat{f_T})'$ are the eigenvectors corresponding to the largest r eigenvalues of $Y' W_T Y$ and $\widehat{\Lambda} = (\widehat{\lambda}_1, \ldots, \widehat{\lambda}_n)' = \frac{1}{T} Y \widehat{F}$.

(5) (Bai and Liao, 2016) Consider

$$y_{it} = \alpha_i + \lambda_i' f_t + u_{it},$$

where α_i is an individual effect, λ_i is an $r \times 1$ vector of factor loadings, f_t is an $r \times 1$ vector of common factors and u_{it} denotes the idiosyncratic component. Let $y_t = (y_{1t}, \ldots, y_{nt})'$, $\Lambda = (\lambda_1, \ldots, \lambda_n)'$, $\alpha = (\alpha_1, \ldots, \alpha_n)'$ and $u_t = (u_{1t}, \ldots, u_{nt})'$. In vector form,

$$y_t = \alpha + \Lambda f_t + u_t.$$

Let $S = \frac{1}{T} \sum_{t=1}^{T} (y_t - \overline{y})(y_t - \overline{y})'$ and $S_f = \frac{1}{T} \sum_{t=1}^{T} (f_t - \overline{f})(f_t - \overline{f})'$ with $\overline{y} = \frac{1}{T} \sum_{t=1}^{T} y_t$ and $\overline{f} = \frac{1}{T} \sum_{t=1}^{T} f_t$. Assume $S_f = I_r$ and $\Lambda' \Sigma_u^{-1} \Lambda$ is diagonal. The quasi-likelihood function is

$$L(\Lambda, \Sigma_u) = \frac{1}{n} \log[\Lambda\Lambda' + \Sigma_u] + \frac{1}{n} tr(S(\Lambda\Lambda' + \Sigma_u)^{-1}),$$

where $\Sigma_u = E(u_t u_t')$. Define

$$(\widehat{\Lambda}, \widehat{\Sigma}_u) = \arg\min_{(\Lambda, \Sigma_u)} L(\Lambda, \Sigma_u) + P_T(\Sigma_u)$$

with

$$P_T(\Sigma_u) = \frac{1}{n} \sum_{i \neq j} \mu_{nT} w_{ij} |\Sigma_{ij}|,$$

where μ_{nT} is a tuning parameter that converges to zero and w_{ij} is an entry-dependent weight parameter. Let

$$\widehat{f_t} = (\widehat{\Lambda}' \widehat{\Sigma}_u \widehat{\Lambda})^{-1} \widehat{\Lambda}' \widehat{\Sigma}_u^{-1} (y_t - \overline{y}).$$

Assume $\log(n) = o(T)$. Show that as $(n, T) \to \infty$

$$\frac{1}{n}\|\widehat{\Sigma}_u - \Sigma_u\|_F^2 \xrightarrow{p} 0,$$

$$\frac{1}{n}\|\widehat{\Lambda} - \Lambda\|_F^2 \xrightarrow{p} 0,$$

and

$$\|\widehat{f}_t - f_t\| \xrightarrow{p} 0$$

for each t where $\|\cdot\|_F$ is the Frobenius norm.

(6) (Fan, Liao, Liu, 2016) Consider

$$y_t = \Lambda f_t + e_t.$$

Assume Λ is known, $\Lambda = l_n$, and $\Sigma_e = E(e_t e_t') = I$, where l_n denotes the n-dimensional column of ones with $\|l_n l_n'\|_2 = n$. Let $\Sigma = E(y_t y_t')$. Then

$$\Sigma = \text{Var}(f_1) l_n l_n' + I$$

and

$$\widehat{\Sigma} = \widehat{\text{Var}}(f_1) l_n l_n' + I.$$

Note $\|\widehat{\Sigma} - \Sigma\|_2 = |\frac{1}{T}\sum_{t=1}^{T}(f_{1t} - \overline{f}_1)^2 - \text{var}(f_{1t})| \times \|l_n l_n'\|_2$ where $\|A\|_2$ denotes the operator norm of a matrix A. Show that $\frac{\sqrt{T}}{n}\|\widehat{\Sigma} - \Sigma\|_2 = O_p(1)$ and $\|\widehat{\Sigma} - \Sigma\|_2 \to \infty$ if $n > \sqrt{T}$.

(7) Consider

$$y_t = \Lambda f_t + e_t,$$

where f_t is an $r \times 1$ vector of common factors, $y_t = (y_{1t}, \ldots, y_{nt})'$, $\Lambda = (\lambda_1, \ldots, \lambda_n)'$ and $e_t = (e_{1t}, \ldots, e_{nt})'$. Let $F = (f_1, \ldots, f_T)'$ and $Y = (y_1, \ldots, y_T)'$. Assume $\frac{\Lambda\Lambda'}{n} \to \Sigma_\Lambda$ which is positive definite, $E(e_t e_t') = \Sigma = \text{diag}(\sigma_1^2, \ldots, \sigma_n^2)$, $\frac{1}{T}F'F = I_r$ and $\Lambda\Lambda'$ is diagonal with distinct entries. Let $\widehat{F}$ be the first r leading eigenvectors of YY' multiplied by $\sqrt{T}$ and $\widehat{\Lambda} = \frac{Y'\widehat{F}}{T}$. Show that for each i

$$\sqrt{T}(\widehat{\lambda}_i - \lambda_i) \xrightarrow{d} N(0, \sigma_i^2 I_r)$$

if $\frac{\sqrt{T}}{n} \to 0$ for each i,

and

$$\sqrt{T}(\widehat{f}_t - f_t) \xrightarrow{d} N(0, \Sigma_\Lambda^{-1} Q \Sigma_\Lambda)$$

if $\frac{\sqrt{n}}{T} \to 0$ for each t, with

$$\frac{1}{n}\Lambda'\Lambda \to \Sigma_\Lambda$$

and

$$\frac{1}{n}\Lambda'\Sigma\Lambda \to Q.$$

Consider a quasi-likelihood function

$$(Y; \Lambda, F, \Sigma) = -nT\log(2\pi) - \frac{T}{2}\log\det\left|\frac{XX'}{T} + \Sigma\right|$$

$$-\frac{1}{2}\mathrm{tr}\left[Y'\left(\frac{XX'}{T} + \Sigma\right)^{-1}Y\right]$$

with $X = \Lambda F'$ and $\frac{XX'}{T} = \Lambda\Lambda'$. Let $\widetilde{\Lambda}$ and $\widetilde{\Sigma}$ be the quasi-maximum likelihood estimates (QMLE) of Λ and Σ. Show that as $(n, T) \to \infty$ for each i

$$\sqrt{T}(\widetilde{\lambda}_i - \lambda_i) \xrightarrow{d} N(0, \sigma_i^2 I_r)$$

and

$$\sqrt{T}(\widetilde{\sigma}_i^2 - \sigma_i^2) \xrightarrow{d} N(0, (2 + \kappa_i)\sigma_i^4)$$

where κ_i is the excess kurtosis of e_{it}. Define

$$\widetilde{f}_t = (\widetilde{\Lambda}'\widetilde{\Sigma}^{-1}\widetilde{\Lambda})^{-1}\widetilde{\Lambda}'\widetilde{\Sigma}^{-1}y_t.$$

Show that

$$\sqrt{n}(\widetilde{f}_t - f_t) \xrightarrow{d} N(0, Q^{-1})$$

if $\frac{n}{T^2} \to 0$.

(8) (*Continued*) Let

$$\widehat{\beta} = (F'F)^{-1}F'\widehat{F} = \frac{F'\widehat{F}}{T}.$$

Show that

$$\widehat{\beta} - 1 = o_p\left(\frac{1}{\sqrt{T}}\right)$$

if factors are strong, i.e., $\frac{\Lambda'\Lambda}{n} \to \Sigma_\Lambda$. Let $Y = \sqrt{T}\widehat{U}\widehat{D}\widehat{V}'$ with $\widehat{D} = \mathrm{diag}(\widehat{d}_1, \ldots, \widehat{d}_{\min(n,T)})$, and $\widehat{U}'\widehat{U} = \widehat{V}'\widehat{V} = I_r$. Define $\Lambda = UD$ with

$U'U = I_r$ and $D = \text{diag}(d_1, \ldots, d_r)$. By assuming factors are weak, i.e., $d_k \to \rho_k < \infty$, show that

$$\widehat{d}_k \xrightarrow{p} \begin{cases} \sqrt{\left(\rho_k + \dfrac{1}{\rho_k}\right)\left(\rho_k + \dfrac{c}{\rho_k}\right)}\,\sigma & \text{if } \rho_k > c^{1/4}\sigma, \\ (1 + \sqrt{c})\sigma & \text{otherwise} \end{cases}$$

and

$$\widehat{\beta}_k \xrightarrow{p} \begin{cases} \sqrt{\dfrac{\rho_k^4 - c}{\rho_k^4 + \rho_k^2}} & \text{if } \rho_k > c^{1/4}\sigma, \\ 0 & \text{otherwise} \end{cases}$$

if $\Sigma = \sigma^2 I_n$ and $\frac{n}{T} \to c$.

(9) Consider a large factor model as in Bai and Ng (2002),

$$y_{it} = \lambda_i' f_t + u_{it} \text{ for } i = 1, \ldots, n \text{ and } t = 1, \ldots, T, \qquad (3.24)$$

to test the null hypothesis of

$$H_0 : \lambda_i = 0 \qquad (3.25)$$

for all i against the alternative that

$$H_1 : \lambda_i \neq 0$$

for some i. To test the null hypothesis in equation (3.25), a standard F-statistic is defined as

$$F_\lambda(r) = \frac{(\text{RRSS} - \text{URSS})/nr}{\text{URSS}/[n(T - r)]}, \qquad (3.26)$$

where RRSS and URSS denote the residual sum of squares from the restricted and unrestricted models, respectively. Show that the F-statistic can be written as a ratio of the average of r largest eigenvalues and the average of the rest $T - r$ eigenvalues,

$$F_\lambda(r) = \frac{\frac{1}{r}\sum_{j=1}^{r} \widehat{l}_j}{\frac{1}{T-r}\sum_{j=r+1}^{T} \widehat{l}_j}$$

where $\widehat{l}_1, \ldots, \widehat{l}_T$ are eigenvalues of $\frac{1}{n}\sum_{i=1}^{n} X_i X_i'$.

(10) Let X_{ij} be i.i.d. standard normal variables. Write

$$S_n = \left(\frac{1}{n} \sum_{k=1}^{n} X_{ik} X_{jk} \right)_{i,j=1}^{p},$$

which can be considered as a sample covariance matrix with n samples of a p-dimensional mean zero random vector with covariance matrix $I_{p \times p}$. Define

$$T_n = \ln(\det S_n)$$

$$= \sum_{j=1}^{p} \ln \lambda_{n,j},$$

where $\lambda_{n,j}$ are the eigenvalues of S_n, $j = 1, \ldots, p$.

(a) Show that when p is fixed, $\lambda_j \xrightarrow{p} 1$ and hence $T_n \xrightarrow{p} 0$.
(b) Show that

$$\sqrt{\frac{n}{p}} T_n \xrightarrow{d} N(0, 2)$$

   for any fixed p.

(c) One may think that the possibility that T_n is asymptotically normal provided $p = O(n)$. However, this is not the case. Explain (no need to show it formally) why

$$\sqrt{\frac{n}{p}} T_n \to -\infty$$

   when $(p, n) \to \infty$.

(11) Suppose $\widetilde{X}_{it}$ is observed with a measurement error ε_{it} in a large factor model

$$\widetilde{X}_{it} = \lambda_i' f_t + e_{it}$$

with

$$\widetilde{X}_{it} = X_{it} + \varepsilon_{it}$$

and

$$\frac{1}{nT} \sum_{i=1}^{n} \sum_{t=1}^{T} \varepsilon_{it} = O_p \left(\frac{1}{\delta_{nT}^2} \right),$$

where $\delta_{nT} = \min(\sqrt{n}, \sqrt{T})$. Show that PC and IC estimators of the number of factors in Bai and Ng (2002) are still consistent. Impose the conditions/assumptions you need as you see fit.

(12) (Kao and Oh, 2017) Consider a factor model

$$y_{it} = \lambda_i' f_t + \varepsilon_{it},$$

$i = 1, \ldots, n$, $t = 1, \ldots, T$, where f_t is an $r \times 1$ vector of factors, λ_i is an $r \times 1$ vector of factor loadings and r is the number of factors, and $\varepsilon_{it} \overset{\text{i.i.d.}}{\sim} N(0, 1)$. Let

$$\text{IC}(k) = \ln S(k) + k \cdot G(n, T)$$

with

$$S(k) = \frac{1}{nT} \sum_{t=1}^{n} \sum_{t=1}^{T} (y_{it} - \widehat{\lambda}_i'^k \widehat{f}_t^k)^2,$$

where $k < \min(n, T)$, $G(n, T)$ is a penalty function, $\widehat{\lambda}_i^k$ and $\widehat{f}_t^k$ are estimated loadings and factors given by the number of factors k, e.g., Bai and Ng (2002). Define

$$\widehat{k}_{\text{IC}} = \arg\min_k \text{IC}(k).$$

Show that $\text{IC}(k)$ in Bai and Ng (2002) can be written as

$$\text{IC}(k) = \ln\left(\frac{1}{n} \sum_{j=k+1}^{n} \ell_j\right) + k \cdot G(n, T),$$

where $\ell_1 \geq \ell_2 \geq \cdots \geq \ell_n$ denotes the n eigenvalues of an $n \times n$ sample covariance matrix $\frac{1}{T} \sum_{t=1}^{T} x_t' x_t$. Let $\Delta \text{IC}(1) = \text{IC}(r) - \text{IC}(r+1) > 0$, where

$$\text{IC}(r) = \ln\left(\frac{1}{n} \sum_{j=r+1}^{n} \ell_j\right) + r \cdot G(n, T)$$

and

$$\text{IC}(r+1) = \ln\left(\frac{1}{n} \sum_{j=r+2}^{n} \ell_j\right) + (r+1) \times G(n, T).$$

Show that the probability of the number of factors would be overestimated by exactly one has the form

$$P(\Delta\mathrm{IC}(1) > 0) = P\left(\frac{\ell_1(W)}{\mathrm{Tr}(W)} > \xi_{n,T}\right) + O_p\left(\frac{1}{n}\right),$$

where W is an $(n-r) \times (n-r)$ Wishart matrix with identity covariance matrix, $\ell_1(W)$ is the largest eigenvalue of W, $\mathrm{Tr}(W)$ is the sum of $n-r$ eigenvalues of W and

$$\xi_{n,T} = -1 + \sqrt{1 + 2G(n,T)}.$$

Chapter 4

Structural Changes in Panel Data Models

Based on Baltagi, Feng and Kao (2016, 2019), this chapter studies the issue of structural changes in large panel data regression models. Parameter instability due to new policy implementation or major technological shocks is more likely to occur over a longer time span. Consequently, ignoring structural changes may lead to inconsistent estimation and invalid inference.

We consider a heterogeneous panel regression model and extend Pesaran's (2006) work on common correlated effect (CCE) estimators for large heterogeneous panels with a general multifactor error structure by allowing for unknown common structural breaks. We propose a general framework that includes heterogeneous panel data models and structural break models as special cases. The least squares method proposed by Bai (1997a, 2010) is applied to estimate the common change points, and the consistency of the estimated change points is established. We find that the CCE estimators have the same asymptotic distribution as if the true change points were known.

Then, we discuss the case of endogenous regressors and structural changes in error factor loadings. Allowing for endogenous regressors makes the proposed panel regression empirically more appealing. An extensive Monte Carlo study is employed to examine the proposed estimator in various scenarios. In addition, an empirical example of infrastructure investment is used to illustrate the estimation of common break date and slope parameters.

Finally, we also review the recent development in this literature, including Lasso-type approaches in Qian and Su (2017) and Okui and Wang (2018).

4.1. Heterogeneous Panels with a Common Structural Break

In a heterogeneous panel data model:

$$y_{it} = x_{it}'\beta_i + e_{it}, \quad i = 1, \ldots, n; \ t = 1, \ldots, T, \tag{4.1}$$

x_{it} is a $p \times 1$ vector of explanatory variables, and the errors are cross-sectionally correlated, modeled by a multifactor structure

$$e_{it} = \gamma_i'f_t + \varepsilon_{it}, \tag{4.2}$$

where f_t is an $m \times 1$ vector of unobserved factors and γ_i is the corresponding loading vector. Here, ε_{it} is the idiosyncratic error independent of x_{it}. However, x_{it} could be affected by the unobservable common effects f_t. Projecting x_{it} on f_t, we obtain

$$x_{it} = \Gamma_i'f_t + v_{it}, \quad i = 1, \ldots, n; \ t = 1, \ldots, T, \tag{4.3}$$

where Γ_i is an $m \times p$ factor loading matrix and v_{it} is a $p \times 1$ vector of disturbances. Due to the correlation between x_{it} and e_{it}, ordinary least squares (OLS) for each individual regression could be inconsistent. Thus, Pesaran (2006) develops the CCE estimator of β_i by least squares using augmented data.

In this chapter, we allow for structural breaks to occur in some or all components of the slopes β_i. Following Bai (2010) and Kim (2011), a structural break at a common unknown date k_0 is assumed. This could be due to a macro policy implementation or a technological shock that affects all markets or firms at the same time. More formally,

$$y_{it} = x_{it}'\beta_i(k_0) + e_{it}, \quad i = 1, \ldots, n; \ t = 1, \ldots, T, \tag{4.4}$$

where some or all components of $\beta_i(k_0)$ are different before and after the date k_0. Following Bai (1997a), this structural break model can be written as

$$y_{it} = \begin{cases} x_{it}'\beta_i + e_{it}, & t = 1, \ldots, k_0, \\ x_{it}'\beta_i + z_{it}'\delta_i + e_{it}, & t = k_0 + 1, \ldots, T, \end{cases} \tag{4.5}$$

$i = 1, \ldots, n$, where $z_{it} = R'x_{it}$ denotes a $q \times 1$ subvector of x_{it} with $R' = (0_{q \times (p-q)}, I_q)$. Here, I_q is the $q \times q$ identity matrix with $q \leq p$. The case where $q < p$ denotes a partial change model, while the case where $q = p$ is for a pure change model. Pauwels, Chan and Mancini-Griffoli (2012) propose a testing procedure for k_0 in this setting.

Substituting $z_{it} = R'x_{it}$ in (4.5), we obtain

$$\beta_i(k_0) = \beta_i + R\delta_i \cdot 1\{t > k_0\}$$

$$= \begin{cases} \beta_{1i} = \beta_i, & t = 1, \ldots, k_0, \\ \beta_{2i} = \beta_i + R\delta_i, & t = k_0 + 1, \ldots, T, \end{cases}$$

so that $\beta_{2i} - \beta_{1i} = R\delta_i$, and δ_i denotes the slope jump for i. When $\delta_i = 0$, there is no structural break in the slope.

The case of multiple break points will be discussed in Section 4.5. In Sections 4.2 and 4.3, we consider the simple case of one common break as in model (4.5). Compared with the heterogeneous panel data model considered in Pesaran (2006), equation (4.5) has the extra component $R\delta_i \cdot 1\{t > k_0\}$ in the slope, involving the unknown structural change point k_0. Thus, ignoring the structural break in the slopes may invalidate the CCE estimator proposed by Pesaran (2006). Compared with the simple mean-shift panel data model in Bai (2010), our model is enriched by adding a regression structure with $x_{it} \neq 1$ in general, as well as cross-sectional dependence characterized by a multifactor structure in the errors. When there are no unobservable common factors f_t, our model (4.4) can also be regarded as an extension of Bai (1997a) to a panel data setting. In addition, the model (4.4) above is similar to Kim (2011), who considered the case of a deterministic time trend with a common break.

Before proceeding to the general model (4.5), we start with a simple case of heterogeneous panels in the absence of common correlated effects f_t and then extend the main results to the general case.

To estimate the common change point k_0, we need the following additional assumptions.

Assumption 4.1. $k_0 = [\tau_0 T]$, where $\tau_0 \in (0, 1)$ and $[\cdot]$ is the greatest integer function.

Note that unlike the time-series model considered by Bai (1997a), the restriction of $\tau_0 \in (0, 1)$ is unnecessary in a panel mean-shift setup considered by Bai (2010) as long as $T/n \to 0$. However, this assumption is required in our heterogeneous panels with general regressors. Enough observations are needed to consistently estimate the slopes in each regime.

Define $\phi_n = \sum_{i=1}^n \delta_i' \delta_i$. For series i, $\delta_i' \delta_i$ measures the magnitude of the structural break, thus ϕ_n is an indicator of the break magnitude for all n series sharing a common break.

Assumption 4.2. $\phi_n \to \infty$ and (i) $\frac{\phi_n}{n}$ is bounded as $n \to \infty$; (ii) $\phi_n \frac{T}{n} \to \infty$ as $(n, T) \to \infty$.

δ_i could be random with a finite variance across i, with Assumption 4.2(i) describing this case. When δ_i is considered as random, Assumption 4.2 means that $\frac{\phi_n}{n}$ is stochastically bounded in part (i), and that $\frac{n}{\phi_n T}$ converges in probability to 0 in part (ii). Alternatively, δ_i could denote fixed parameters. Since Assumption 4.2(i) allows for the case where $\frac{\phi_n}{n} \to 0$ as $n \to \infty$, Assumption 4.2(ii) implies that it cannot converge to 0 too fast. Consequently, Assumption 4.2(i) imposes an upper bound on $\frac{\phi_n}{n}$, while Assumption 4.2(ii) imposes a lower bound on $\frac{\phi_n}{n}$.

In case T grows at a comparable rate or faster than n, i.e., $T = O(n^\psi)$ with $\psi \geq 1$, Assumption 4.2(ii) implies that ϕ_n can diverge at any rate. When ϕ_n increases at a rate less than n, Assumption 4.2(ii) allows for the possibility of no structural break in some series. Assumption $\phi_n \to \infty$ rules out the case where there is no structural break in the slopes in all series.

4.2. Model 1: No Common Correlated Effects

In this section, we assume that there are no unobserved common effects f_t in the errors and regressors. Or the loading vectors γ_i and Γ_i are equal to zero. For $i = 1, \ldots, n$,

$$
y_{it} = \begin{cases} x_{it}' \beta_i + \varepsilon_{it}, & t = 1, \ldots, k_0, \\ x_{it}' \beta_i + z_{it}' \delta_i + \varepsilon_{it}, & t = k_0 + 1, \ldots, T. \end{cases} \tag{4.6}
$$

This is the special case of cross-sectionally independent errors, where a common break k_0 occurs in the heterogeneous slopes. This model generalizes Bai's (1997a, 2010) and Pesaran and Smith's (1995) models. When $n = 1$, equation (4.6) is the time-series model considered in Bai (1997a). When $x_{it} = 1$, this model reduces to the one in Bai (2010). In case the lagged-dependent variable is included in x_{it} and $\delta_i = 0$, equation (4.6) turns out to be the setup in Pesaran and Smith (1995).

Assumption 4.3. (i) The disturbances $\varepsilon_{it}, i = 1, \ldots, n$, are cross-sectionally independent; (ii) for each series i, ε_{it} is independent of x_{it} for all i and t; (iii) ε_{it} is a stationary process with absolute summable autocovariances,

$$\varepsilon_{it} = \sum_{l=0}^{\infty} a_{il} \zeta_{i,t-l},$$

where $\{\zeta_{it}, t = 1, \ldots, T\}$ are i.i.d. random variables with finite fourth-order cumulants. Assume $0 < \text{Var}(\varepsilon_{it}) = \sum_{l=0}^{\infty} a_{il}^2 = \sigma_i^2 < \infty$. Also, for the $T \times 1$ vector $\varepsilon_i = (\varepsilon_{i1}, \varepsilon_{i2}, \ldots, \varepsilon_{iT})'$, $\text{Var}(\varepsilon_i) = \Sigma_{\varepsilon,i}$.

When ε_{it} is serially uncorrelated, lagged-dependent variables are predetermined and can be included as regressors in (4.6).

Assumption 4.4. For $i = 1, \ldots, n$, the matrices $(1/j) \sum_{t=1}^{j} x_{it} x_{it}'$, $(1/j) \sum_{t=T-j+1}^{T} x_{it} x_{it}'$, $(1/j) \sum_{t=k_0-j+1}^{k_0} x_{it} x_{it}'$ and $(1/j) \sum_{t=k_0+1}^{k_0+j} x_{it} x_{it}'$ are stochastically bounded and have minimum eigenvalues bounded away from zero in probability for all large j. In addition, for each i, $(1/T) \sum_{t=1}^{T} x_{it} x_{it}'$ converges in probability to a nonrandom and positive definite matrix as $T \to \infty$.

This assumption is borrowed from Assumptions A3 and A4 in Bai (1997a). Its counterpart across the cross-sectional dimension is also needed.

Assumption 4.5. For any positive finite integer s, the matrices $\frac{1}{n} \sum_{i=1}^{n} \sum_{t=k_0-s+1}^{k_0} x_{it} x_{it}'$ and $\frac{1}{n} \sum_{i=1}^{n} \sum_{t=k_0+1}^{k_0+s} x_{it} x_{it}'$, $i = 1, \ldots, n$, are stochastically bounded, with minimum eigenvalues bounded away from zero in probability for large n. In addition, for each t, $(1/n) \sum_{i=1}^{n} x_{it} x_{it}'$ is stochastically bounded as $n \to \infty$.

Assumption 4.6. $\{\delta_i, i = 1, \ldots, n\}$ are drawn independently of $\{x_{it}, i = 1, \ldots, n\}$.

Let $b_i = (\beta_i', \delta_i')', i = 1, \ldots, n$, denote the slope parameters. In the random coefficient model considered by Pesaran and Smith (1995) and Pesaran (2006), we assume the following.

Assumption 4.7. For $i = 1, \ldots, n$,

$$b_i = b + v_{b,i}, v_{b,i} \sim \text{i.i.d.}(0, \Sigma_b), \tag{4.7}$$

where $b = (\beta', \delta')'$, $v_{b,i} = \begin{pmatrix} v_{\beta,i} \\ v_{\delta,i} \end{pmatrix}$ and $\Sigma_b = \begin{pmatrix} \Sigma_\beta & 0 \\ 0 & \Sigma_\delta \end{pmatrix}$ for $i = 1, 2, \ldots, n$, where $\|b\| < \infty$, $\|\Sigma_b\| < \infty$, and the random deviations $v_{b,i}$ are independent of x_{it} and ε_{jt} for all i, j and t.

For any matrix or vector A, the norm of A is defined as $\|A\| = \sqrt{\mathrm{tr}(AA')}$. This assumption is a simplified version of Assumption 4 of Pesaran (2006). Under Assumption 4.6, $\{\delta_i, i = 1, \ldots, n\}$ are not necessarily random. When $\{\delta_i, i = 1, \ldots, n\}$ are considered as random, as part of Assumption 4.7, Assumption 4.6 becomes redundant. Under Assumption 4.7, $\Sigma_\delta \neq 0$ implies a structural break in the slope.

By (4.4),

$$y_{it} = x'_{it}\beta_i + x'_{it}R\delta_i 1\{t > k_0\} + \varepsilon_{it},$$

if the structural break is ignored, the term $x'_{it}R\delta_i 1\{t > k_0\}$ is absorbed in the error term $\hat{\varepsilon}_{it} = x'_{it}R\delta_i 1\{t > k_0\} + \varepsilon_{it}$. This leads to inconsistency of OLS for each series due to endogeneity. Thus, estimating k_0 first is essential.

Let $Y_i = (y_{i1}, \ldots, y_{iT})'$, $X_i = (x_{i1}, \ldots, x_{iT})'$ and $\varepsilon_i = (\varepsilon_{i1}, \varepsilon_{i2}, \ldots, \varepsilon_{iT})'$ denote the stacked data and errors for individual $i = 1, \ldots, n$ over the time periods observed. Similarly, define $Z_{0i} = (0, \ldots, 0, z_{i,k_0+1}, \ldots, z_{iT})'$. Equation (4.6) can be written in matrix form as

$$Y_i = X_i\beta_i + Z_{0i}\delta_i + \varepsilon_i, \quad i = 1, \ldots, n. \tag{4.8}$$

The parameters of interest are β_i, δ_i and the change point k_0. We first estimate k_0 using least squares as proposed by Bai (1997a, 2010). For any possible change point $k = 1, \ldots, T - 1$, define the matrices $X_{2i}(k) = (0, \ldots, 0, x_{i,k+1}, \ldots, x_{iT})'$, and $Z_{2i}(k) = (0, \ldots, 0, z_{i,k+1}, \ldots, z_{iT})'$. When k happens to be the true change point k_0, $Z_{2i}(k_0) = Z_{0i}$. Define $X_{0i} = X_{2i}(k_0)$, thus $Z_{0i} = X_{0i}R$. To make the notation more compact, we let $\mathbb{X}_i(k) = (X_i, Z_{2i}(k))$ and $\mathbb{X}_{0i} = (X_i, Z_{0i})$. Thus, (4.8) becomes

$$Y_i = X_i\beta_i + Z_{0i}\delta_i + \varepsilon_i = \mathbb{X}_{0i}b_i + \varepsilon_i, \quad i = 1, \ldots, n. \tag{4.9}$$

Given any $k = 1, \ldots, T - 1$, one can estimate b_i by least squares,

$$\hat{b}_i(k) = \begin{pmatrix} \hat{\beta}_i(k) \\ \hat{\delta}_i(k) \end{pmatrix} = [\mathbb{X}_i(k)'\mathbb{X}_i(k)]^{-1}\mathbb{X}_i(k)'Y_i, \quad i = 1, \ldots, n. \tag{4.10}$$

The corresponding sum of squared residuals is given by

$$\text{SSR}_i(k) = [Y_i - \mathbb{X}_i(k)\hat{b}_i(k)]'[Y_i - \mathbb{X}_i(k)\hat{b}_i(k)]$$
$$= [Y_i - X_i\hat{\beta}_i(k) - Z_{2i}(k)\hat{\delta}_i(k)]'[Y_i - X_i\hat{\beta}_i(k) - Z_{2i}(k)\hat{\delta}_i(k)],$$

$i = 1, \dots, n$. Note that both $\hat{b}_i(k)$ and $\text{SSR}_i(k)$ depend on k. For each series i, k_0 can be estimated by $\arg\min_{1 \leq k \leq T-1} \text{SSR}_i(k)$ as in Bai (1997a). Given that the structural break occurs at a common date for all cross-sectional units in the panel setup, the least squares estimator of k_0 is defined as

$$\hat{k} = \arg \min_{1 \leq k \leq T-1} \sum_{i=1}^{n} \text{SSR}_i(k). \tag{4.11}$$

In Baltagi *et al.* (2016), different weights are used in the sum (4.11) above to allow for the possibility of different magnitudes, e.g., different variances, across series.

When $n = 1$, $\hat{k}$ defined in (4.11) boils down to the change-point estimator considered by Bai (1997a) in a time-series setting, with $\hat{k} - k_0 = O_p(1)$ for large T. In time-series models, only the break fraction $\tau_0 = k_0/T$, instead of k_0 itself, can be consistently estimated. In a multivariate time series setup, Bai, Lumsdaine and Stock (1998) show that the width of the confidence interval of the estimated change point decreases with the number of time series. This result implies that cross-sectional observations with common breaks improve the accuracy of the estimated change point. In fact, Bai (2010) shows that the least squares estimator of the change point is consistent in a panel mean-shift model, i.e., $\hat{k} - k_0 = o_p(1)$. A similar result is also obtained by Kim (2011) in a panel deterministic time trend model. In our heterogeneous panel regression model, equation (4.11) combines the information from each series by summing up $\text{SSR}_i(k)$. With a large n, $\hat{k}$ uses more information provided by the multiple time series sharing a common break. Consequently, the panel data estimator $\hat{k}$ is more accurate than the time-series estimator and achieves consistency, i.e., $\hat{k} - k_0 \xrightarrow{p} 0$ as $(n, T) \to \infty$.

Theorem 4.1. *Under Assumptions 4.1–4.6 (or 4.7),* $\lim_{(n,T) \to \infty} P(\hat{k} = k_0) = 1$.

Given the estimated change point $\hat{k}$, the corresponding estimator of the slopes is $\hat{b}_i = \hat{b}_i(\hat{k})$, $i = 1, \dots, n$. When b_i, $i = 1, \dots, n$, are considered as random variables under Assumption 4.7, the cross-sectional mean b can be consistently estimated by the mean group estimator proposed by Pesaran and Smith (1995) and Pesaran (2006):

$$\hat{b}_{\mathrm{MG}} = \frac{1}{n}\sum_{i=1}^{n}\hat{b}_i = \frac{1}{n}\sum_{i=1}^{n}[\mathbb{X}_i(\hat{k})_i'\mathbb{X}_i(\hat{k})]_i^{-1}\mathbb{X}_i(\hat{k})'Y_i. \tag{4.12}$$

4.3. Model 2: Common Correlated Effects

In this section, we extend Model 1 to the general model with common correlated effects (4.5): for $i = 1, \ldots, n$,

$$
\begin{aligned}
y_{it} &= x_{it}'\beta_i(k_0) + e_{it} \\
&= \begin{cases} x_{it}'\beta_i + e_{it}, & t = 1, \ldots, k_0, \\ x_{it}'\beta_i + z_{it}'\delta_i + e_{it}, & t = k_0 + 1, \ldots, T, \end{cases}
\end{aligned}
$$

where $e_{it} = \gamma_i'f_t + \varepsilon_{it}$. The regressors x_{it}, $i = 1, \ldots, n$, are allowed to be correlated with the unobservable factors f_t modeled in (4.3), $x_{it} = \Gamma_i'f_t + v_{it}$. When $\delta_i = 0$, the model reduces to the one considered by Pesaran (2006). Kim (2011) considers the special case of $x_{it} = (1, t)'$. Recently, a simplified model with $x_{it} = 1$ and fixed T is considered by Westerlund (2019). In this heterogeneous panel data model with a common break k_0, the parameters of interest are $b_i = (\beta_i', \delta_i')'$, $i = 1, \ldots, n$, and the change point k_0. The following assumptions are needed.

Assumption 4.8. Common factors f_t, $t = 1, \ldots, T$, are covariance stationary with absolute summable autocovariances, independent of errors ε_{is} and v_{is} for all i, s, t.

Assumption 4.9. Errors ε_{is} and v_{jt} are independent for all i, j, s, t. Moreover, v_{it}, $i = 1, \ldots, n$, are linear stationary processes with absolute summable autocovariances, $v_{it} = \sum_{l=0}^{\infty} S_{il}v_{i,t-l}$, where $(\zeta_{it}, v_{it}')'$ are $(p+1) \times 1$ vectors of i.i.d. random variables with variance–covariance matrix I_{p+1} and finite fourth-order cumulants, and

$$\mathrm{Var}(v_{it}) = \sum_{l=0}^{\infty} S_{il}S_{il}' = \Sigma_{i,v}, \quad \text{and} \quad 0 < \|\Sigma_{i,v}\| < \infty.$$

Assumption 4.10. Factor loadings γ_i and Γ_i are i.i.d. across i, and independent of ε_{jt}, v_{jt} and f_t for all i, j, t. Assume $\gamma_i = \gamma + \eta_i$, $\eta_i \sim$ i.i.d.$(0, \Omega_\eta)$

and $\Gamma_i = \Gamma + \xi_i$, $\xi_i \sim$ i.i.d.$(0, \Omega_\xi)$, $i = 1, \ldots, n$, where the means γ, Γ are nonzero and fixed and the variances Ω_η, Ω_ξ are finite.

Together with Assumptions 4.3 and 4.7, Assumptions 4.8–4.10 given above are the same as Assumptions 1–3 of Pesaran (2006), with the additional restrictions $\gamma \neq 0$ and $\Gamma \neq 0$.

The correlation between x_{it} and e_{it} due to unobserved common factors f_t renders OLS inconsistent. If f_t were observable, it could be treated as a regressor, and this correlation can be removed using a partitioned regression. Let $F = (f_1, f_2, \ldots, f_T)'$, then the corresponding orthogonal projection matrix is given by $M_f = I_T - F(F'F)^{-1}F'$. In this case, equation (4.5) can be written in matrix form as

$$Y_i = X_i\beta_i + Z_{0i}\delta_i + F\gamma_i + \varepsilon_i, \quad i = 1, \ldots, n. \tag{4.13}$$

Premultiplying (4.13) by M_f, we get

$$\breve{Y}_i = \breve{X}_i\beta_i + \breve{Z}_{0i}\delta_i + \breve{\varepsilon}_i, \quad i = 1, \ldots, n, \tag{4.14}$$

which is of the same form as equation (4.8) considered in Model 1 of no factor structure above, with transformed data $\breve{Y}_i = M_f Y_i$, $\breve{X}_i = M_f X_i = M_f V_i$, $\breve{Z}_{0i}(k_0) = M_f Z_{0i}$ and $\breve{\varepsilon}_i = M_f \varepsilon_i$. For each $i = 1, \ldots, n$, the $T \times p$ vector V_i denotes $(v_{i1}, \ldots, v_{iT})'$. Conditional on F, $(\breve{X}_i, \breve{Z}_{0i})$ and $\breve{\varepsilon}_i$ are uncorrelated under Assumption 4.9.

However, f_t, $t = 1, \ldots, T$, are unobservable. To proceed, we follow Pesaran's (2006) idea of using the cross-sectional averages of y_{it} and x_{it} as proxies for f_t. Combining (4.5) and (4.3) yields

$$\underset{(p+1)\times 1}{w_{it}} = \begin{pmatrix} y_{it} \\ x_{it} \end{pmatrix} = \underset{(p+1)\times m}{C_i(k_0)'} \underset{m\times 1}{f_t} + \underset{(p+1)\times 1}{u_{it}(k_0)}, \tag{4.15}$$

where

$$\underset{m\times(p+1)}{C_i(k_0)} = (\gamma_i, \Gamma_i) \begin{pmatrix} 1 & 0 \\ \beta_i(k_0) & I_p \end{pmatrix},$$

$$u_{it}(k_0) = \begin{pmatrix} \varepsilon_{it} + v'_{it}\beta_i(k_0) \\ v_{it} \end{pmatrix}.$$

Note that like $\beta_i(k_0)$, the slope $C_i(k_0)$ in (4.15) also shifts at k_0.

$$C_i(k_0) = \begin{cases} C_{1i} = (\gamma_i + \Gamma_i\beta_{1i}, \ \Gamma_i), & t = 1, \ldots, k_0, \\ C_{2i} = (\gamma_i + \Gamma_i\beta_{2i}, \ \Gamma_i), & t = k_0 + 1, \ldots, T. \end{cases} \tag{4.16}$$

Common break k_0 splits the data generating process for all individuals into two regimes, and each regime has the same structure as that considered in Pesaran (2006). Consequently, unobserved common factors f_t can be partialled out by using cross-sectional averages in the same spirit.

Let $\bar{w}_t = \sum_{i=1}^{n} \theta_i w_{it}$ be the cross-sectional averages of w_{it} using weights θ_i, $i = 1, \ldots, n$. In particular,

$$\bar{w}_t = \bar{C}(k_0)' f_t + \bar{u}_t(k_0), \tag{4.17}$$

where

$$\bar{C}(k_0) = \sum_{i=1}^{n} \theta_i C_i(k_0) = \begin{cases} \bar{C}_1 = \sum_{i=1}^{n} \theta_i C_{1i}, & t = 1, \ldots, k_0, \\ \bar{C}_2 = \sum_{i=1}^{n} \theta_i C_{2i}, & t = k_0 + 1, \ldots, T. \end{cases}$$

The common break assumption is needed, otherwise $\bar{C}(k_0)$ is not well defined. Now $\bar{u}_t(k_0)$ is defined as

$$\bar{u}_t(k_0) = \sum_{i=1}^{n} \theta_i u_{it}(k_0)$$

$$= \begin{cases} \left(\begin{array}{c} \bar{\varepsilon}_t + \sum_{i=1}^{n} \theta_i v_{it}' \beta_{1i} \\ \bar{v}_t \end{array} \right), & t = 1, \ldots, k_0, \\ \\ \left(\begin{array}{c} \bar{\varepsilon}_t + \sum_{i=1}^{n} \theta_i v_{it}' \beta_{2i} \\ \bar{v}_t \end{array} \right), & t = k_0 + 1, \ldots, T. \end{cases} \tag{4.18}$$

As in Pesaran (2006), the weights θ_i, $i = 1, \ldots, n$, satisfy conditions: $\theta_i = O(\frac{1}{n})$, $\sum_{i=1}^{n} \theta_i = 1$ and $\sum_{i=1}^{n} |\theta_i| < \infty$.

Assumption 4.11. $\text{Rank}(\bar{C}_1) = \text{Rank}(\bar{C}_2) = m \leq p + 1$.

We assume that the rank condition is satisfied. Pesaran (2006) shows that in the case of deficient rank, it is impossible to obtain consistent estimators of the individual slope coefficients, but their cross-sectional mean can be consistently estimated. When $\bar{C}(k_0)$ is of full rank, f_t can be written as

$$f_t = \left[\bar{C}(k_0)\bar{C}(k_0)'\right]^{-1} \bar{C}(k_0)(\bar{w}_t - \bar{u}_t(k_0)).$$

From (4.16), the matrix $\bar{C}(k_0)\bar{C}(k_0)'$ has two regimes, shifting at k_0,

$$\bar{C}(k_0)\bar{C}(k_0)' = \begin{cases} \bar{C}_1'\bar{C}_1, & t = 1, \ldots, k_0, \\ \bar{C}_2'\bar{C}_2, & t = k_0 + 1, \ldots, T. \end{cases}$$

Assumption 4.11 implies that $\bar{C}(k_0)\bar{C}(k_0)'$ is invertible. As shown in Lemma 1 of Pesaran (2006), the cross-sectional average of the errors vanish in both regimes as $n \to \infty$, where $\bar{\varepsilon}_t = \sum_{i=1}^n \theta_i \varepsilon_{it}$, $\bar{v}_t = \sum_{i=1}^n \theta_i v_{it}$, yielding

$$f_t - \left[\bar{C}(k_0)\bar{C}(k_0)'\right]^{-1} \bar{C}(k_0)\bar{w}_t \overset{p}{\to} 0. \tag{4.19}$$

This suggests that it is asymptotically valid to use $\bar{w}_t$ as observable proxies for f_t. Let $\bar{W} = (\bar{w}_1, \bar{w}_2, \ldots, \bar{w}_T)'$ denote the $T \times (p + 1)$ matrix of cross-sectional averages. Denote the $T \times T$ matrix M_w by $M_w = I_T - \bar{W}(\bar{W}'\bar{W})^{-1}\bar{W}'$. Thus, similar to the result $M_f F = 0$, by (4.19) it is expected that the terms involving $M_w F$ are ignorable asymptotically as $n \to \infty$.

Premultiplying (4.13) by M_w instead of M_f, we obtain

$$M_w Y_i = M_w X_i \beta_i + M_w Z_{0i} \delta_i + M_w F \gamma_i + M_w \varepsilon_i, \quad i = 1, \ldots, n. \tag{4.20}$$

Let the $T \times p$ matrix $\tilde{X}_i = M_w X_i = (\tilde{x}_{i1}, \ldots, \tilde{x}_{iT})'$ denote the transformed regressors. Similarly, define $\tilde{Y}_i = M_w Y_i$, $\tilde{Z}_{0i} = M_w Z_{0i}$ and $\tilde{\varepsilon}_i = M_w \varepsilon_i$. Thus, equation (4.20) becomes

$$\begin{aligned} \tilde{Y}_i &= \tilde{X}_i \beta_i + \tilde{Z}_{0i} \delta_i + M_w F \gamma_i + \tilde{\varepsilon}_i \\ &= \tilde{X}_i \beta_i + \tilde{Z}_{0i} \delta_i + \tilde{\varepsilon}_i^0, \quad i = 1, \ldots, n, \end{aligned} \tag{4.21}$$

where $\tilde{\varepsilon}_i^0 = M_w F \gamma_i + \tilde{\varepsilon}_i$.

Lemma 4.5 in Section 4.8 shows that each element of $M_w F \gamma_i$ is of order $O_p(\frac{1}{\sqrt{n}})$ and vanishes as $(n, T) \to \infty$, implying that $\tilde{\varepsilon}_i^0$ can be treated as $\tilde{\varepsilon}_i$ asymptotically. Based on this intuition, we can follow the procedure proposed in Model 1 above to estimate k_0 and $b_i = (\beta_i', \delta_i')'$, using transformed data $\{\tilde{Y}_i, \tilde{X}_i, i = 1, \ldots, n\}$.

For any possible change point $k = 1, \ldots, T-1$, define matrices $\tilde{Z}_{2i}(k) = M_w Z_{2i}(k)$, $\tilde{\mathbb{X}}_i(k) = (\tilde{X}_i, \tilde{Z}_{2i}(k))$ and $\tilde{\mathbb{X}}_{0i} = (\tilde{X}_i, \tilde{Z}_{0i})$. With new notation, equation (4.21) becomes

$$\tilde{Y}_i = \tilde{\mathbb{X}}_{0i} b_i + \tilde{\varepsilon}_i^0, \quad i = 1, \ldots, n. \tag{4.22}$$

Given k, slope b_i can be estimated by least squares,

$$\tilde{b}_i(k) = \begin{pmatrix} \tilde{\beta}_i(k) \\ \tilde{\delta}_i(k) \end{pmatrix} = [\tilde{\mathbb{X}}_i(k)'\tilde{\mathbb{X}}_i(k)]^{-1}\tilde{\mathbb{X}}_i(k)'\tilde{Y}_i, \quad i = 1, \ldots, n. \tag{4.23}$$

The resulting sum of squared residuals is

$$\begin{aligned}
\widetilde{\text{SSR}}_i(k) &= [\tilde{Y}_i - \tilde{\mathbb{X}}_i(k)\tilde{b}_i(k)]'[\tilde{Y}_i - \tilde{\mathbb{X}}_i(k)\tilde{b}_i(k)] \\
&= [\tilde{Y}_i - \tilde{X}_i\tilde{\beta}_i(k) - \tilde{Z}_{2i}(k)\tilde{\delta}_i(k)]' \\
&\quad \times [\tilde{Y}_i - \tilde{X}_i\tilde{\beta}_i(k) - \tilde{Z}_{2i}(k)\tilde{\delta}_i(k)], \quad i = 1, \ldots, n,
\end{aligned}$$

and the estimator of k_0 is defined similarly as

$$\tilde{k} = \arg \min_{1 \leq k \leq T-1} \sum_i \widetilde{\text{SSR}}_i(k). \tag{4.24}$$

Assumption 4.12. For $i = 1, \ldots, n$, the matrices $\frac{1}{T}X_i'M_wX_i$ and $\frac{1}{T}X_i'M_fX_i$ are nonsingular, and their inverses have finite second-order moments.

This assumption of identifying b_i and b is adopted from Pesaran (2006). Let $\tilde{x}_{it}'$ be the tth element of matrix $\tilde{X}_i$, $i = 1, \ldots, n$. To identify k_0, we need a modified version of Assumptions 4.4–4.6.

Assumption 4.13. For $i = 1, \ldots, n$, the matrices $(1/j)\sum_{t=1}^{j} \tilde{x}_{it}\tilde{x}_{it}'$, $(1/j)\sum_{t=T-j+1}^{T} \tilde{x}_{it}\tilde{x}_{it}'$, $(1/j)\sum_{t=k_0-j+1}^{k_0} \tilde{x}_{it}\tilde{x}_{it}'$ and $(1/j)\sum_{t=k_0+1}^{k_0+j} \tilde{x}_{it}\tilde{x}_{it}'$ are stochastically bounded and have minimum eigenvalues bounded away from zero in probability for all large j. In addition, for each i, $(1/T)\sum_{t=1}^{T} \tilde{x}_{it}\tilde{x}_{it}'$ converges in probability to a nonrandom and positive definite matrix as $T \to \infty$.

Assumption 4.14. For any positive finite integer s, the matrices $\frac{1}{n}\sum_{i=1}^{n}\sum_{t=k_0-s+1}^{k_0} \tilde{x}_{it}\tilde{x}_{it}'$ and $\frac{1}{n}\sum_{i=1}^{n}\sum_{t=k_0+1}^{k_0+s} \tilde{x}_{it}\tilde{x}_{it}'$, $i = 1, \ldots, n$, are stochastically bounded, with minimum eigenvalues bounded away from zero in probability for large n. In addition, for each t, $(1/n)\sum_{i=1}^{n} \tilde{x}_{it}\tilde{x}_{it}'$ is stochastically bounded as $n \to \infty$.

Assumption 4.15. $\{\delta_i, i = 1, \ldots, n\}$ are drawn independently of the process of $\{\tilde{x}_{it}, i = 1, \ldots, n\}$.

Alternatively, under a random coefficient model, we have a slightly different version of Assumption 4.7.

Assumption 4.16. For $i = 1, \ldots, n$,

$$b_i = b + v_{b,i}, v_{b,i} \sim \text{i.i.d.}(0, \Sigma_b),$$

where $b = (\beta', \delta')'$, $v_{b,i} = \begin{pmatrix} v_{\beta,i} \\ v_{\delta,i} \end{pmatrix}$ and $\Sigma_b = \begin{pmatrix} \Sigma_\beta & 0 \\ 0 & \Sigma_\delta \end{pmatrix}$ for $i = 1, 2, \ldots, n$, where $\|b\| < \infty$, $\|\Sigma_b\| < \infty$, and the random deviations $v_{b,i}$ are independent of γ_j, Γ_j, ε_{jt}, and v_{jt} for all i, j and t.

Under Assumption 4.16, b_i is independent of Γ_j, implying that as $n \to \infty$, $\bar{C}_1 = \sum_{i=1}^{n} \theta_i C_{1i} \xrightarrow{P} E(C_{1i}) = (\gamma + \Gamma\beta, \Gamma)$ and $\bar{C}_2 \xrightarrow{P} E(C_{2i}) = (\gamma + \Gamma(\beta + R\delta), \Gamma)$. In this case, rank condition (Assumption 4.11) requires nonzero means for γ and Γ in Assumption 4.10 when n is large. Similarly in Model 1, when $\{\delta_i, i = 1, \ldots, n\}$ are considered as random, as part of Assumption 4.16, Assumption 4.15 becomes redundant.

After the transformation (4.20), it can be shown that the change point estimator $\tilde{k}$ is still consistent in a linear model with a multifactor error structure (4.5), i.e., $\tilde{k} - k_0 = o_p(1)$.

Theorem 4.2. *Under Assumptions* 4.1–4.3, 4.8–4.15 (*or* 4.16), $\lim_{(n,T) \to \infty} P(\tilde{k} = k_0) = 1$.

Theorem 4.2 can be proved similarly to Theorem 4.1, see the technical details in Section 4.8.

Given the change point estimator $\tilde{k}$, the CCE estimator of the slope coefficients can be written as

$$\tilde{b}_i = \tilde{b}_i(\tilde{k}) = [\tilde{X}_i(\tilde{k})'\tilde{X}_i(\tilde{k})]^{-1}\tilde{X}_i(\tilde{k})'\tilde{Y}_i, \quad i = 1, \ldots, n.$$

With the consistency of $\tilde{k}$, the asymptotics of $\tilde{b}_i$ can be established.

Proposition 4.1. *Under Assumptions* 4.1–4.3, 4.8–4.15, *and* $\sqrt{T}/n \to 0$ *as* $(n,T) \to \infty$, *for each* i,

$$\sqrt{T}(\tilde{b}_i - b_i) \xrightarrow{d} N\left(0, \Sigma_{\tilde{X},i}^{-1} \Sigma_{\tilde{X}\tilde{\varepsilon},i} \Sigma_{\tilde{X},i}^{-1}\right),$$

where

$$\Sigma_{\tilde{\mathbb{X}},i} = \plim_{T\to\infty} \frac{1}{T}\tilde{\mathbb{X}}'_{0i}\tilde{\mathbb{X}}_{0i},$$

$$\Sigma_{\tilde{\mathbb{X}}\tilde{\varepsilon},i} = \plim_{T\to\infty} \frac{1}{T}\tilde{\mathbb{X}}'_{0i}\Sigma_{\varepsilon,i}\tilde{\mathbb{X}}_{0i}, \quad i = 1,\ldots,n.$$

An additional condition $\sqrt{T}/n \to 0$ as $(n,T) \to \infty$ is required here, due to the fact that $M_w F\gamma_i$ is included in $\tilde{\varepsilon}^0_i = M_w F\gamma_i + \tilde{\varepsilon}_i$, the error term of transformed model (4.21) using cross-sectional averages. This yields an extra term in $\sqrt{T}(\tilde{b}_i - b_i)$ whose order is $O_p(\sqrt{T}/n) + O_p(1/\sqrt{n})$ which is asymptotically ignorable when $\sqrt{T}/n \to 0$ as $(n,T) \to \infty$. See the Supplementary Appendix.

As discussed above, Assumption 4.2 allows that T can grow faster than n, i.e., $T = O(n^\psi)$ with $\psi \geq 1$. Here, the relative speed of n and T, $\sqrt{T}/n \to 0$ as $(n,T) \to \infty$ imposes an upper bound on ψ, i.e., $\psi < 2$. Therefore, in the case of $T = O(n^\psi)$ with $1 \leq \psi < 2$, both Assumption 4.2 and $\sqrt{T}/n \to 0$ as $(n,T) \to \infty$ required by Proposition 4.1 are satisfied.

As discussed by Pesaran (2006), a consistent Newey–West-type estimator of $\Sigma_{\tilde{\mathbb{X}}\tilde{\varepsilon},i}$ can be obtained using the transformed data,

$$\tilde{\Sigma}_{\tilde{\mathbb{X}}\tilde{\varepsilon},i} = \tilde{\Lambda}_{i0} + \sum_{j=1}^{\omega}\left(1 - \frac{j}{\omega+1}\right)(\tilde{\Lambda}_{ij} + \tilde{\Lambda}'_{ij}),$$

$$\tilde{\Lambda}_{ij} = \frac{1}{T}\sum_{t=j+1}^{\omega}\tilde{e}_{it}\tilde{e}_{i,t-j}\mathbb{X}_{it}(\hat{k})\mathbb{X}_{it}(\hat{k})',$$

where ω is the window size. $\tilde{e}_{it}$ is the tth element of $\tilde{e}_i = \tilde{Y}_i - \tilde{\mathbb{X}}_i(\tilde{k})\tilde{b}_i$ and $\tilde{\mathbb{X}}_{it}(\tilde{k})$ is the tth row of $\tilde{\mathbb{X}}_i(\tilde{k})$. Since $\Sigma_{\tilde{\mathbb{X}},i}$ can be consistently estimated by $\frac{1}{T}\tilde{\mathbb{X}}_i(\tilde{k})'\tilde{\mathbb{X}}_i(\tilde{k})$. Thus, a consistent estimator of $\Sigma^{-1}_{\tilde{\mathbb{X}},i}\Sigma_{\tilde{\mathbb{X}}\tilde{\varepsilon},i}\Sigma^{-1}_{\tilde{\mathbb{X}},i}$ is given by

$$\left[\frac{1}{T}\tilde{\mathbb{X}}_i(\tilde{k})'\tilde{\mathbb{X}}_i(\tilde{k})\right]^{-1}\tilde{\Sigma}_{\tilde{\mathbb{X}}\tilde{\varepsilon},i}\left[\frac{1}{T}\tilde{\mathbb{X}}_i(\tilde{k})'\tilde{\mathbb{X}}_i(\tilde{k})\right]^{-1}. \tag{4.25}$$

Since $\tilde{b}_i(\tilde{k})$ has the same limiting distribution as $\tilde{b}_i(k_0)$, parameters b_i, $i = 1,\ldots,n$, in model (4.5) can be inferred as if k_0 were known.

The mean group estimator with a common break can be defined similarly:

$$\tilde{b}_{\mathrm{MG}} = \frac{1}{n}\sum_{i=1}^{n}\tilde{b}_i = \frac{1}{n}\sum_{i=1}^{n}[\tilde{\mathbb{X}}_i(\tilde{k})'\tilde{\mathbb{X}}_i(\tilde{k})]^{-1}\tilde{\mathbb{X}}_i(\tilde{k})'\tilde{Y}_i. \tag{4.26}$$

Proposition 4.2. *Under the Assumptions* 4.1–4.3, 4.8–4.14, 4.16,

$$\sqrt{n}(\tilde{b}_{\mathrm{MG}} - b) \xrightarrow{d} N(0, \Sigma_b).$$

As in Pesaran (2006), Σ_b can be consistently estimated by

$$\frac{1}{n-1} \sum_{i=1}^{n} (\tilde{b}_i - \tilde{b}_{\mathrm{MG}})(\tilde{b}_i - \tilde{b}_{\mathrm{MG}})'.$$

For detailed proofs of Propositions 4.1 and 4.2, see the Supplementary Appendix. Unlike Pesaran (2006), an additional step is needed, that of estimating k_0. As shown in the propositions above, with the consistency of $\tilde{k}$, the convergence rate of $\tilde{k}$ is not required for deriving the asymptotic distributions of $\tilde{b}_i$, for $i = 1, \ldots, n$, and $\tilde{b}_{\mathrm{MG}}$.

4.4. Multiple Common Break Points

When multiple common break points $k_0^{(1)}, \ldots, k_0^{(B_k)}$, occur in the slopes, there are $B_k + 1$ regimes for each individual:

$$y_{it} = \begin{cases} x_{it}'\beta_i + e_{it}, & t = 1, \ldots, k_0^{(1)}, \\ x_{it}'\beta_i + z_{it}'\delta_{1i} + e_{it}, & t = k_0^{(1)} + 1, \ldots, k_0^{(2)}, \\ \quad \vdots & \quad \vdots \\ x_{it}'\beta_i + z_{it}'\delta_{B_k,i} + e_{it}, & t = k_0^{(B_k)} + 1, \ldots, T, \end{cases} \tag{4.27}$$

for $i = 1, \ldots, n$.

Estimation of multiple break points has been discussed by Bai (1997b) and Chong (1995) in a mean-shift model, Bai and Perron (1998) in linear regression models and Bai (2010) in a panel mean-shift model. To deal with this issue in the model (4.27), we can follow the sequential or one at-a-time approach discussed by Bai (1997b, 2010). The number of common breaks, B_k, is assumed *known*. The idea of the sequential approach is to estimate break points one by one. For example, if $B_k = 3$, the estimation of $k_0^{(1)}, k_0^{(2)}$ and $k_0^{(3)}$ can be completed in three steps. In the first step, one break point is assumed as in Model 1 (or Model 2) above, and can be estimated by (4.11) (or (4.24)), denoted by $\hat{k}^{(1)}$ (or $\tilde{k}^{(1)}$). In the second step, in each of the two sub-panels split by $\hat{k}^{(1)}$ (or $\tilde{k}^{(1)}$), the same procedure (4.11) (or (4.24)) is applied. Thus, two single break estimators are obtained in these two sub-panels. Moreover, $\hat{k}^{(2)}$ (or $\tilde{k}^{(2)}$) is defined as the one associated with a larger reduction in the sum of squared residuals. Similarly, $\hat{k}^{(1)}$ and $\hat{k}^{(2)}$ (or $\tilde{k}^{(1)}$ and $\tilde{k}^{(2)}$) yield three sub-panels. In the third step, in each of these three sub-panels, one break point can be estimated as in Model 1 (or 2). Among these three break estimators, we choose the one associated with the largest reduction of sum of squared residuals, denoted as $\hat{k}^{(3)}$ (or $\tilde{k}^{(3)}$). As suggested by Bai (2010), it can be shown that after rearranging $(\hat{k}^{(1)}, \hat{k}^{(2)}, \hat{k}^{(3)})$ (or $(\tilde{k}^{(1)}, \tilde{k}^{(2)}, \tilde{k}^{(3)})$) in temporal order, $(\hat{k}^{(1)}, \hat{k}^{(2)}, \hat{k}^{(3)})$ (or $(\tilde{k}^{(1)}, \tilde{k}^{(2)}, \tilde{k}^{(3)})$ in Model 2) is consistent for $(k_0^{(1)}, k_0^{(2)}, k_0^{(3)})$ as long as the assumptions listed in Section 4.2 (or 4.3) hold in each of the sub-panels.

Once the consistent estimators of $(k_0^{(1)}, \ldots, k_0^{(B_k)})$ are obtained, the parameters $\beta_i, \delta_{1i}, \ldots, \delta_{B_k,i}$, $i = 1, \ldots, n$, can be estimated by least squares as in (4.10) (or (4.23)). Thus, their mean group estimators can be obtained similarly.

4.5. Endogenous Regressors and Break in Factors

In the empirical studies using the CCE and iterated principal component (IPC) approaches, there are two main concerns. First, to apply these two approaches, long panel data sets are usually required. However, over a long span, parameter instability due to structural breaks is possible. Second, with the exception of Temple and Van de Sijpe (2017), and Chirinko and Wilson (2017), endogeneity due to the correlation between the regressors and the idiosyncratic errors could bias the resulting estimates. Though an error factor structure can be used to control for the correlation between the regressors and the unobserved factors or loadings, the correlation between the regressors and the idiosyncratic errors could still be present due to reverse causality or other sources. This endogeneity is common in empirical studies using aggregate data, for example, the return of public infrastructure as surveyed by Gramlich (1994) and Calderon, Moral-Benito and Serven (2015).

In this section, we show that the model (4.4) considered in Section 4.5 can be extended to allow for endogenous regressors and structural changes in error factor loadings. Thus, based on Pesaran's (2006) heterogeneous panels we provide an appealing panel data regression model with four empirical features: (i) slope heterogeneity, (ii) cross-sectional dependence modeled by an error factor structure, (iii) endogenous regressors and (iv) structural changes in slopes and error factor loadings.

Specifically, the model considered here is

$$y_{it} = x'_{it}\beta_i(k_0) + e_{it}$$

$$= \begin{cases} x'_{it}\beta_{1i} + e_{it}, & t = 1, \ldots, k_0, \\ x'_{it}\beta_{2i} + e_{it}, & t = k_0 + 1, \ldots, T, \end{cases}$$

$$e_{it} = \gamma_i(k_1)' f_t + \varepsilon_{it}, \quad x_{it} = \Gamma'_i f_t + v_{it}.$$

Here $\text{Cov}(\varepsilon_{it}, v_{it}) \neq 0$. The case of partial changes in slopes can be easily accommodated as in (4.6) of Model 1 in Section 4.2. Assume there are q instruments z_{it} with $q \geq p$. The instruments z_{it} could be affected by f_t. The key differences of this model from (4.4) are (i) endogenous regressors and (ii) a common break k_1 in factor loading $\gamma_i(k_1)$.

To deal with endogeneity, we start with a simplified case without considering the error factor structure. Different from the assumption in Sections 4.2 and 4.3, here ε_{it} is allowed to be correlated with x_{it}.

Let $b_i = (\beta'_{1i}, \beta'_{2i})', i = 1, \ldots, n$. For every i, and $k = 1, \ldots, T - 1$, define $X_{1i}(k) = (x_{i1}, \ldots, x_{i,k})'$ and $X_{2i}(k) = (x_{i,k+1}, \ldots, x_{iT})'$. Similarly, define $Y_{1i}(k) = (y_{i1}, \ldots, y_{i,k})'$ and $Y_{2i}(k) = (y_{i,k+1}, \ldots, y_{iT})'$. Let $Y_i = (y_{i1}, \ldots, y_{iT})'$ and $\varepsilon_i = (\varepsilon_{i1}, \varepsilon_{i2}, \ldots, \varepsilon_{iT})'$ denote the stacked data and errors over time, thus $Y_i = (Y_{1i}(k)', Y_{2i}(k)')'$. Using the notation $\mathbb{X}_i(k) = \begin{pmatrix} X_{1i}(k) & 0 \\ 0 & X_{2i}(k) \end{pmatrix}$, equation (4.6) can be written in matrix form as

$$Y_i = \mathbb{X}_i(k_0) b_i + \varepsilon_i, \quad i = 1, \ldots, n. \tag{4.28}$$

Following Perron and Yamamoto (2015), we can project ε_i on the column space spanned by $\mathbb{X}_i(k_0)$ such that the new error term ε_i^* (defined below) is uncorrelated with $\mathbb{X}_i(k_0)$. Rewrite equation (4.8) as follows:

$$Y_i = \mathbb{X}_i(k_0)\beta_i^*(k_0) + \varepsilon_i^*, \tag{4.29}$$

where $\varepsilon_i^* = (I - P_{\mathbb{X}})\varepsilon_i = (\varepsilon_{i1}^*, \ldots, \varepsilon_{iT}^*)'$ and $P_{\mathbb{X}}$ is the projection matrix based on $\mathbb{X}_i(k_0)$, and

$$\beta_i^*(k_0) = \begin{pmatrix} \beta_{1i}^* \\ \beta_{2i}^* \end{pmatrix} = b_i + [\mathbb{X}_i(k_0)'\mathbb{X}_i(k_0)]^{-1} \mathbb{X}_i(k_0)'\varepsilon_i.$$

As argued by Perron and Yamamoto (2015) in a time-series model, a structural change in the original parameter $\beta_i(k_0)$ implies a shift in the new parameter, the probability limit of $\beta_i^*(k_0)$, at the same break date k_0, except for a knife-edge case.

Since the new errors ε_{it}^* are uncorrelated with x_{it}, equation (4.29) becomes Model 1 in Section 4.2. Following the same lines of proof as in Theorem 1, it can be shown that $\hat{k}$ is consistent for k_0, i.e., $\hat{k} - k_0 = o_p(1)$, under appropriate assumptions.

In the general model,

$$Y_i = \mathbb{X}_i(k_0)b_i + F\gamma_i(k_1) + \varepsilon_i, \quad i = 1, \ldots, n.$$

The new complication is the additional term $F\gamma_i(k_1)$. Besides nonzero $\text{Cov}(v_{it}, \varepsilon_{it})$, this unobserved factors create an additional source of endogeneity due to the unobservable common factors f_t that affect both $x_{it} = \Gamma_i' f_t + v_{it}$ and e_{it}.

With endogenous regressors x_{it}, this general model with a multifactor error structure can still fit into the simplified case discussed in the previous subsection. Hence, we can still use OLS to estimate k_0. However, due to the common f_t, errors e_{it} are no longer cross-sectionally independent. This is a major difference. As pointed out by Kim (2011), the cross-sectional correlation in the errors could offset the information across the cross-sectional dimension under the common break assumption. Thus, $\hat{k} - k_0 = o_p(1)$ is not necessarily achieved without controlling for f_t. It depends on the magnitude of the cross-sectional correlation governed by the unobservable loadings.

As shown in Baltagi, Feng and Kao (2019), the CCE approach is still valid in this general model. Since f_t are unobservable, we follow Pesaran's (2006) idea of using the cross-sectional averages of y_{it} and x_{it} as proxies for f_t. Combining (4.3) and (4.5) yields

$$\underset{(p+1)\times 1}{w_{it}} = \begin{pmatrix} y_{it} \\ x_{it} \end{pmatrix} = \underset{(p+1)\times m}{C_i(k_0, k_1)'} \underset{m\times 1}{f_t} + \underset{(p+1)\times 1}{u_{it}(k_0)},$$

where

$$\underset{m\times(p+1)}{C_i(k_0, k_1)} = (\gamma_i(k_1), \Gamma_i) \begin{pmatrix} 1 & 0 \\ \beta_i(k_0) & I_p \end{pmatrix},$$

$$u_{it}(k_0) = \begin{pmatrix} \varepsilon_{it} + v_{it}'\beta_i(k_0) \\ v_{it} \end{pmatrix}.$$

In the case that the instruments z_{it} are affected by f_t, z_{it} can be included in the vector w_{it}. Note that like $\beta_i(k_0)$, the slope $C_i(k_0, k_1)$ in (4.15) also shifts at k_0, and k_1. Without loss of generality, we assume $k_1 > k_0$. Thus,

$$
C_i(k_0, k_1) = \begin{cases}
C_{1i} = (\gamma_{1i} + \Gamma_i\beta_{1i}, \ \Gamma_i), & t = 1, \ldots, k_0, \\
C_{2i} = (\gamma_{1i} + \Gamma_i\beta_{2i}, \ \Gamma_i), & t = k_0 + 1, \ldots, k_1, \\
C_{3i} = (\gamma_{2i} + \Gamma_i\beta_{2i}, \ \Gamma_i), & t = k_1 + 1, \ldots, T.
\end{cases}
$$

Common break k_0 splits the data generating process for all individuals into two regimes, and in each regime the unobserved common factors f_t can be partialled out by using cross-sectional averages in Pesaran (2006). Let $\bar{w}_t = \sum_{i=1}^{n} \theta_i w_{it}$ be the cross-sectional average of w_{it} using weights θ_i, $i = 1, \ldots, n$. In particular,

$$
\bar{w}_t = \bar{C}(k_0, k_1)' f_t + \bar{u}_t(k_0), \tag{4.30}
$$

where

$$
\bar{C}(k_0, k_1) = \sum_{i=1}^{N} \theta_i C_i(k_0, k_1)
$$

$$
= \begin{cases}
\bar{C}_1 = \sum_{i=1}^{n} \theta_i C_{1i}, & t = 1, \ldots, k_0, \\
\bar{C}_2 = \sum_{i=1}^{n} \theta_i C_{2i}, & t = k_0 + 1, \ldots, k_1, \\
\bar{C}_3 = \sum_{i=1}^{n} \theta_i C_{3i}, & t = k_1 + 1, \ldots, T,
\end{cases} \tag{4.31}
$$

and

$$
\bar{u}_t(k_0) = \sum_{i=1}^{n} \theta_i u_{it}(k_0)
$$

$$
= \begin{cases}
\begin{pmatrix} \bar{\varepsilon}_t + \sum_{i=1}^{n} \theta_i v_{it}' \beta_{1i} \\ \bar{v}_t \end{pmatrix}, & t = 1, \ldots, k_0, \\
\begin{pmatrix} \bar{\varepsilon}_t + \sum_{i=1}^{n} \theta_i v_{it}' \beta_{2i} \\ \bar{v}_t \end{pmatrix}, & t = k_0 + 1, \ldots, T,
\end{cases} \tag{4.32}
$$

where $\bar{\varepsilon}_t = \sum_{i=1}^{n} \theta_i \varepsilon_{it}$, $\bar{v}_t = \sum_{i=1}^{n} \theta_i v_{it}$.

For equation (4.30), when $\bar{C}(k_0, k_1)$ is of full rank, f_t can be written as

$$f_t = \left[\bar{C}(k_0, k_1)\bar{C}(k_0, k_1)'\right]^{-1} \bar{C}(k_0, k_1)(\bar{w}_t - \bar{u}_t(k_0)). \qquad (4.33)$$

For simplicity, we assume that the rank condition is satisfied.

Assumptions 4.10 and 4.11 imply that $\bar{C}(k_0, k_1)\bar{C}(k_0, k_1)'$ is invertible. As shown in Lemma 1 of Pesaran (2006), in (4.18), the cross-sectional averages of the errors $\bar{\varepsilon}_t$, $\bar{v}_t$, $\sum_{i=1}^{n} \theta_i v_{it}' \beta_{1i}$ and $\sum_{i=1}^{n} \theta_i v_{it}' \beta_{2i}$ all vanish as $n \to \infty$, thus

$$\bar{u}_t(k_0) \xrightarrow{p} 0$$

in both regimes as $n \to \infty$, regardless of the correlation between ε_{it} and v_{it}, yielding

$$f_t - \left[\bar{C}(k_0, k_1)\bar{C}(k_0, k_1)'\right]^{-1} \bar{C}(k_0, k_1)\bar{w}_t \xrightarrow{p} 0. \qquad (4.34)$$

This suggests that it is asymptotically valid to use $\bar{w}_t$ as observable proxies for f_t. This finding also shows that the CCE approach proposed by Pesaran (2006) is robust to endogeneity and structural changes in slopes and factor structures. Same as Model 2 above, OLS of k_0 using the CCE transformed data is consistent, i.e., $\tilde{k} - k_0 = o_p(1)$.

4.6. Monte Carlo Simulations

This section employs Monte Carlo simulations to examine the consistency of the estimated break points $\hat{k}$ and $\tilde{k}$ summarized in Theorems 4.1 and 4.2. Since the CCE estimators in Model 2 have the same asymptotic distributions as if the true common breaks were known, their asymptotic properties are not examined here. Two different designs are used for Models 1 and 2, respectively. In Model 1, there are no common correlated effects in the errors and regressors, so least squares can be run for each individual series. While in Model 2, the regressors and errors are correlated due to common correlated effects f_t. A transformation, using cross-sectional averages of the dependent variable and regressors proposed by Pesaran (2006), is needed to remove such effects asymptotically.

In the following experiments, the focus is on the histograms of $\hat{k}$ and $\tilde{k}$ in setups with different combinations of (n, T).

4.6.1. Model 1: No common correlated effects

The data generating process (DGP) of Model 1 is modified from that in Pesaran (2004, p. 24):

$$y_{it} = \alpha_i + \beta_i(k_0)y_{i,t-1} + e_{it}, \quad i = 1,\ldots,n; t = 1,\ldots,T;$$

$$e_{it} = \gamma_i f_t + \varepsilon_{it}.$$

Here we set $\gamma_i = 0$, so there is no cross-sectional dependence in the errors. Instead, in this dynamic heterogeneous panel model, there is a common break $k_0 = 0.5T$ in the slopes β_i, for $i = 1,\ldots,n$, i.e.,

$$\beta_i(k_0) = \begin{cases} \beta_{1i}, & t = 1,\ldots,k_0, \\ \beta_{2i} = \beta_{1i} + \delta_i, & t = k_0 + 1,\ldots,T, \end{cases}$$

where δ_i is the jump in the slope for each series. We assume $\beta_{1i} \sim$ i.i.d. $U(0, 0.8)$ and $\delta_i \sim$ i.i.d. $U(0, 0.2)$. We set $\alpha_i = \mu_i(1 - \beta_{1i})$, $\mu_i = \varepsilon_{0i} + \eta_i$ where $\varepsilon_{0i} \sim$ i.i.d. $N(0, 1)$ and $\eta_i \sim$ i.i.d. $N(1, 2)$. In addition, we assume $y_{i,0} \sim$ i.i.d. $N(0, 1)$ and $\varepsilon_{it} \sim$ i.i.d. $N(0, \sigma_i^2)$, with $\sigma_i^2 \sim \chi_2^2/2$.

In (4.11), for any possible change point $k = 1,\ldots,T-1$, the estimated change point $\hat{k}$ is the one that minimizes the sum of n individual sum of squared residuals. 1000 replications are performed to obtain the histogram of $\hat{k}$ for each setup.

Panel A of Fig. 4.1 reports the histograms of $\hat{k}$ for $T = 50$ and $n = 10, 50, 200$. The frequency of choosing the true value k_0 increases from 17% for $n = 10$ to almost 90% for $n = 200$. It shows that the distribution of $\hat{k}$ shrinks with n. This finding supports Theorem 4.1, confirming that multiple individual series provide additional information on k_0, and that $\hat{k}$ converges to k_0 as the number of series goes to infinity.

To consider the case where there is no structural break in slopes in some series, we set $\delta_i = 0$ in $[n/4]$ series, implying that ϕ_N increases with n at a rate of $O(n^{3/4})$. Panel B of Fig. 4.1 reports the histograms of $\hat{k}$ for this case with $T = 50$. Similar to Panel A, the pattern that $\hat{k}$ converges to k_0 as n increases remains. However, the frequency of choosing the true value k_0 is significantly smaller than that in Panel A of Fig. 4.1. For example, for $n = 50$, the frequency of choosing the true value k_0 drops from 44% in Panel A to 34% in Panel B. This suggests that for the accuracy of the estimated change point, allowing for no break in some series is equivalent to reducing the number of series or the magnitude of break ϕ_N.

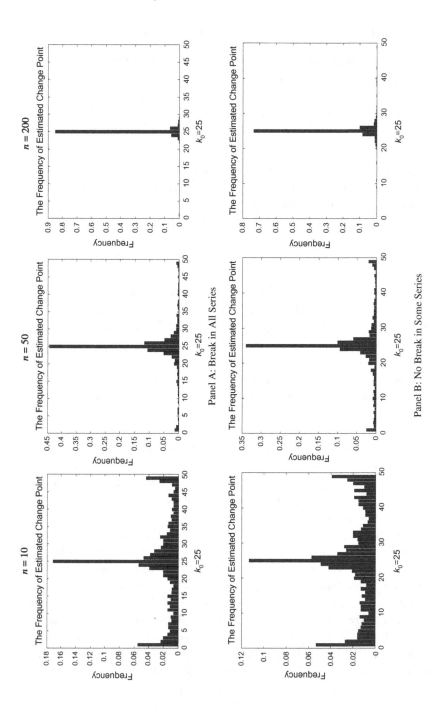

Fig. 4.1.   Histograms of $\hat{k}$ in Model 1: $T = 50$.

4.6.2. Model 2: Common correlated effects

The data generating process for Model 2 is as follows:

$$y_{it} = \alpha_i + \beta_i(k_0)x_{i,t} + e_{it}, \quad i = 1, \ldots, n; \ t = 1, \ldots, T,$$

$$e_{it} = \gamma_{1i}f_t + \varepsilon_{it},$$

where $\alpha_i \overset{\text{i.i.d.}}{\sim} N(1,1)$ and $\gamma_{1i} \overset{\text{i.i.d.}}{\sim} N(1, 0.2)$. The idiosyncratic errors are generated as $\varepsilon_{it} \overset{\text{i.i.d.}}{\sim} N(0, \sigma_i^2)$ and $\sigma_i^2 \overset{\text{i.i.d.}}{\sim} U(0.5, 1.5)$. There is a common break in the individual slopes:

$$\beta_i(k_0) = \begin{cases} \beta_{1i}, & t = 1, \ldots, k_0, \\ \beta_{2i} = \beta_{1i} + \delta_i, & t = k_0 + 1, \ldots, T, \end{cases} \quad k_0 = 0.5T,$$

where $\beta_{1i} = 1 + \eta_i, \eta_i \overset{\text{i.i.d.}}{\sim} N(0, 0.04)$ and $\delta_i \overset{\text{i.i.d.}}{\sim} N(0, 0.04)$.

Unlike Model 1, the error e_{it} and the regressor x_{it} contain the common correlated effect f_t:

$$x_{it} = a_i + \gamma_{2i}f_t + v_{it},$$

where $a_i \overset{\text{i.i.d.}}{\sim} N(0.5, 0.5)$, $\gamma_{2i} \overset{\text{i.i.d.}}{\sim} N(0.5, 0.5)$ and $v_{it} \overset{\text{i.i.d.}}{\sim} N(0, 1 - \rho_{vi}^2)$, with $\rho_{vi} = 0.5$. The factor f_t is generated by the stationary process:

$$f_t = \rho_f f_{t-1} + v_{ft}, \quad t = -49, \ldots, 0, 1, \ldots, T;$$

$$\rho_f = 0.5, v_{ft} \overset{\text{i.i.d.}}{\sim} N(0, 1 - \rho_f^2), f_{-50} = 0.$$

The correlation between x_{it} and e_{it} renders OLS inconsistent in the individual regressions. Thus, transformation (4.20) using cross-sectional averages of y_{it} and x_{it} is needed to remove f_t before conducting least squares estimation of k_0.

The setup above is a simplified version of the design in Pesaran (2006). First, as in model (4.4), the observed factors are omitted for simplicity. Second, the number of regressors and unobservable factors are reduced to 1, respectively. Third, the correlation structures in v_{it} and ε_{it} are removed. The only new feature of this model is that there is a common break at k_0, specified as $0.5T$.

The first row of Fig. 4.2 presents the histograms of the estimated change point $\tilde{k}$ for $T = 50$. It replicates the pattern in Fig. 4.1, showing that after the transformation, the frequency of choosing the true value k_0 increases significantly with n. Figure 4.2 also reports, in the second row, the histograms of the estimated change point $\hat{k}$ without conducting

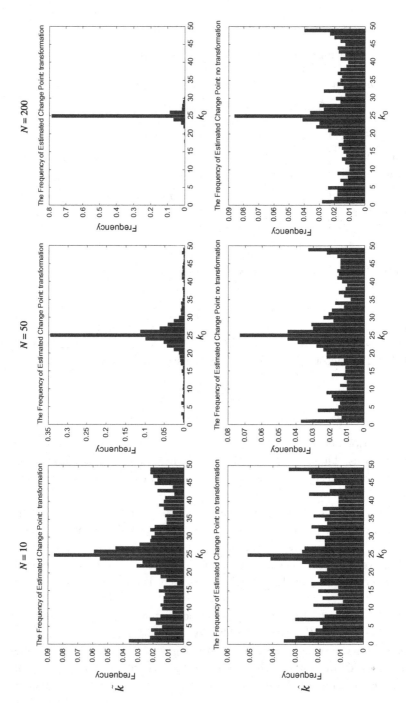

Fig. 4.2.   Histograms of $\tilde{k}$ and $\hat{k}$ in Model 2: $T = 50$.

transformation (4.20). It indicates that in the presence of common correlated effects, cross-sectional information using multiple series fails to improve the accuracy of the estimated change point.

Figure 4.3 reports the histograms of $\tilde{k}$ and $\hat{k}$ for $T = 200$. The same pattern emerges, suggesting that the distribution of $\tilde{k}$ shrinks to k_0 as $n \to \infty$. Different from Fig. 4.2, the frequency of $\hat{k}$, the estimator without conducting transformation (4.20), choosing the true break date increases with n in Fig. 4.3 when T is large, although not at a rate as high as that of $\tilde{k}$ using the transformed data. Whether $|\hat{k} - k_0|$ shrinks to 0 or not as $(n, T) \to \infty$ depends upon the correlation between x_{it} and e_{it}. In Fig. 4.4, we increase this correlation by changing the distribution of γ_{1i} from $N(1, 0.2)$ to $N(2, 0.2)$. In this case, the cross-sectional information using multiple series fails to improve the accuracy of the estimated change point $\hat{k}$. This is consistent with the findings of Kim (2011).

4.6.3. *Case of endogenous regressors*

We also check the impact of endogeneity on the consistency of the break point estimator using various experiments. The DGP used here is a modified design of Model 2. The main difference is that e_{it} is correlated with x_{it} (or v_{it}) by adding a term $\rho_{e,i} v_{it}$ in the process of e_{it}:

$$e_{it} = \gamma_{1i}(k_1) f_t + \rho_{e,i} v_{it} + (1 - \rho_e^2)^{1/2} \varepsilon_{it}, \qquad (4.35)$$

where $\rho_{e,i}$ denotes the correlation between x_{it} and e_{it}. We also allow a break in the factor loading $\gamma_{1i}(k_1)$ at a different time point $k_1 = [0.7T]$:

$$\gamma_{1i}(k_1) = \begin{cases} \gamma_{1i}, & t = 1, \ldots, k_1, \\ \gamma_{1i} + \Delta\gamma_{1i}, & t = k_1 + 1, \ldots, T. \end{cases}$$

In the process generating e_{it}, the loadings $\gamma_{1i} \sim$ i.i.d. $N(1, 0.2)$, $\Delta\gamma_{1i} \sim$ i.i.d. $N(0.5, 0.5)$, $\rho_{e,i} \sim$ i.i.d. $U(-0.5, 0.5)$ and $\varepsilon_{it} \sim$ i.i.d. $N(0, \sigma_i^2)$ with $\sigma_i^2 \sim$ i.i.d. $U(0.5, 1.5)$.

In the error structure (4.35), there are two sources of endogeneity due to the unobserved factor f_t and the random component v_{it}. For simplicity, we first ignore the break in factor loading $\gamma_{1i}(k_1)$ and set $\Delta\gamma_{1i} = 0$ in Fig. 4.5. As pointed out by Perron and Yamamoto (2015), the break fraction $\tau_0 = k_0/T$ can be consistently estimated by OLS even in the presence of correlation between x_{it} and e_{it} in a time-series regression. However, in a panel data setup, the cross-sectional correlation in the errors due to the

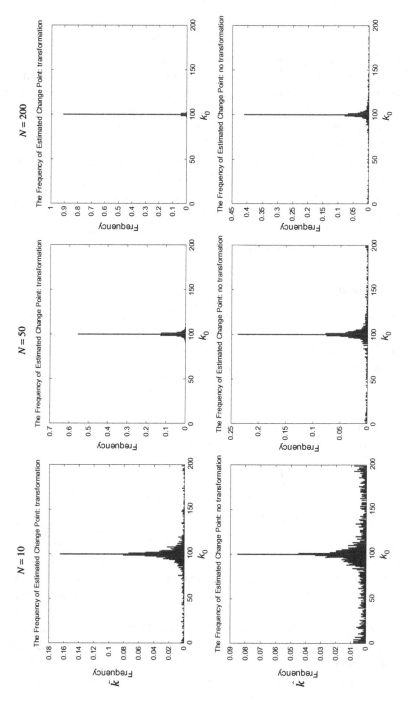

Fig. 4.3.   Histograms of $\tilde{k}$ and $\hat{k}$ in Model 2: $T = 200$.

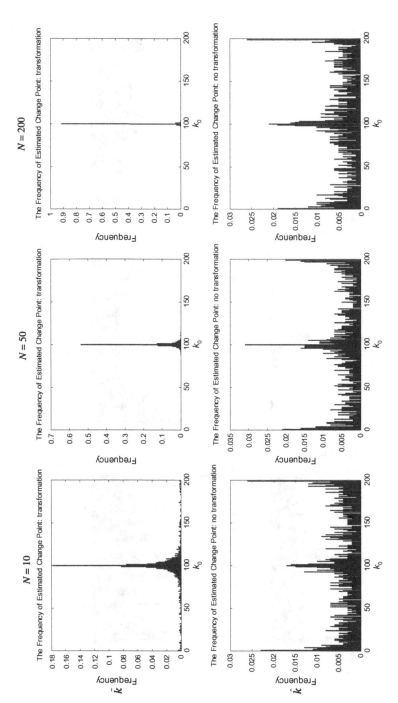

Fig. 4.4. Histograms of $\tilde{k}$ and $\hat{k}$ in Model 2 (with increased correlation between x_{it} and e_{it}): $T = 200$.

Note: The DGP is the same as in Fig. 4.2, except that the correlation between x_{it} and e_{it} increases by changing the distribution of γ_{i1} from i.i.d. $N(1, 0.2)$ to i.i.d. $N(2, 0.2)$. $k_0 = 0.5T = 100$.

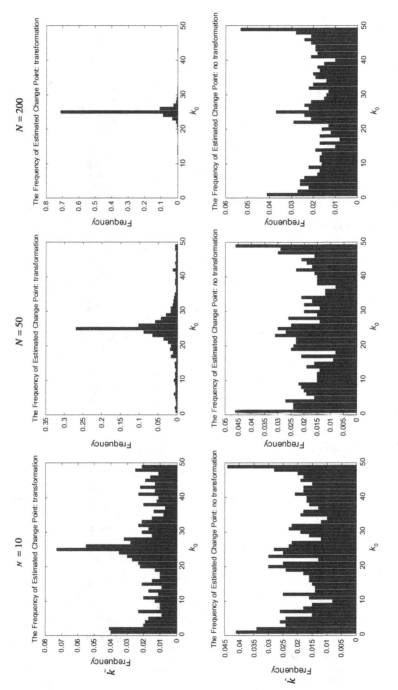

Fig. 4.5.　Histograms of $\check{k}$ and $\hat{k}$ in the general case with endogenous regressors ($T = 50$).

common f_t could fail to improve the accuracy of the OLS estimator of k_0, as pointed out by Theorem 1A(iii) of Kim (2011) and Fig. 4.4. Thus, the transformation (4.20) using cross-sectional averages of y_{it} and x_{it} is needed to remove f_t before conducting least squares.

The first row of Fig. 4.5 presents the histograms of the estimated change point $\tilde{k}$ for $T = 50$. The frequency of choosing the true value k_0 increases significantly with n. It confirms the finding that the distribution of $\tilde{k}$ collapses to k_0 as $n \to \infty$ in the presence of endogenous regressors. The second row of Fig. 4.5 also reports the histograms of the estimated change point $\hat{k}$ without conducting the CCE transformation (4.20). It indicates that in the presence of common correlated effects, cross-sectional information using multiple series fails to improve the accuracy of the estimated change point.

Figure 4.6 presents the case when there is a common break in the factor loading $\gamma_{1i}(k_1)$, with $k_1 = [0.7T] > k_0$. Consistent with our theory $\tilde{k}$, our estimator of the break point in the slope parameters is robust to a break in the error factor loadings γ_{1i}. This holds since f_t is asymptotically removed by the CCE transformation (4.20). However, as shown in the second row of Fig. 4.6, the break point in factor loadings could lead to a spurious break in the slope parameters if we ignore the unobserved factors in the errors. In Fig. 4.7, we reduce the correlation between x_{it} and e_{it} by changing the distribution of the loading γ_{2i} from $N(0.5, 0.5)$ to $N(0.1, 0.1)$, increasing n does not improve the frequency of $\hat{k}$ choosing k_0.

Figure 4.8 reports the case of rank deficiency. By changing the distribution of γ_{2i} from $N(0.5, 0.5)$, the matrix $\bar{C}(k_0)$ is not of full rank asymptotically. The first panel of Fig. 4.8 shows that the consistency of $\tilde{k}$ remains in the case of rank deficiency. As N increases, the probability of choosing the true value k_0 increases.

In Fig. 4.9, we also compare the efficiency of the proposed OLS and IV estimators of k_0. An IV estimator is used in the first step, instead of OLS, in a simplified case without an error factor structure. The DGP is similar to the one used in Fig. 4.5 except that there are no factors and an instrument is introduced and regressor x_{it} is generated in a slightly different way, similar to Hall *et al.* (2012). As expected, the IV estimator $\check{k}$ is also consistent, and its probability of choosing the true value k_0 increases with n (and T). However, a comparison between the histograms of $\hat{k}$ and $\check{k}$ suggests that OLS yields more accuracy in terms of the probability of finding the true value k_0 than the IV estimator.

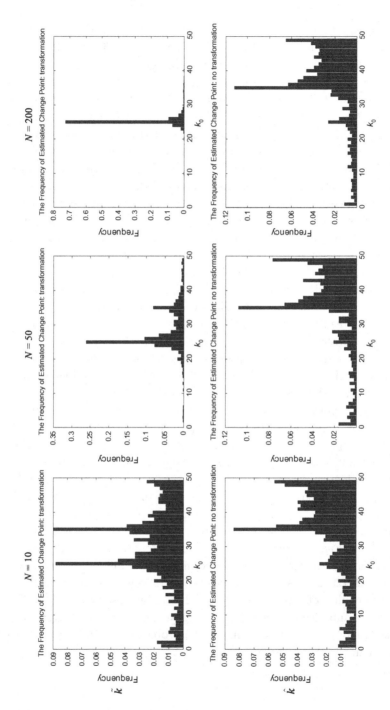

Fig. 4.6.   Histograms of $\tilde{k}$ and $\hat{k}$ with endogenous regressors and a structural change in the error factor loading ($T = 50$).

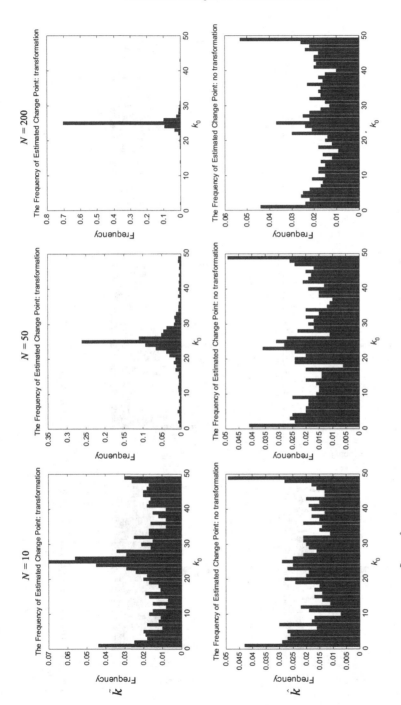

Fig. 4.7. Histograms of $\tilde{k}$ and $\hat{k}$ in the general case with reduced endogeneity ($T = 50$).

Note: The DGP is the same as the one in Fig. 4.5, except for reducing the correlation between $x_{i,t}$ and $e_{i,t}$ by changing the distribution of the loading γ_{2i} from i.i.d. $N(0.5, 0.5)$ to i.i.d. $N(0.1, 0.1)$.

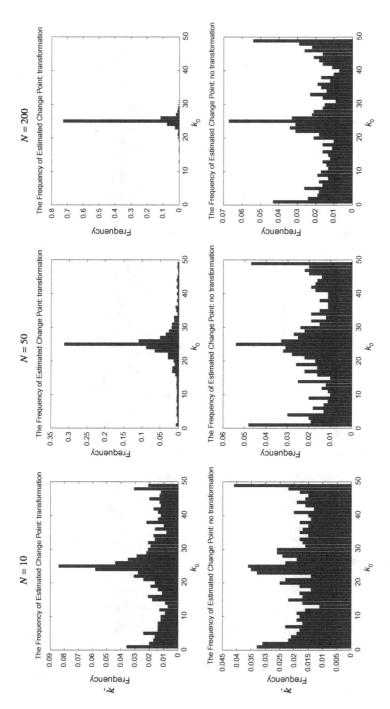

Fig. 4.8.   Histograms of $\tilde{k}$ and $\hat{k}$ in the general case with rank deficiency ($T = 50$).

Note: The means of γ_{i2} and a_i change to zero, i.e., $\gamma_{i2} \sim$ i.i.d. $N(0, 0.5)$, $a_i \sim$ i.i.d. $N(0, 0.5)$, so the rank condition is not satisfied asymptotically.

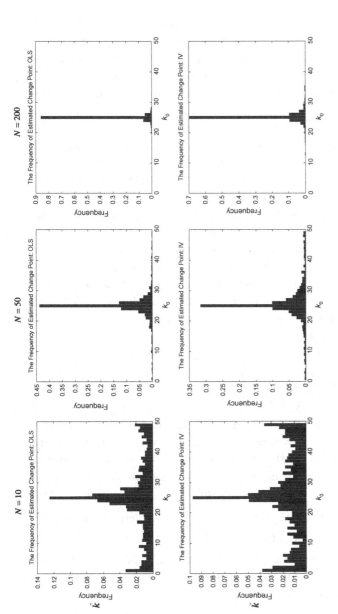

Fig. 4.9.   Histograms of the OLS estimator $\hat{k}$ and IV estimator $\check{k}$ in a simplified case without a factor structure in the errors ($T = 50$).

Note: In this simplified case, there is no factor structure in the errors. The instrument $z3_{it}$ is introduced and regressor x_{it} is generated in a slightly different way (similar to Hall et al., 2012). $z3_{it} = 2a_i + \gamma_{3i} f_t + v2_{it}$ where $\gamma_{3i} \sim$ i.i.d. $N(1, 0.5)$, $v2_{it} \sim$ i.i.d. $N(0, 1)$, and $v2_{it}$ is independent of v_{it} and ε_{it}.

$x_{it} = 0.5 z3_{it} + v_{it}$; $\varepsilon_{it} = \rho_{e,i} v_{it} + (1 - \rho_{e,i}^2)^{1/2} \varepsilon_{it}$, $\rho_{e,i} \sim$ i.i.d. $U(-0.5, 0.5)$, $\varepsilon_{it} \sim$ i.i.d. $N(0, \sigma_i^2)$, $\sigma_i^2 \sim$ i.i.d. $U(0.5, 1.5)$, $\gamma_{1i} \sim$ i.i.d. $N(1, 0.2)$, $\gamma_{2i} \sim$ i.i.d. $N(0.5, 0.5)$, $a_i \sim$ i.i.d. $N(0.5, 0.5)$, $v_{it} \sim$ i.i.d. $N(0, 1, -\rho_{vi}^2)$, $\rho_{vi} = 0.5$. These variables are mutually independent. The replication number is 1000. $T = 50$, $k_0 = 25$.

$\hat{k}$: The OLS estimator of the change point.

$\check{k}$: The IV estimator of the change point: the IV estimator is used in the first step, instead of OLS.

4.7. An Empirical Example

In Section 3.6, CCE, IPC and likelihood approaches are illustrated by using China's provincial panel data during 1996–2015 to estimate the output elasticity with respect to public infrastructure in an aggregate production function. In this section, based on Feng (2020), we empirically investigate how to deal with common factors and common breaks using the estimators proposed in this chapter.

Baltagi, Feng and Kao (2016, 2019) extend Pesaran's (2006) CCE approach by allowing for unknown common structural changes in slopes and error factor structure and endogenous regressors in large heterogeneous panels. They find that Pesaran's CCE approach is still valid when dealing with unobservable common factors in the presence of common breaks in slopes and error factor loadings and endogenous regressors. Given that there are no empirical investigations of the proposed estimators available, this section aims to compare these estimators to Bai's (2009) IPC estimator and Pesaran's (2006) CCE mean group estimator in the context of China's provincial infrastructure investment covering the period 1996–2015. In this specific empirical context, the trade-offs of allowing for endogeneity and common structural breaks in heterogeneous panels with an error factor structure can be illustrated.

Consider the general model,

$$Y_i = \mathbb{X}_i(k_0)b_i + F\gamma_i(k_1) + \varepsilon_i, \quad i = 1, \ldots, n.$$

Denote $w_{it} = (y_{it}, x'_{it})'$, $\bar{w}_t = \frac{1}{n}\sum_{i=1}^n w_{it}$, $\bar{W} = (\bar{w}'_1, \bar{w}'_2, \ldots, \bar{w}'_T)'$ and $M_w = I_T - \bar{W}(\bar{W}'\bar{W})^{-1}\bar{W}'$. Baltagi, Feng and Kao (2019) argue that $\bar{W}$ can be treated as exogenous asymptotically when n is large, and that it can be included as the first-stage regressors along with instruments z_{it}. Similar to the definition of $\mathbb{X}_i(k)$, we define the instrument matrix $\mathbb{Z}_i(k) = \begin{pmatrix} Z_{1i}(k) & 0 \\ 0 & Z_{2i}(k) \end{pmatrix}$ where $Z_{1i}(k) = (z'_{i1}, \ldots, z'_{ik})'$ and $Z_{2i}(k) = (z'_{ik+1}, \ldots, z'_{iT})'$. Denote $Z_i^+(k) = (\mathbb{Z}_i(k), \bar{W})$. The predicted value of $\mathbb{X}_i(\tilde{k})$ is $\widehat{\mathbb{X}}_i(\tilde{k}) = P_{Z_i^+(\tilde{k})}\mathbb{X}_i(\tilde{k})$. Given the OLS estimator of the break date, $\tilde{k}$, the IV estimator of b_i is given by $[\widehat{\mathbb{X}}_i(\tilde{k})'M_w\widehat{\mathbb{X}}_i(\tilde{k})]^{-1}\widehat{\mathbb{X}}_i(\tilde{k})'M_wY_i$, $i = 1, \ldots, n$, and the mean group estimator of the cross-sectional mean of b_i, $i = 1, \ldots, n$, is defined in Baltagi, Feng and Kao (2019) by

$$\frac{1}{n}\sum_{i=1}^n [\widehat{\mathbb{X}}_i(\tilde{k})'M_w\widehat{\mathbb{X}}_i(\tilde{k})]^{-1}\widehat{\mathbb{X}}_i(\tilde{k})'M_wY_i, \tag{4.36}$$

which is labeled as CCEMG-IV-b here.

In this example, we make use of China's institutional context to obtain an instrument to deal with endogeneity issue. The endogeneity due to the reverse causality between output and infrastructure has been widely documented in the literature (Gramlich, 1994). In Section 3.6, Table 3.1 reports FD estimates of output elasticity of infrastructure, β_b, in a homogeneous model assuming exogenous regressors:

$$\Delta g_{it} = \beta_b \Delta b_{it} + \beta_k \Delta k_{it} + \Delta \lambda_t + \Delta \epsilon_{it}. \tag{4.37}$$

Here, we consider the case that Δb_{it} and Δk_{it} are endogenous due to reverse causality. Thus, first-differenced instrumental variable (FDIV) estimation is reported in Table 4.1. Δenb_{it}, the infrastructure capital per labor in two economically neighboring provinces, and lagged values Δk_{it-2} in differenced form are used as instruments for Δb_{it} and Δk_{it}. The validity of instruments has been discussed in Feng and Wu (2018). In line with Feng and Wu (2018), after controlling for endogeneity, there is no strong evidence on a large and significant estimate of β_b. In addition, comparisons between columns (2) and (3), and between (4) and (5) also confirm the finding in Table 3.1 of potential cross-region heterogeneity and structural change.

Besides endogeneity, we also consider three other empirical features in various cases: slope heterogeneity, common factors and a common break in

Table 4.1. Output elasticities estimates: Endogenous regressors.

Dependent variable: Output per labor

			FD IV		
Independent variables	(1)	(2)	(3)	(4)	(5)
Infrastructure per labor	0.077	−0.070	0.033	0.202	−0.202**
	(0.150)	(0.316)	(0.137)	(0.199)	(0.244)
Noninfrastructure per labor	0.250***	0.245*	0.286***	0.099	0.438***
	(0.079)	(0.133)	(0.074)	(0.126)	(0.128)
Regions	All	Noneastern	Eastern	All	All
Periods	All	All	All	1997–2007	2008–2015
Year effects	Yes	Yes	Yes	Yes	Yes
No. of observations	569	322	187	269	240
Overall R^2	0.704	0.614	0.742	0.687	0.510
Instruments			$\Delta enb_t, \Delta k_{t-2}$		
First-stage regression coefficients	0.256	0.153	0.287	0.241	0.283
First-stage t-ratio	(4.61)	(2.02)	(3.92)	(3.15)	(3.45)

slopes. In Table 4.2, columns (1)–(3) of Panel A consider the case of exogenous regressors, including mean group (MG) estimates without considering unobserved factors in column (1), Pesaran's (2006) CCE mean group (CCEMG) estimates in column (2), CCEMG allowing for a common break in slopes (CCEMG-b) in column (3). Column (1) of Table 4.2 estimates a heterogeneous model to allow for different elasticities across provinces:

$$\Delta g_{it} = \beta_{b,i}\Delta b_{it} + \beta_{k,i}\Delta k_{it} + \Delta\lambda_t + \Delta\epsilon_{it}. \tag{4.38}$$

Pesaran's (2006) CCEMG reported in column (8) of Table 3.1 is included as column (2) of Table 4.2 as a reference, assuming a factor structure in the error $\Delta\epsilon_{it} = \gamma_i' f_t + \varepsilon_{it}$ in equation (4.38). Column (3) extends Pesaran's (2006) approach by allowing for a common break k_0 in the slopes:

$$\Delta g_{it} = \beta_{b,i}(k_0)\Delta b_{it} + \beta_{k,i}(k_0)\Delta k_{it} + \Delta\lambda_t + \Delta\epsilon_{it}, \Delta\epsilon_{it} = \gamma_i' f_t + \varepsilon_{it}. \tag{4.39}$$

Compared with the first-difference estimates in column (1) of Table 3.1, CCEMG in column (2) of Table 4.2 accommodates two empirical features: slope heterogeneity and cross-sectional dependence. CCEMG-b in column (3) adds one more feature of parameter structural change to CCEMG in column (2). In column (3) of Table 4.2, using the estimation procedure in Baltagi, Feng and Kao (2016), the estimated common break 2004 splits β_b and β_k in two regimes of 1997–2004 and 2005–2015. The CCEMG-b estimates of β_b and β_k deviate moderately from their CCEMG counterparts in column (2) of Table 4.2 in different directions.

Columns (4)–(6) of Panel B of Table 4.2 are the IV versions of columns of (1)–(3) of Table 4.2 assuming that $\Delta b_{it}, \Delta k_{it}$ are endogenous. MG-IV in column (4) is the IV version of MG without considering unobserved common factors. In the simplified case without unobserved common factors, $Y_i = \mathbb{X}_i(k_0)b_i + \varepsilon_i, i = 1, \ldots, N$, Baltagi, Feng and Kao (2019) show that the OLS estimator $\hat{k}$, b_i can be consistently estimated by the IV estimator

$$\hat{b}_{i,IV}(\hat{k}) = [\mathbb{X}_i(\hat{k})' P_{\mathbb{Z}_i(\hat{k})}\mathbb{X}_i(\hat{k})]^{-1}\mathbb{X}_i(\hat{k})' P_{\mathbb{Z}_i(\hat{k})}Y_i,$$

where the projection matrix $P_{\mathbb{Z}_i(\hat{k})} = \mathbb{Z}_i(\hat{k})[\mathbb{Z}_i(\hat{k})'\mathbb{Z}_i(\hat{k})]^{-1}\mathbb{Z}_i(\hat{k})'$. The cross-sectional mean of b_i can be consistently estimated by a mean group (called MG-IV) estimator $\frac{1}{N}\sum_{i=1}^{N} \hat{b}_{i,IV}(\hat{k})$. CCEMG-IV in column (5) refers to the estimator (4.36) assuming no break. Column (6) is the IV version of CCEMG with an estimated common break in the slopes. The instruments $\Delta enb_{it}, \Delta k_{it-2}$ are used for the endogenous $\Delta b_{it}, \Delta k_{it}$. Compared to the

Table 4.2. Output elasticities estimates: Common factors and common break.

Dependent variable: Output per labor

	Panel A: exogeneity				Panel B: endogeneity			
	MG	CCEMG	CCEMG-b		MG-IV	CCEMG-IV	CCEMG-IV-b	
	(1)	(2)	(3)		(4)	(5)	(6)	
Independent variables								
Infrastructure per labor	0.205***	0.194***	0.252***	0.179***	0.156	0.165	0.289*	0.468
	(0.025)	(0.023)	(0.044)	(0.036)	(0.132)	(0.137)	(0.137)	(0.418)
Noninfrastructure per labor	0.361***	0.407***	0.386***	0.441***	0.231*	0.286*	0.527***	−0.370
	(0.031)	(0.037)	(0.052)	(0.047)	(0.149)	(0.174)	(0.168)	(0.597)
Periods	All	All	1997–2004	2005–2015	All	All	1997–2004	2005–2015
Year effects	Yes	Yes	Yes		Yes	Yes	Yes	
No. of observations	569	569	239	330	509	509	179	330
Overall R^2	0.65	0.72	0.78					
Empirical features								
Slope heterogeneity	Yes	Yes	Yes		Yes	Yes	Yes	
Cross-sectional dependence	No	Yes	Yes		No	Yes	Yes	
Structural break	No	No	Yes		No	No	Yes	
Endogeneity	No	No	No		Yes	Yes	Yes	

* and *** for 10% and 1% significance, respectively.

FDIV estimates in column (1) of Table 4.1, the CCEMG-IV estimates in column (5) of Table 4.2 show a positive and significant β_k, but weak evidence on the productivity of infrastructure.

In column (6) of Table 4.2, as suggested by Theorem 1 of Baltagi, Feng and Kao (2019), with endogenous regressors the estimated common break date remains the same as 2004 in column (3). Interestingly, CCEMG-IV-b estimates of β_b and β_k in the period 1997–2004 are 0.289, 0.527 and significant, but no longer significant in the period 2005–2015. Compared with the case of exogenous regressors in column (3), the IV estimates in column (6) have much bigger standard errors.

To look at the effect of choosing structural break on coefficient estimates, we also use the imposed break date of 2007 as in the subsample estimates in columns (4) and (5) of Table 4.1. In this case, the CCEMG-IV-b estimate of β_k becomes 0.765 and significant over the period 2008–2015, but the coefficient of β_b is still insignificant.

This application shows that the proposed panel data model has the advantage of accommodating more empirical features in the data than existing models considered the literature in Panel A of Table 4.2. However, the trade-off seems also pronounced, especially when the endogeneity issue arises. The estimates in Panel B of Table 4.2 become less accurate especially when the sample size is not very big. From this point of view, applied researchers have to strike a balance between model flexibility and data constraints.

4.8. Recent Development

In this section, we review other approaches on estimating panel regression models with structural changes in the recent literature. Specifically, we introduce the Lasso-type approaches proposed by Qian and Su (2016), Li, Qian and Su (2016) and Okui and Wang (2018).

To facilitate the discussion, we start with a simple setup of time-series regression with endogenous regressors and multiple structural changes discussed by Qian and Su (2014):

$$y_t = x_t'\beta_t + \varepsilon_t, \quad t = 1, \ldots, T, \tag{4.40}$$

where slopes β_t vary over time. In this setup, structural breaks in slopes are modeled by time-varying coefficients $\{\beta_1, \ldots, \beta_T\}$, and the sequential changes in β_t are assumed to be sparse. Assume there are m unknown break points $\mathcal{T}_m = \{T_1, \ldots, T_m\}$ in slopes that slit the time span into $m + 1$ intervals, i.e.,

$$\beta_t = \alpha_j \quad \text{for } t = T_{j-1}, \ldots, T_j - 1 \quad \text{and} \quad j = 1, \ldots, m + 1 \qquad (4.41)$$

with $T_0 = 1$ and $T_{m+1} = T$.

To estimate the number of breaks m, break dates $\mathcal{T}_m$, Qian and Su (2014) apply the group-fused Lasso approach in a two-step procedure based on a penalized lease squares

$$\min_{\{\beta_t\}} \frac{1}{T} \sum_{t=1}^{T} (y_t - x_t'\beta_t)^2 + \lambda \sum_{t=2}^{T} \|\beta_t - \beta_{t-1}\|, \qquad (4.42)$$

where λ is the tuning parameter and $\|\cdot\|$ denotes the Frobenius norm. In Step 1, the break date estimates $\tilde{\mathcal{T}}_{\hat{m}_\lambda} = \{\tilde{T}_1, \ldots, \tilde{T}_{\hat{m}_\lambda}\}$ can be obtained by the solution $\{\hat{\beta}_t\}$ to (4.42) such that $\hat{\beta}_t = \hat{\beta}_s$ for t, $s \in [\hat{T}_{j-1}, \hat{T}_j - 1]$ and $\hat{\beta}_{\hat{T}_j} \neq \hat{\beta}_{\hat{T}_{j-1}}$ for $j = 1, \ldots, \hat{m}_\lambda + 1$, where $\hat{m}_\lambda$ denotes the estimated number of breaks.

Qian and Su (2014) prove that if $\hat{m}_\lambda$ is equal to the true number of breaks, $\tilde{\mathcal{T}}_{\hat{m}_\lambda}$ is consistent under certain assumptions. In addition, given that λ is chosen properly by minimizing a BIC-type information criterion, $\hat{m}_\lambda$ can be consistently estimated with a probability approaching to one. In Step 2, regime-specific parameters $\alpha_m = (\alpha_1', \ldots, \alpha_{m+1}')'$ can be consistently estimated by applying the post-Lasso GMM procedure.

Recently, Qian and Su (2016) extend their work from a time-series regression model to a panel data model with exogenous regressors:

$$y_{it} = \mu_i + x_{it}'\beta_t + u_{it}, \quad i = 1, \ldots, n; t = 1, \ldots, T \geq 2, \qquad (4.43)$$

where time-varying coefficients $\{\beta_1, \ldots, \beta_T\}$ follow the same modeling setup (4.41) with parameters of interest: $\mathcal{T}_m = \{T_1, \ldots, T_m\}$, number of breaks m and $\alpha_m = (\alpha_1', \ldots, \alpha_{m+1}')'$. In this panel data model, first differencing is used to remove μ_i,

$$\Delta y_{it} = x_{it}'\beta_t - x_{i,t-1}'\beta_{t-1} + \Delta u_{it}$$
$$= \Delta x_{it}'\beta_t + x_{i,t-1}'(\beta_t - \beta_{t-1}) + \Delta u_{it}.$$

As in Qian and Su (2014), a two-step procedure is applied to estimate parameters of interest. In Step 1, a penalized least squares (PLS) is used to obtain shrinkage estimators of breaks $\widetilde{\mathcal{T}}_{\hat{m}} = \left\{\tilde{T}_1, \ldots, \tilde{T}_{\hat{m}_\lambda}\right\}$ and $\hat{m}_\lambda$:

$$\min_{\{\beta_t\}} \frac{1}{n} \sum_{i=1}^{n} \sum_{t=2}^{T} (\triangle y_{it} - x_{it}'\beta_t + x_{i,t-1}'\beta_{t-1})^2 + \lambda \sum_{t=2}^{T} \dot{w}_t \left\|\beta_t - \beta_{t-1}\right\|,$$

$$(4.44)$$

where λ_1 is the tuning parameter. In this adaptive group-fused lasso (AGFL) approach, weights $\dot{w}_t$ are used and treated as known by using preliminary estimates of $\{\beta_t\}$. The new features in this panel data model include transformed equation due to first differencing and additional dimension $\sum_{i=1}^{n}$ due to the data along the cross-sectional dimension.

Similar to the time-series model (4.42), the estimators of breaks $\widetilde{\mathcal{T}}_{\hat{m}} = \left\{\tilde{T}_1, \ldots, \tilde{T}_{\hat{m}_\lambda}\right\}$ and $\hat{m}_\lambda$ are shown to be consistent under certain conditions given that tuning parameter λ is carefully chosen. In Step 2, post-Lasso estimation is applied to obtain consistent estimator of slopes $\tilde{\alpha}_{\hat{m}}^{p} = \tilde{\alpha}_{\hat{m}}^{p}(\widetilde{\mathcal{T}}_{\hat{m}_\lambda}) = \{\hat{\alpha}_j\}$ for each regime, $j = 1, \ldots, \hat{m} + 1$, based on $\widetilde{\mathcal{T}}_{\hat{m}_\lambda} = \left\{\tilde{T}_1, \ldots, \tilde{T}_{\hat{m}_\lambda}\right\}$ in Step 1:

$$\min_{\alpha_m} \frac{1}{n} \sum_{j=1}^{m+1} \sum_{t=T_{j-1}}^{T_j-1} \sum_{i=1}^{n} (\triangle y_{it} - \triangle x_{it}'\beta_t - x_{i,t-1}'(\beta_t - \beta_{t-1}))^2$$

$$= \min_{\alpha_m} \frac{1}{n} \sum_{j=1}^{m+1} \sum_{t=T_{j-1}}^{T_j-1} \sum_{i=1}^{n} (\triangle y_{it} - \triangle x_{it}'\alpha_j)^2$$

or

$$\min_{\alpha_m} \frac{1}{n} \sum_{j=1}^{m+1} \sum_{t=T_{j-1}}^{T_j-1} \sum_{i=1}^{n} (\triangle y_{it} - \triangle x_{it}'\alpha_j)^2$$

$$+ \frac{1}{n} \sum_{j=1}^{m} \sum_{i=1}^{n} (\triangle y_{iT_j} - x_{iT_j}'\alpha_{j+1} + x_{i,T_j-1}'\alpha_j)^2$$

where the second term is used for asymptotic efficiency.

By generalizing the fixed effects μ_i in (4.43) to interactive fixed effects modeled by a factor structure $\lambda_i'f_t$, Li, Qian and Su (2016) extend Bai's (2009) model to the case of multiple breaks in slopes:

$$y_{it} = x_{it}'\beta_t + \lambda_i'f_t + \varepsilon_{it}, \quad i = 1, \ldots, n; t = 1, \ldots, T, \qquad (4.45)$$

where $\{\beta_1, \ldots, \beta_T\}$ follow the same modeling setup (4.41) with break dates $\mathcal{T}_m = \{T_1, \ldots, T_m\}$, number of breaks m and $\alpha_m = (\alpha_1', \ldots, \alpha_{m+1}')'$.

Here, f_t denote unobserved factors and λ_i are corresponding loading vectors. To deal with the latent factor structure, a novel penalized principal component (PPC) estimation procedure is introduced:

$$\min_{\{\beta_t, f_t, \lambda_i\}} \frac{1}{nT} \sum_{j=1}^{m+1} \sum_{t=T_{j-1}}^{T_j - 1} \sum_{i=1}^{n} (y_{it} - x_{it}'\beta_t - \lambda_i' f_t)^2 + \frac{\lambda}{T} \sum_{t=2}^{T} \dot{w}_t \, \|\beta_t - \beta_{t-1}\|.$$

(4.46)

The latent factor structure in (4.46) brings rich empirical features, e.g., cross-sectional dependence, at a cost of additional unknown parameters $\{f_t, \lambda_i\}$ to estimate, besides $\{\beta_t\}$ in (4.42) in a time-series setup and in (4.44) in a panel data model. Thus, an iteration procedure similar to Bai's (2009) IPC approach is applied to the first term of estimate $\{\beta_t, f_t, \lambda_i\}$. Then, the rest procedure falls into the framework of (4.44).

Okui and Wang (2018) consider a group pattern of heterogeneity and structural breaks in slopes in a panel data model:

$$y_{it} = x_{it}'\beta_{i,t} + \varepsilon_{it}, \quad i = 1, \dots, n; \ t = 1, \dots, T,$$

where $\beta_{i,t}$ are group specific and time-varying within the group $g_i, \{\beta_{g,1}, \dots, \beta_{g,T}\}$, i.e.,

$$y_{it} = x_{it}'\beta_{g_i,t} + \varepsilon_{it}.$$

In this model, slopes $\beta_{g_i,t}$ vary across groups and over time. The AGFL approach proposed by Qian and Su (2016) is applied to estimate the group structure and slopes.

In these Lasso-type papers discussed above, structural breaks in slopes are modeled by time-varying parameters. Compared with the traditional modeling of structural breaks by allowing one or very a few jumps in slopes in time-series literature, this modeling approach is more like a top-down strategy by allowing changes in any time periods with a sparsity restriction. The model flexibility of this top-down strategy could accommodate more empirical features in the data than existing methods, and the phenomenon of structural breaks in slopes is considered as *a* model among a set of models dependent on values of model parameters. In this way, identifying structural breaks and parameters is equivalent to a model selection procedure, and shrinkage or Lasso approaches are thus applied to estimate slope parameters, break dates, and number of breaks all together.

Compared with the traditional structural break literature, the Lasso-type approaches have been proved to be more flexible in modeling, but, at a cost of being less straightforward to implement the proposed estimation procedures. In addition, the consistency of Lasso estimators of breaks and slope parameters depends on a proper choice of tuning parameters, which requires certain conditions. In empirical studies, it seems unclear whether the required conditions are guaranteed.

4.9. Technical Details

This section provides technical details required to prove the main findings above. Since the panel data model (4.6) considered here includes the time-series model in Bai (1997a) as a special case of $n = 1$, it can be shown similarly that $\hat{k} - k_0 = O_p(1)$. In the proofs that follow, we assume $\hat{k} - k_0$ is stochastically bounded. With more information along the cross-sectional dimension under the common break assumption, we further show that $\hat{k} - k_0 \xrightarrow{p} 0$ as $(n, T) \to \infty$.

For $i = 1, \ldots, n$, let SSR_i be the sum of squared residuals of regressing Y_i on X_i in case there is no break, i.e., $Z_{2i}(k) = 0_{T \times q}$. Using the identity

$$\text{SSR}_i - \text{SSR}_i(k) = [Y_i - X_i\hat{\beta}_i(k) - Z_{2i}(k)\hat{\delta}_i(k)]'[Y_i - X_i\hat{\beta}_i(k) - Z_{2i}(k)\hat{\delta}_i(k)]$$

$$- [Y_i - X_i\hat{\beta}_i(k)]'[Y_i - X_i\hat{\beta}_i(k)]$$

$$= \hat{\delta}_i(k)'[Z_{2i}(k)'M_iZ_{2i}(k)]\hat{\delta}_i(k)$$

with $M_i = I - X_i(X_i'X_i)^{-1}X_i'$,

$$\hat{k} = \arg \min_{1 \le k \le T-1} \sum_{i=1}^{n} \text{SSR}_i(k) = \arg \max_{1 \le k \le T-1} \sum_{i=1}^{n} SV_i(k)$$

$$= \arg \max_{1 \le k \le T-1} \sum_{i=1}^{n} [SV_i(k) - SV_i(k_0)],$$

where $SV_i(k) = \hat{\delta}_i(k)'[Z_{2i}(k)'M_iZ_{2i}(k)]\hat{\delta}_i(k)$. Note that $SV_i(k_0) = \hat{\delta}_i(k_0)'[Z_{0i}'M_iZ_{0i}]\hat{\delta}_i(k_0)$ is not a function of k.

To prove Theorem 4.1, $\sum_{i=1}^{n}[SV_i(k) - SV_i(k_0)]$ can be decomposed into a deterministic part and a stochastic one. Partitioned regression gives

$$\hat{\delta}_i(k) = [Z_{2i}(k)'M_iZ_{2i}(k)]^{-1} Z_{2i}(k)'M_iY_i, \quad i = 1, \ldots, n.$$

Substituting $Y_i = X_i\beta_i + Z_{0i}\delta_i + \varepsilon_i$ into the equation above, we obtain

$$\hat{\delta}_i(k) = [Z_{2i}(k)'M_i Z_{2i}(k)]^{-1} Z_{2i}(k)'M_i Z_{0i}\delta_i$$
$$+ [Z_{2i}(k)'M_i Z_{2i}(k)]^{-1} Z_{2i}(k)'M_i \varepsilon_i$$

and $\hat{\delta}_i(k_0) = \delta_i + (Z'_{0i}M_i Z_{0i})^{-1} Z_{0i}'M_i \varepsilon_i$.

To simplify notation, k is suppressed in $\hat{\delta}_i(k)$ and $Z_{2i}(k)$ when no confusion arises. Since

$$SV_i(k) = \hat{\delta}'_i(Z'_{2i}M_i Z_{2i})\hat{\delta}_i$$
$$= \delta'_i(Z'_{0i}M_i Z_{2i})(Z'_{2i}M_i Z_{2i})^{-1}(Z'_{2i}M_i Z_{0i})\delta_i$$
$$+ 2\delta'_i(Z'_{0i}M_i Z_{2i})(Z'_{2i}M_i Z_{2i})^{-1}Z'_{2i}M_i \varepsilon_i$$
$$+ \varepsilon'_i M_i Z_{2i}(Z'_{2i}M_i Z_{2i})^{-1}Z'_{2i}M_i \varepsilon_i,$$

it follows that

$$SV_i(k) - SV_i(k_0)$$
$$= -\delta'_i[(Z'_{0i}M_i Z_{0i}) - (Z'_{0i}M_i Z_{2i})(Z'_{2i}M_i Z_{2i})^{-1}(Z'_{2i}M_i Z_{0i})]\delta_i \quad (4.47)$$
$$+ 2\delta'_i(Z'_{0i}M_i Z_{2i})(Z'_{2i}M_i Z_{2i})^{-1}Z'_{2i}M_i \varepsilon_i - 2\delta'_i Z'_{0i}M_i \varepsilon_i \quad (4.48)$$
$$+ \varepsilon'_i M_i Z_{2i}(Z'_{2i}M_i Z_{2i})^{-1}Z'_{2i}M_i \varepsilon_i - \varepsilon'_i M_i Z_{0i}(Z'_{0i}M_i Z_{0i})^{-1}Z'_{0i}M_i \varepsilon_i. \quad (4.49)$$

The deterministic part is denoted by

$$J_{1i}(k) = \delta'_i[(Z'_{0i}M_i Z_{0i}) - (Z'_{0i}M_i Z_{2i})(Z'_{2i}M_i Z_{2i})^{-1}(Z'_{2i}M_i Z_{0i})]\delta_i, \quad (4.50)$$

and the stochastic part is denoted by

$$J_{2i}(k) = 2\delta'_i(Z'_{0i}M_i Z_{2i})(Z'_{2i}M_i Z_{2i})^{-1}Z'_{2i}M_i \varepsilon_i$$
$$- 2\delta'_i Z'_{0i}M_i \varepsilon_i + \varepsilon'_i M_i Z_{2i}(Z'_{2i}M_i Z_{2i})^{-1}Z'_{2i}M_i \varepsilon_i$$
$$- \varepsilon'_i M_i Z_{0i}(Z'_{0i}M_i Z_{0i})^{-1}Z'_{0i}M_i \varepsilon_i.$$

Thus $SV_i(k) - SV_i(k_0) = -J_{1i}(k) + J_{2i}(k)$ and

$$\hat{k} = \arg\max_{1 \le k \le T-1} \sum_{i=1}^{n}[SV_i(k) - SV_i(k_0)]$$

$$= \arg\max_{1 \le k \le T-1} \left[-\sum_{i=1}^{n} J_{1i}(k) + \sum_{i=1}^{n} J_{2i}(k) \right].$$

Define

$$X_{\Delta i} = \begin{cases} X_{2i} - X_{0i} = (0, \ldots, 0, x_{i,k+1}, \ldots, x_{i,k_0}, 0, \ldots, 0)' & \text{for } k < k_0, \\ -(X_{2i} - X_{0i}) = (0, \ldots, 0, x_{i,k_0+1}, \ldots, x_{i,k}, 0, \ldots, 0)' & \text{for } k \geq k_0, \end{cases}$$

and $Z_{\Delta i}$ can be defined similarly.

For a finite large number C_k and arbitrarily small positive number $a < \tau_0$, define the set $K(C_k) = \{k : 1 \leq |k - k_0| < C_k, aT < k < (1-a)T\}$. Since $\hat{k} - k_0$ is stochastically bounded, we only consider the values of k that belong to set $K(C_k)$.

Let $\lambda_1(k)$ be the minimum eigenvalue of $\frac{1}{n} \sum_{i=1}^n R'(X'_{\Delta i} X_{\Delta i}) R$. Define $\lambda_1 = \min_{k \in K(C_k)} \lambda_1(k)$. Under Assumption 4.5, $\lambda_1(k) > 0$ and $\lambda_1 > 0$.

Lemma 4.1. *Under Assumptions* 4.1–4.7, *for all large n and T, with probability tending to 1,*

$$\inf_{K(C_k)} \sum_{i=1}^n J_{1i}(k) \geq \lambda_1 \phi_N.$$

This lemma is similar to Lemma A.2 in Bai (1997a).

Lemma 4.2. *Under Assumptions* 4.1–4.7, *uniformly on $K(C_k)$,*

(i) $\sum_{i=1}^n \delta'_i Z'_{\Delta i} \varepsilon_i = O_p(\sqrt{\phi_N})$;

(ii) $\frac{1}{\sqrt{T}} \sum_{i=1}^n \delta'_i Z'_{\Delta i} X_i (\frac{X'_i X_i}{T})^{-1} \frac{X'_i \varepsilon_i}{\sqrt{T}} = O_p(\sqrt{\frac{\phi_N}{T}})$;

(iii) $\frac{1}{\sqrt{T}} \sum_{i=1}^n \delta'_i (Z'_{\Delta i} M_i Z_{2i}) (\frac{Z'_{2i} M_i Z_{2i}}{T})^{-1} \frac{Z'_{2i} M_i \varepsilon_i}{\sqrt{T}} = O_p(\sqrt{\frac{\phi_N}{T}})$;

(iv) $\frac{1}{T} \sum_{i=1}^n \varepsilon'_i M_i Z_{\Delta i} (\frac{Z'_{2i} M_i Z_{2i}}{T})^{-1} Z'_{\Delta i} M_i \varepsilon_i = O_p(\frac{n}{T})$;

(v) $\frac{1}{T} \sum_{i=1}^n \varepsilon'_i M_i Z_{0i} (\frac{Z'_{2i} M_i Z_{2i}}{T})^{-1} Z'_{\Delta i} M_i \varepsilon_i = O_p(\frac{n}{T}) + O_p(\sqrt{\frac{n}{T}})$;

(vi) $\sum_{i=1}^n \frac{\varepsilon'_i M_i Z_{0i}}{\sqrt{T}} \left[(\frac{Z'_{2i} M_i Z_{2i}}{T})^{-1} - (\frac{Z'_{0i} M_i Z_{0i}}{T})^{-1} \right] \frac{Z'_{0i} M_i \varepsilon_i}{\sqrt{T}} = O_p(\frac{n}{T})$.

Proof of Lemma 4.2. (i) Under Assumption 4.3, for large n,

$$\text{Var} \left(\sum_{i=1}^n \delta'_i Z'_{\Delta i} \varepsilon_i \right) = \sum_{i=1}^n \delta'_i Z'_{\Delta i} \Sigma_{\varepsilon,i} Z_{\Delta i} \delta_i.$$

It can be shown equal to $O(\phi_N)$ under Assumptions 4.4–4.7, implying $\sum_{i=1}^n \delta'_i Z'_{\Delta i} \varepsilon_i = O_p(\sqrt{\phi_N})$ on $K(C_k)$.

The proofs of Lemma 4.2(ii)–(vi) are similar. $\qquad\qquad\square$

With these lemmas, we are ready to prove Theorem 4.1.

Proof of Theorem 4.1. To prove $\lim_{(N,T)\to\infty} P(\hat{k} = k_0) = 1$, it is equivalent to show that, for any given $\epsilon > 0$, for both large T and n, $P(|\hat{k} - k_0| \geq 1) < \epsilon$. It is sufficient to show that $P(\sup_{K(C_k)} \sum_{i=1}^{n}[SV_i(k) - SV_i(k_0)] \geq 0) < \epsilon$, or

$$P\left(\sup_{K(C_k)} \left|\sum_{i=1}^{n} J_{2i}(k)\right| \geq \inf_{K(C_k)} \sum_{i=1}^{n} J_{1i}(k)\right) < \epsilon.$$

By Lemma 4.1, it suffices to show $P(\sup_{K(C_k)} \frac{1}{\phi_N} |\sum_{i=1}^{n} J_{2i}(k)| \geq \lambda_1) < \epsilon$. For any $k \in K(C_k)$,

$$\left|\sum_{i=1}^{n} J_{2i}(k)\right| \leq \left|\sum_{i=1}^{n} \left[2\delta_i'(Z_{0i}'M_i Z_{2i})(Z_{2i}'M_i Z_{2i})^{-1}Z_{2i}'M_i\varepsilon_i - 2\delta_i'Z_{0i}'M_i\varepsilon_i\right]\right|$$

$$+ \left|\sum_{i=1}^{n} \left[\varepsilon_i'M_i Z_{2i}(Z_{2i}'M_i Z_{2i})^{-1}Z_{2i}'M_i\varepsilon_i\right.\right.$$

$$\left.\left.- \varepsilon_i'M_i Z_{0i}(Z_{0i}'M_i Z_{0i})^{-1}Z_{0i}'M_i\varepsilon_i\right]\right|.$$

Consider the first term, $Z_{2i} = Z_{0i} + Z_{\Delta i}$ for $k < k_0$,

$$\left|\sum_{i=1}^{n} \left[2\delta_i'(Z_{0i}'M_i Z_{2i})(Z_{2i}'M_i Z_{2i})^{-1}Z_{2i}'M_i\varepsilon_i - 2\delta_i'Z_{0i}'M_i\varepsilon_i\right]\right|$$

$$= \left|\sum_{i=1}^{n} \left[2\delta_i'Z_{\Delta i}'M_i\varepsilon_i - 2\delta_i'(Z_{\Delta i}'M_i Z_{2i})(Z_{2i}'M_i Z_{2i})^{-1}Z_{2i}'M_i\varepsilon_i\right]\right|$$

$$\leq 2\left|\sum_{i=1}^{n} \delta_i'Z_{\Delta i}'\varepsilon_i\right| + \frac{2}{\sqrt{T}}\left|\sum_{i=1}^{n} \delta_i'Z_{\Delta i}'X_i\left(\frac{X_i'X_i}{T}\right)^{-1}\frac{X_i'\varepsilon_i}{\sqrt{T}}\right|$$

$$+ \frac{2}{\sqrt{T}}\left|\sum_{i=1}^{n} \delta_i'\left[(Z_{\Delta i}'M_i Z_{2i})\left(\frac{Z_{2i}'M_i Z_{2i}}{T}\right)^{-1}\frac{Z_{2i}'M_i\varepsilon_i}{\sqrt{T}}\right]\right|.$$

By (i), (ii) and (iii) of Lemma 4.2, the first term

$$\left|\sum_{i=1}^{n} \left[2\delta_i'(Z_{0i}'M_i Z_{2i})(Z_{2i}'M_i Z_{2i})^{-1}Z_{2i}'M_i\varepsilon_i - 2\delta_i'Z_{0i}'M_i\varepsilon_i\right]\right| = O_p(\sqrt{\phi_N}).$$

$$(4.51)$$

Now consider the second term

$$\left| \sum_{i=1}^{n} \left[\varepsilon_i' M_i Z_{2i} (Z_{2i}' M_i Z_{2i})^{-1} Z_{2i}' M_i \varepsilon_i - \varepsilon_i' M_i Z_{0i} (Z_{0i}' M_i Z_{0i})^{-1} Z_{0i}' M_i \varepsilon_i \right] \right|$$

$$\leq \frac{1}{T} \left| \sum_{i=1}^{n} \varepsilon_i' M_i Z_{\Delta i} \left(\frac{Z_{2i}' M_i Z_{2i}}{T} \right)^{-1} Z_{\Delta i}' M_i \varepsilon_i \right|$$

$$+ 2 \frac{1}{\sqrt{T}} \left| \sum_{i=1}^{n} \frac{\varepsilon_i' M_i Z_{0i}}{\sqrt{T}} \left(\frac{Z_{2i}' M_i Z_{2i}}{T} \right)^{-1} Z_{\Delta i}' M_i \varepsilon_i \right|$$

$$+ \left| \sum_{i=1}^{n} \frac{\varepsilon_i' M_i Z_{0i}}{\sqrt{T}} \left[\left(\frac{Z_{2i}' M_i Z_{2i}}{T} \right)^{-1} - \left(\frac{Z_{0i}' M_i Z_{0i}}{T} \right)^{-1} \right] \frac{Z_{0i}' M_i \varepsilon_i}{\sqrt{T}} \right|.$$

Similarly, by (iv), (v) and (vi) of Lemma 4.2, the second term

$$\left| \sum_{i=1}^{N} \left[\varepsilon_i' M_i Z_{2i} (Z_{2i}' M_i Z_{2i})^{-1} Z_{2i}' M_i \varepsilon_i - \varepsilon_i' M_i Z_{0i} (Z_{0i}' M_i Z_{0i})^{-1} Z_{0i}' M_i \varepsilon_i \right] \right|$$

$$= O_p \left(\frac{n}{T} \right) + O_p \left(\sqrt{\frac{n}{T}} \right). \tag{4.52}$$

Combining (4.51) and (4.52), we obtain

$$\frac{1}{\phi_N} \left| \sum_{i=1}^{n} J_{2i}(k) \right| = \frac{1}{\phi_N} \left[O_p(\sqrt{\phi_N}) + O_p \left(\frac{n}{T} \right) + O_p \left(\sqrt{\frac{n}{T}} \right) \right]$$

$$= O_p \left(\frac{1}{\sqrt{\phi_N}} \right) + \frac{1}{\phi_N} \left[O_p \left(\frac{n}{T} \right) + O_p \left(\sqrt{\frac{n}{T}} \right) \right].$$

Under Assumption 4.2, $\frac{1}{\phi_N} \left| \sum_{i=1}^{n} J_{2i}(k) \right|$ vanishes for any $k \in K(C_k)$, so does its maximum. $\square$

Proof of Theorem 4.2. Compared with (4.8) of Model 1, equation (4.21) of Model 2 has the same form using transformed data $\{\tilde{Y}_i, \tilde{X}_i, i = 1, \ldots, n\}$, except for the additional term $M_w F \gamma_i$. The focus of the proof of Theorem 4.2 is on showing that $M_w F \gamma_i$ can be ignored asymptotically as $(n, T) \to \infty$.

For $i = 1, \ldots, n$, let $\widetilde{\text{SSR}}_i$ be the sum of squared residuals of regressing $\tilde{Y}_i$ on $\tilde{X}_i$ alone. Using the identity $\widetilde{\text{SSR}}_i - \widetilde{\text{SSR}}_i(k) = \tilde{\delta}_i(k)'[\tilde{Z}_{2i}(k)'\tilde{M}_i\tilde{Z}_{2i}(k)]\tilde{\delta}_i(k)$ with $\tilde{M}_i = I - \tilde{X}_i(\tilde{X}_i'\tilde{X}_i)^{-1}\tilde{X}_i'$, we obtain

$$\hat{k} = \arg\min_{1 \leq k \leq T-1} \sum_{i=1}^{n} \widetilde{\text{SSR}}_i(k) = \arg\max_{1 \leq k \leq T-1} \sum_{i=1}^{n} \widetilde{SV}_i(k)$$

$$= \arg\max_{1 \leq k \leq T-1} \sum_{i=1}^{n} [\widetilde{SV}_i(k) - \widetilde{SV}_i(k_0)],$$

where $\widetilde{SV}_i(k) = \tilde{\delta}_i(k)'[\tilde{Z}_{2i}(k)'\tilde{M}_i\tilde{Z}_{2i}(k)]\tilde{\delta}_i(k)$.

Partitioned regression gives

$$\tilde{\delta}_i(k) = \left[\tilde{Z}_{2i}(k)'\tilde{M}_i\tilde{Z}_{2i}(k)\right]^{-1}\tilde{Z}_{2i}(k)'\tilde{M}_i\tilde{Y}_i.$$

Substituting $\tilde{Y}_i = \tilde{X}_i\beta_i + \tilde{Z}_{0i}\delta_i + \tilde{\varepsilon}_i^0$ into the equation above, we obtain

$$\tilde{\delta}_i(k) = \left[\tilde{Z}_{2i}(k)'\tilde{M}_i\tilde{Z}_{2i}(k)\right]^{-1}\tilde{Z}_{2i}(k)'\tilde{M}_i\tilde{Z}_{0i}\delta_i$$

$$+ \left[\tilde{Z}_{2i}(k)'\tilde{M}_i\tilde{Z}_{2i}(k)\right]^{-1}\tilde{Z}_{2i}(k)'\tilde{M}_i\tilde{\varepsilon}_i^0$$

and $\tilde{\delta}_i(k_0) = \delta_i + \left(\tilde{Z}_{0i}'\tilde{M}_i\tilde{Z}_{0i}\right)^{-1}\tilde{Z}_{0i}'\tilde{M}_i\tilde{\varepsilon}_i^0$.

The rest of proof can proceed in the same way as that of Theorem 4.1 using the new notations with "~". Note that there is an additional term $M_w F\gamma_i$ in $\tilde{\varepsilon}_i^0 = M_w F\gamma_i + \tilde{\varepsilon}_i$ in Model 2. In what follows, we show that each element of $M_w F\gamma_i$ is of order $O_p(\frac{1}{\sqrt{n}})$, which implies that $\tilde{\varepsilon}_i^0$ behaves as ε_i as in Model 1 asymptotically as $n \to \infty$. $\square$

To examine the effect of this extra term on the estimated $\tilde{k}$ and $\tilde{b}_i$, we introduce some new matrix notation. Since $x_{it} = \Gamma_i'f_t + v_{it}$ in (4.3), we write

$$\underset{T \times p}{X_i} = \underset{T \times m}{F} \underset{m \times p}{\Gamma_i} + \underset{T \times p}{V_i},$$

where $V_i = (v_{i1}, \ldots, v_{iT})'$. Denote $F_0 = (0, \ldots, 0, f_{k_0+1}, \ldots, f_T)'$ and $V_{0i} = (0, \ldots, 0, v_{i,k_0+1}, \ldots, v_{i,T})'$. Thus,

$$X_{0i} = (0, \ldots, 0, x_{i,k_0+1}, \ldots, x_{i,T})'$$

$$= (0, \ldots, 0, \Gamma_i'f_{k_0+1} + v_{i,k_0+1}, \ldots, \Gamma_i'f_T + v_{i,T})'$$

$$= F_0\Gamma_i + V_{0i}.$$

For the error term (4.18), denote

$$\bar{u}_t = \begin{pmatrix} \bar{\varepsilon}_t + \sum_{i=1}^{n} \theta_i v_{it}' \beta_i \\ \bar{v}_t \end{pmatrix} \quad \text{and}$$

$$\Delta \bar{u}_t(k_0) = \begin{cases} \begin{pmatrix} 0 \\ 0 \end{pmatrix}, & t = 1, \ldots, k_0, \\ \begin{pmatrix} \sum_{i=1}^{n} \theta_i v_{it}' R \delta_i \\ 0 \end{pmatrix}, & t = k_0 + 1, \ldots, T. \end{cases}$$

Thus, $\bar{u}_t(k_0) = \sum_{i=1}^{n} \theta_i u_{it}(k_0) = \bar{u}_t + \Delta \bar{u}_t(k_0)$. Denote $\bar{U} = (\bar{u}_1, \ldots, \bar{u}_T)'$ and

$$\Delta \bar{U}(k_0) = \left(\begin{pmatrix} 0 \\ 0 \end{pmatrix}, \ldots, \begin{pmatrix} 0 \\ 0 \end{pmatrix}, \begin{pmatrix} \sum_{i=1}^{n} \theta_i v_{i,k_0+1}' R \delta_i \\ 0 \end{pmatrix}, \ldots, \begin{pmatrix} \sum_{i=1}^{n} \theta_i v_{i,T}' R \delta_i \\ 0 \end{pmatrix} \right)'.$$

Thus, stacking cross-sectional averages $\bar{w}_t = \bar{C}(k_0)' f_t + \bar{u}_t(k_0)$, we obtain

$$\underset{T \times (p+1)}{\bar{W}} = (\bar{w}_1, \ldots, \bar{w}_{k_0}, \bar{w}_{k_0+1}, \ldots, \bar{w}_T)'$$

$$= (\bar{C}_1' f_1 + \bar{u}_1, \ldots, \bar{C}_1' f_{k_0} + \bar{u}_{k_0}, \bar{C}_2' f_{k_0+1} + \bar{u}_{k_0+1}, \ldots, \bar{C}_2' f_T + \bar{u}_T)'$$

$$= F \bar{C}_1 + F_0 (\bar{C}_2 - \bar{C}_1) + \bar{U} + \Delta \bar{U}(k_0).$$

Denote

$$\underset{T \times 2m}{\mathbb{F}} = (F, F_0), \quad \underset{2m \times (p+1)}{\overline{\mathbb{C}}} = (\bar{C}_1', (\bar{C}_2 - \bar{C}_1)')' \quad \text{and} \quad \underset{T \times (p+1)}{\overline{\mathbb{U}}} = \bar{U} + \Delta \bar{U}(k_0).$$

Therefore,

$$\bar{W} = \mathbb{F} \overline{\mathbb{C}} + \overline{\mathbb{U}}. \tag{4.53}$$

With this notation, we obtain lemmas, which can be proved similarly to Lemmas 1–3 in Pesaran (2006).

Lemma 4.3. *Under Assumptions* 4.1, 4.2, 4.8–4.15, *uniformly on* $K(C_k)$,

(i) $\bar{u}_t = O_p(\frac{1}{\sqrt{n}})$, $\Delta \bar{u}_t(k_0) = O_p(\frac{1}{\sqrt{n}})$;

(ii) $\frac{1}{T}\bar{\mathbb{U}}'\bar{\mathbb{U}} = O_p(\frac{1}{n})$; $\frac{1}{T}\mathbb{F}'\bar{\mathbb{U}} = O_p(\frac{1}{\sqrt{nT}})$, $\frac{1}{T}V_i'\mathbb{F} = O_p(\frac{1}{\sqrt{T}})$;

(iii) $\frac{1}{T}V_i'\bar{\mathbb{U}} = O_p(\frac{1}{n}) + O_p(\frac{1}{\sqrt{nT}})$, $\frac{1}{T}\varepsilon_i'\bar{\mathbb{U}} = O_p(\frac{1}{n}) + O_p(\frac{1}{\sqrt{nT}})$, $\frac{1}{T}V_{0i}'\bar{\mathbb{U}} = O_p(\frac{1}{n}) + O_p(\frac{1}{\sqrt{nT}})$;

(iv) $\frac{1}{T}X_i'\bar{\mathbb{U}} = O_p(\frac{1}{n}) + O_p(\frac{1}{\sqrt{nT}})$; $\frac{1}{T}X_{0i}'\bar{\mathbb{U}} = O_p(\frac{1}{n}) + O_p(\frac{1}{\sqrt{nT}})$.

Lemma 4.4. *Under Assumptions* 4.1, 4.2, 4.8–4.15, *uniformly on* $K(C_k)$,

(i) $\frac{1}{T}\mathbb{F}'\mathbb{F} = O_p(1)$; $\frac{1}{T}\mathbb{F}'F = O_p(1)$;

(ii) $\frac{1}{T}X_i'\mathbb{F} = O_p(1)$; $\frac{1}{T}\mathbb{X}_i(k)'\mathbb{F} = O_p(1)$.

Proof. Item (i) is obvious by Assumption 4.8.

(ii) Since $X_i = F\Gamma_i + V_i = (F, F_0)(\Gamma_i', 0)' + V_i$, $\frac{1}{T}X_i'\mathbb{F}$ can be written as $(\Gamma_i', 0)(\frac{1}{T}\mathbb{F}'\mathbb{F}) + \frac{1}{T}V_i'\mathbb{F}$. By (i) and Lemma 4.3(iv), $\frac{1}{T}X_i'\mathbb{F} = O_p(1)$. Similarly, $\frac{1}{T}\mathbb{X}_i(k)'\mathbb{F} = O_p(1)$. $\square$

With Lemmas 4.3 and 4.4, we are ready to establish the property of the $T \times m$ matrix $M_w F\gamma_i$, which will be frequently used in the derivations below. Denote

$$\underset{(p+1)\times(p+1)}{E} = \frac{1}{T}\overline{\mathbb{C}}'\mathbb{F}'\bar{\mathbb{U}} + \frac{1}{T}\bar{\mathbb{U}}'\mathbb{F}\overline{\mathbb{C}} + \frac{1}{T}\bar{\mathbb{U}}'\bar{\mathbb{U}};$$

$$\underset{(p+1)\times(p+1)}{f(E)} = \sum_{k=1}^{\infty}(-1)^{k+1}\left[\left(\frac{1}{T}\overline{\mathbb{C}}'\mathbb{F}'\mathbb{F}\overline{\mathbb{C}}\right)^{-1}E\right]^k\left(\frac{1}{T}\overline{\mathbb{C}}'\mathbb{F}'\mathbb{F}\overline{\mathbb{C}}\right)^{-1}.$$

By Lemma 4.4(v), $E = O_p(\frac{1}{n}) + O_p(\frac{1}{\sqrt{nT}})$, thus $f(E) = O_p(\frac{1}{n}) + O_p(\frac{1}{\sqrt{nT}})$. In addition, denote

$$\underset{2m\times m}{D_1} = -\overline{\mathbb{C}}f(E)\overline{\mathbb{C}}'\frac{\mathbb{F}'F}{T} + \overline{\mathbb{C}}\left[\left(\overline{\mathbb{C}}'\frac{\mathbb{F}'\mathbb{F}}{T}\overline{\mathbb{C}}\right)^{-1} + f(E)\right]\frac{\bar{\mathbb{U}}'F}{T} \quad (4.54)$$

and

$$\underset{(p+1)\times m}{D_2} = -\left[\left(\overline{\mathbb{C}}'\frac{\mathbb{F}'\mathbb{F}}{T}\overline{\mathbb{C}}\right)^{-1} + f(E)\right]\left(\overline{\mathbb{C}}'\frac{\mathbb{F}'F}{T} + \frac{\bar{\mathbb{U}}'F}{T}\right). \quad (4.55)$$

Since $\overline{\mathbb{C}} = O(1)$, $\frac{\mathbb{F}'F}{T}$ and $\frac{\mathbb{F}'\mathbb{F}}{T}$ are $O_p(1)$, $f(E) = O_p(\frac{1}{n}) + O_p(\frac{1}{\sqrt{nT}})$, and $\frac{\bar{\mathbb{U}}'F}{T} = O_p(\frac{1}{\sqrt{nT}})$,

$$
D_1 = O_p(1) \left[O_p\left(\frac{1}{n}\right) + O_p\left(\frac{1}{\sqrt{nT}}\right) \right] O_p(1)
$$
$$
+ O_p(1) \left[O_p(1) + O_p\left(\frac{1}{n}\right) + O_p\left(\frac{1}{\sqrt{nT}}\right) \right] O_p\left(\frac{1}{\sqrt{nT}}\right)
$$
$$
= O_p\left(\frac{1}{n}\right) + O_p\left(\frac{1}{\sqrt{nT}}\right).
$$

Similarly,

$$
D_2 = \left[O_p(1) + O_p\left(\frac{1}{n}\right) + O_p\left(\frac{1}{\sqrt{nT}}\right) \right] \left[O_p(1) + O_p\left(\frac{1}{\sqrt{nT}}\right) \right]
$$
$$
= O_p(1).
$$

Lemma 4.5. *Under Assumptions* 4.1, 4.2, 4.8–4.15, *uniformly on* $K(C_k)$,

$$
M_w F \gamma_i = \mathbb{F} D_1 \gamma_i + \bar{\mathbb{U}} D_2 \gamma_i.
$$

By Lemma 4.3(i) *where each element of* $\bar{\mathbb{U}}$ *is* $O_p(\frac{1}{\sqrt{n}})$, *each element of* $M_w F \gamma_i$ *is of order* $O_p(\frac{1}{\sqrt{n}})$.

Proof. Plugging in (4.53), we obtain

$$
\frac{1}{T}\bar{W}'\bar{W} = \frac{1}{T}\overline{\mathbb{C}}'\mathbb{F}'\mathbb{F}\overline{\mathbb{C}} + \frac{1}{T}\overline{\mathbb{C}}'\mathbb{F}'\bar{\mathbb{U}} + \frac{1}{T}\bar{\mathbb{U}}'\mathbb{F}\overline{\mathbb{C}} + \frac{1}{T}\bar{\mathbb{U}}'\bar{\mathbb{U}}
$$
$$
= \frac{1}{T}\overline{\mathbb{C}}'\mathbb{F}'\mathbb{F}\overline{\mathbb{C}} + E.
$$

By Lemma 4.4(i), $\frac{1}{T}\overline{\mathbb{C}}'\mathbb{F}'\mathbb{F}\overline{\mathbb{C}}$ is $O_p(1)$. Since $E = O_p(\frac{1}{n}) + O_p(\frac{1}{\sqrt{nT}})$, it could be very small when both n and T are large. By Horn and Johnson (1985, p. 335)

$$
\left(\frac{1}{T}\overline{\mathbb{C}}'\mathbb{F}'\mathbb{F}\overline{\mathbb{C}} \right)^{-1} - \left(\frac{1}{T}\bar{W}'\bar{W} \right)^{-1}
$$
$$
= \left(\frac{1}{T}\overline{\mathbb{C}}'\mathbb{F}'\mathbb{F}\overline{\mathbb{C}} \right)^{-1} - \left(\frac{1}{T}\overline{\mathbb{C}}'\mathbb{F}'\mathbb{F}\overline{\mathbb{C}} + E \right)^{-1}
$$

$$= \left(\frac{1}{T}\overline{\mathbb{C}}'\mathbb{F}'\mathbb{F}\overline{\mathbb{C}}\right)^{-1} - \left[I + \left(\frac{1}{T}\overline{\mathbb{C}}'\mathbb{F}'\mathbb{F}\overline{\mathbb{C}}\right)^{-1}E\right]^{-1}\left(\frac{1}{T}\overline{\mathbb{C}}'\mathbb{F}'\mathbb{F}\overline{\mathbb{C}}\right)^{-1}$$

$$= \sum_{k=1}^{\infty}(-1)^{k+1}\left[\left(\frac{1}{T}\overline{\mathbb{C}}'\mathbb{F}'\mathbb{F}\overline{\mathbb{C}}\right)^{-1}E\right]^{k}\left(\frac{1}{T}\overline{\mathbb{C}}'\mathbb{F}'\mathbb{F}\overline{\mathbb{C}}\right)^{-1} = f(E).$$

This yields

$$\left(\frac{1}{T}\bar{W}'\bar{W}\right)^{-1} = \left(\frac{1}{T}\overline{\mathbb{C}}'\mathbb{F}'\mathbb{F}\overline{\mathbb{C}}\right)^{-1} + f(E).$$

It follows that

$$M_w F = \left[I_T - \bar{W}\left(\frac{1}{T}\bar{W}'\bar{W}\right)^{-1}\frac{1}{T}\bar{W}'\right]F$$

$$= \left[I_T - (\mathbb{F}\overline{\mathbb{C}} + \bar{\mathbb{U}})\left[\left(\frac{1}{T}\overline{\mathbb{C}}'\mathbb{F}'\mathbb{F}\overline{\mathbb{C}}\right)^{-1} + f(E)\right]\frac{1}{T}(\mathbb{F}\overline{\mathbb{C}} + \bar{\mathbb{U}})'\right]F$$

$$= [I_T - (\mathbb{F}\overline{\mathbb{C}})(\overline{\mathbb{C}}'\mathbb{F}'\mathbb{F}\overline{\mathbb{C}})^{-1}(\mathbb{F}\overline{\mathbb{C}})']F - (\mathbb{F}\overline{\mathbb{C}})\left\{f(E)\left(\frac{1}{T}\mathbb{F}\overline{\mathbb{C}}\right)'\right.$$

$$+ \left[\left(\frac{1}{T}\overline{\mathbb{C}}'\mathbb{F}'\mathbb{F}\overline{\mathbb{C}}\right)^{-1} + f(E)\right]\frac{1}{T}\bar{\mathbb{U}}'\right\}F$$

$$- \bar{\mathbb{U}}\left[\left(\frac{1}{T}\overline{\mathbb{C}}'\mathbb{F}'\mathbb{F}\overline{\mathbb{C}}\right)^{-1} + f(E)\right]\left(\frac{1}{T}\mathbb{F}\overline{\mathbb{C}} + \frac{1}{T}\bar{\mathbb{U}}\right)'F.$$

As discussed in Pesaran (2006), $M_{\mathbb{F}\overline{\mathbb{C}}} = I_T - (\mathbb{F}\overline{\mathbb{C}})(\overline{\mathbb{C}}'\mathbb{F}'\mathbb{F}\overline{\mathbb{C}})^{-1}(\mathbb{F}\overline{\mathbb{C}})' = I_T - \mathbb{F}(\mathbb{F}'\mathbb{F})^{-1}\mathbb{F}$ under the rank assumption. This implies that the first term is 0. Therefore, plugging in (4.54) and (4.55), we obtain

$$M_w F\gamma_i = \mathbb{F}D_1\gamma_i + \bar{\mathbb{U}}D_2\gamma_i. \tag{4.56}$$

$\square$

4.10. Exercises

(1) (Westerlund, 2019) Consider a panel model

$$y_{it} = \alpha_{1i}1\,(t \le k_0) + \alpha_{2i}1\,(t > k_0) + \lambda_i f_t + \varepsilon_{it},$$

where $1\,(A)$ is the indicator function, k_0 is the breakpoint, f_t is a the common factor and λ_i is the loading. We can use the common correlated effects (CCE) of Pesaran (2006) to approximate f_t by $\overline{y}_t$

$$\overline{y}_t = \overline{\alpha}_1 1\,(t \le k) + \overline{\alpha}_2 1\,(t > k) + \overline{\lambda} f_t + \overline{\varepsilon}_i,$$

and

$$f_t = \overline{\lambda}^{-1} [\overline{y}_t - \overline{\alpha}_1 1\,(t \le k) - \overline{\alpha}_2 1\,(t > k) - \overline{\varepsilon}_i].$$

Then

$$y_{it} = \delta_{1i} 1\,(t \le k) + \delta_{2i} 1\,(t > k) + \lambda_i \overline{\lambda}^{-1} \overline{y}_t + \epsilon_{it}$$

with

$$\delta_{1i} = \alpha_{1i} - \lambda_i \overline{\lambda}^{-1} \overline{\alpha}_1,$$

$$\delta_{2i} = \alpha_{2i} - \lambda_i \overline{\lambda}^{-1} \overline{\alpha}_2,$$

and

$$\epsilon_{it} = \varepsilon_{it} - \lambda_i \overline{\lambda}^{-1} \overline{\varepsilon}_t.$$

Define

$$\widehat{k} = \arg \min_{1 \le k < T-1} \mathrm{RRS}_n(k)$$

with

$$\mathrm{RRS}_n(k) = \sum_{i=1}^{n} \left[y_i - D(k)\widehat{\delta}_i \right]' M_{\overline{y}} \left[y_i - D(k)\widehat{\delta}_i \right],$$

where

$$y_i = \delta_{1i} D_1(k) + \delta_{2i} D_2(k) + \lambda_i \overline{\lambda}^{-1} \epsilon_t;$$

$y_i = [y_{i1}, \ldots, y_{iT}]'$, $\overline{y}_i = [\overline{y}_1, \ldots, \overline{y}_T]'$, and $\epsilon_i = [\epsilon_{i1}, \ldots, \epsilon_{iT}]'$. Also $\delta_i = [\delta_{1i}, \delta_{2i}]$, $D\,(k) = [D_1(k), D_2(k)]$, $D_1(k) = [1_k', 0_{T-k}']'$, $D_2(k) = [0_k', 1_{T-k}']'$, $M_A = I_T - A(A'A)^{-1}A'$. Show that

$$P\big(\widehat{k} = k\big) \to 1$$

as $n \to \infty$ for any fixed T.

(2) (Pestova and Pesta, 2017) Consider

$$y_{it} = \alpha_i 1\,(t > k) + \sigma_i \varepsilon_{it},$$

where $\sigma_i > 0$. Define

$$\widehat{k} = \arg\min_k \sum_{i=1}^{n} \left\{ \frac{1}{w(t)} \sum_{t=1}^{k} (y_{it} - \overline{y}_{ik})^2 + \frac{1}{w(T-k)} \sum_{t=k+1}^{T} (y_{it} - \widetilde{y}_{ik})^2 \right\},$$

where $w(t)$ is a weight, $\overline{y}_{ik}$ is the average of the first k and $\widetilde{y}_{ik}$ is the average of the last $T - k$ observations for each i. Show that if $\frac{1}{n} \sum_{i=1}^{n} \delta_i^2 \to \infty$

$$P(\widehat{k} = k) \to 1$$

as $n \to \infty$ for a fixed T.

(3) (Bhattacharjee, Banerjee and Michailidis, 2017) Consider

$$x_{it} = \begin{cases} \mu_{i1} + \varepsilon_{it}, & t = 1, 2, \ldots, [T\tau], \\ \mu_{i2} + \varepsilon_{it}, & t = [T\tau] + 1, 2, \ldots, T. \end{cases}$$

Define

$$\widehat{\tau} = \arg\min_k \sum_{i=1}^{n} \left[\sum_{t=1}^{[T\tau]} (x_{it} - \widehat{\mu}_{i1}(\tau))^2 + \sum_{t=[T\tau]+1}^{T} (x_{it} - \widehat{\mu}_{i2}(\tau))^2 \right]$$

with

$$\widehat{\mu}_{i1}(\tau) = \frac{1}{[T\tau]} \sum_{t=1}^{[T\tau]} x_{it}$$

and

$$\widehat{\mu}_{i2}(\tau) = \frac{1}{T - [T\tau]} \sum_{t=[T\tau]+1}^{T} x_{it}.$$

Let

$$\mu_1 = (\mu_{11}, \ldots, \mu_{n1})$$

and

$$\mu_2 = (\mu_{12}, \ldots, \mu_{n2}).$$

Show that

$$T \|\mu_1 - \mu_2\|_2^2 (\widehat{\tau} - \tau) = O_p(1).$$

(4) (Aue, Hormann, Horvath and Reimherr, 2009) Let $\{y_t\}_{t=1}^{T}$ be a time series of dimension n with $E(y_t) = 0$ and $\Sigma = E(y_t y_t')$. Define

$$S_k = \frac{1}{\sqrt{T}} \left(\sum_{t=1}^{k} \text{vech}[y_t y_t'] - \frac{k}{T} \sum_{t=1}^{k} \text{vech}[y_t y_t'] \right),$$

$$\Lambda_T = \max_k S_k' \widehat{\Sigma}_T^{-1} S_k,$$

and

$$\Omega_n = \frac{1}{T} \sum_{k=1}^{T} S_k' \widehat{\Sigma}_T^{-1} S_k$$

with

$$\left| \widehat{\Sigma}_T - \Sigma \right|_E = o_p(1)$$

$k = 1, \ldots, T$, where, for an $n \times n$ matrix M, $|M|_E = \sup_{x \neq 0} \frac{|Mx|}{|x|}$ denotes the matrix norm induced by the Euclidean norm on R^n. Show that under the null as $T \to \infty$

$$H_0 : \text{Cov}(y_1) = \cdots = \text{Cov}(y_T)$$

$$\Lambda_T \xrightarrow{d} \Lambda(d) = \sup_r \sum_{l=1}^{d} B_l^2(r)$$

and

$$\Omega_T \xrightarrow{d} \Omega(d) = \sum_{l=1}^{d} B_l^2(r) \, dr,$$

where $d = \frac{n(n+1)}{2}$, $B_l(r)$, $1 \leq l \leq d$, are independent standard Brownian bridges.

(5) (Kao, Trapani and Urga, 2018) Let

$$w_t = \text{vec}(y_t, y_t'),$$

$$\overline{w}_t = \text{vec}(y_t, y_t' - \Sigma),$$

$$\widehat{\Sigma}_\tau = \frac{1}{[T\tau]} \sum_{t=1}^{[T\tau]} y_t y_t',$$

and

$$\widehat{\Sigma}_{1-\tau} = \frac{1}{[T(1-\tau)]} \sum_{t=[T\tau]+1}^{T} y_t y_t'.$$

Define

$$\widehat{V}_{\Sigma,\tau} = \frac{1}{T} \sum_{t=1}^{T} w_t w_t' - \left\{ \begin{array}{l} \tau \left[\text{vec}(\widehat{\Sigma}_\tau) \right] \left[\text{vec}(\widehat{\Sigma}_\tau) \right]' \\ + (1-\tau) \left[\text{vec}(\widehat{\Sigma}_{1-\tau}) \right] \left[\text{vec}(\widehat{\Sigma}_{1-\tau}) \right]' \end{array} \right\},$$

$$\widetilde{V}_{\Sigma,\tau} = \left(\widehat{\Psi}_{0,\tau} + \widehat{\Psi}_{0,1-\tau} \right) + \sum_{l=1}^{m} \left(1 - \frac{l}{m} \right) \left[\left(\widehat{\Psi}_{l,\tau} + \widehat{\Psi}_{l,\tau}' \right) \left(\widehat{\Psi}_{l,1-\tau} + \widehat{\Psi}_{l,1-\tau} \right) \right]$$

with

$$\widehat{\Psi}_{l,\tau} = \frac{1}{T} \sum_{t=l+1}^{[T\tau]} \left[w_t - \text{vec}(\widehat{\Sigma}_\tau) \right] \left[w_{t-l} - \text{vec}(\widehat{\Sigma}_\tau) \right]$$

and

$$\widehat{\Psi}_{l,1-\tau} = \frac{1}{T(1-\tau)} \sum_{t=[T\tau]+1}^{T} \left[w_t - \text{vec}(\widehat{\Sigma}_{1-\tau}) \right] \left[w_{t-l} - \text{vec}(\widehat{\Sigma}_{1-\tau}) \right].$$

Let

$$\Lambda_T(\tau) = R \times D_{\lambda r}.$$

Show that

$$\sup_{[Tr]} \| V \|.$$

(6) (Yao and Davis, 1986) Consider $x_1, \ldots, x_k \overset{\text{i.i.d.}}{\sim} N\left(\mu, \sigma^2\right)$ and $x_{k+1}, \ldots, x_n \overset{\text{i.i.d.}}{\sim} N\left(\mu + \theta, \sigma^2\right)$. We want to test $H_0 : k = n$ versus $H_a : k < n$. Define

$$T_n = \max_k \frac{\left| \frac{S_k}{\sqrt{n}} - \frac{k}{n} \frac{S_n}{\sqrt{n}} \right|}{\sqrt{\left(\frac{k}{n}\right)\left(1 - \frac{k}{n}\right)}}$$

with

$$S_k = x_1 + \cdots + x_k.$$

Show that under the null

$$\lim_{n \to \infty} P\left(\frac{1}{a_n}(T_n - b_n) \le c \right) = \exp(-2\pi^{-1/2} e^{-c})$$

with

$$a_n = \frac{1}{\sqrt{2\ln_2 n}},$$

$$b_n = \frac{1}{a_n} + \frac{1}{2}a_n \ln_3 n$$

and $\ln_k$ is the kth iterated logarithm, where $-\infty < c < \infty$.

(7) (Bai, Han and Shi, 2019) Consider

$$y_{it} = \begin{cases} \lambda'_{i1} f_t + \varepsilon_{it}, & t = 1, \ldots, k_0, \\ \lambda'_{i2} f_t + \varepsilon_{it}, & t = k_0 + 1, \ldots, T, \end{cases}$$

where $k_0 = [T\tau_0]$, f_t is a $r \times 1$ vector of unobserved factors, k_0 is the unknown break date, λ_{i1} and λ_{i2} are the pre- and post-break factor loadings, and ε_{it} is the idiosyncratic error. Let

$$y_t = \begin{cases} \Lambda_1 f_t + \varepsilon_t, & t = 1, \ldots, k_0, \\ \Lambda_2 f_t + \varepsilon_t, & t = k_0 + 1, \ldots, T \end{cases}$$

with

$$y_t = (y_{1t}, \ldots, y_{nt})',$$
$$\Lambda_1 = (\lambda_{11}, \ldots, \lambda_{n1})',$$

and

$$\Lambda_2 = (\lambda_{12}, \ldots, \lambda_{n2})'.$$

Let $\widetilde{F}_k^{(1)}$ denote $\sqrt{k}$ times the first r eigenvalues of $Y_k^{(1)} Y_k^{(1)'}$ and $\widetilde{F}_k^{(2)}$ denote $\sqrt{T-k}$ times the first r eigenvalues of $Y_k^{(2)} Y_k^{(2)'}$, where

$$Y_k^{(1)} = (x_1, \ldots, x_k)'$$

and

$$Y_k^{(2)} = (x_{k+1}, \ldots, x_T)'.$$

Let $\widetilde{f}_t$ denote the transpose of the tth row of $\widetilde{F} = \left[\widetilde{F}_k^{(1)}, \widetilde{F}_k^{(2)} \right]$. Define

$$\widetilde{k} = \arg\min_k \mathrm{SSR}(k, \widetilde{F})$$

with

$$\mathrm{SSR}(k, \widetilde{F}) = \sum_{i=1}^{n} \sum_{t=1}^{k} \left(y_{it} - \widetilde{f}_t' \widetilde{\lambda}_{i1} \right)^2 + \sum_{i=1}^{n} \sum_{t=k+1}^{T} \left(y_{it} - \widetilde{f}_t' \widetilde{\lambda}_{i2} \right)^2,$$

$$\widetilde{\lambda}_{i1} = \frac{\widetilde{F}_k^{(1)'} Y_{k,i}^{(1)}}{k},$$

$$\widetilde{\lambda}_{i2} = \frac{\widetilde{F}_k^{(2)'} Y_{k,i}^{(2)}}{T - k},$$

$$Y_{k,i}^{(1)} = (y_{i1}, \ldots, y_{ik})',$$

$$Y_{k,i}^{(1)} = (y_{i1}, \ldots, y_{iT})'.$$

Show that

(a) if

$$\frac{n^{1-\alpha} \log\log T}{T} \to 0,$$

$$\frac{\log\log T}{n} \to 0,$$

and

$$\frac{\log\log n}{T} \to 0,$$

then

$$\lim_{(n,T) \to \infty} P(\widetilde{k} = k_0) = 1,$$

where $0 < \alpha \le 1$.

(b) if $\alpha = 0$, $\frac{n \log\log T}{T} \to 0$ and $\frac{\log\log T}{n} \to 0$, then

$$\widetilde{k} - k_0 = O_p(1).$$

(8) (Chen, 2015) Consider

$$y_t = \begin{cases} \Lambda_1 f_t + \varepsilon_t, & t = 1, \ldots, k_0, \\ \Lambda_2 f_t + \varepsilon_t, & t = k_0 + 1, \ldots, T. \end{cases}$$

Define the least squares (LS) estimator of the break point as

$$\widehat{k} = \arg\min_{k} \left[\min_{\Lambda_1, \Lambda_2, F} S_{nt}\left(k, F, \Lambda_1, \Lambda_2\right) \right]$$

with

$$S_{nt}\left(k, F, \Lambda_1, \Lambda_2\right) = \sum_{t=1}^{k} \left\| y_t - \Lambda_1 f_t \right\|^2 + \sum_{t=k+1}^{T} \left\| y_t - \Lambda_2 f_t \right\|^2.$$

Let $\widehat{\tau} = \frac{\widehat{k}}{T}$. Show that $\widehat{\tau} - \tau = O_p\left(\frac{1}{\delta_{nt}}\right)$ where $\delta_{nt} = \min\{\sqrt{n}, \sqrt{T}\}$.

Chapter 5

Latent-Grouped Structure in Panel Data Models

5.1. Panel Latent Group Structure Models

In this chapter, we study the issues of homogeneity pursuit in panel models. How to control for unobserved heterogeneity is critical to economists. This chapter considers panel models where individuals may be grouped at different levels. Panel data models with grouped heterogeneity have gained popularity to model the unobserved heterogeneity recently, e.g., Bonhomme and Magresa (2015), Su, Shi and Phillips (2016), Vogt and Linton (2017). Suppose we observe panel data (y_{it}, x_{it}), $i = 1, \ldots, n$, $t = 1, \ldots, T$, where y_{it} is the scalar-dependent variable and x_{it} is a covariate vector

$$y_{it} = x'_{it}\beta + \alpha_{it} + \varepsilon_{it},$$

where α_{it} are unit-specific effects such as, e.g.,

$$\alpha_{it} = \eta_i + \delta_t.$$

We assume that the individual units are grouped into K groups so that

$$\alpha_{it} = \alpha_{g_i t},$$

where $g_i \in \{1, \ldots, K\}$ denotes group membership and $(\alpha_{g1}, \ldots, \alpha_{gT})$ are K group-specific sequences of time effects.

Bonhomme and Manresa (2015) consider a panel model with grouped fixed effects (GFE)

$$y_{it} = x'_{it}\beta^0 + \alpha^0_{g^0_i t} + \varepsilon_{it}. \tag{5.1}$$

Model (5.1) contains three types of parameters: the common parameter β; the group-specific time effects α_{gt} for all $g_i \in \{1, \ldots, K\}$; and the group membership variable g_i for all i. We denote α as the set of all α_{gt}'s, and γ as the set of all g_i's.

The grouped fixed effect estimator in model (5.1) is defined as

$$\left(\widehat{\beta}, \widehat{\alpha}, \widehat{\gamma}\right) = \arg \min_{(\theta, \alpha, \gamma)} \sum_{i=1}^{n} \sum_{t=1}^{T} \left(y_{it} - x_{it}'\beta - \alpha_{g_i t}\right)^2,$$

where the minimum is taken over all possible groupings $\gamma = \{g_1, \ldots, g_n\}$ of the n units into K groups, common parameters β, and group-specific time effects α.

5.2. *K*-means Clustering

K-means clustering is a method of vector quantization, originally from signal processing, that is popular for cluster analysis in data mining. K-means is one of the most popular clustering algorithms. K-means stores k centroids that it uses to define clusters. K-means finds the best centroids by alternating between (1) assigning data points to clusters based on the current centroids and (2) choosing centroids (points which are the center of a cluster) based on the current assignment of data points to clusters. Let us consider the K-means clustering method where there are no covariates in the model, i.e., $\beta = 0$. Denote

$$y_i = (y_{i1}, \ldots, y_{iT})'.$$

Let

$$\alpha_g = (\alpha_{g1}, \alpha_{g2}, \ldots, \alpha_{gT})'$$

and

$$\alpha = (\alpha_1', \alpha_1', \ldots, \alpha_K')'$$

be a $KT \times 1$ vector that stacks all α_{gt}'s. The K-means grouping procedure prescribes a criterion for partitioning a set of points into K groups: to divide points $y_1, \ldots, y_n$ in R^T according to this criterion, first choose cluster centers $\alpha_1, \ldots, \alpha_G$ in R^T to minimize

$$Q_n = \sum_{i=1}^{n} \min_{g \in \{1, \ldots, K\}} \|y_i - \alpha_g\|^2$$

$$= \sum_{i=1}^{n} \min_{g \in \{1, \ldots, K\}} \sum_{t=1}^{T} (y_{it} - \alpha_{gt})^2,$$

i.e.,

$$\widehat{\alpha} = \arg \min_{\alpha} Q_n, \tag{5.2}$$

where $\| \cdot \|$ denotes the usual Euclidean norm, then assign each y_i to its nearest group center. Note that the global minimization is NP-hard and requires integer programming due to the discrete feature of $g \in \{1, \ldots, K\}$. There are almost K^n ways to partition n observations into K groups. That is, in practice, finding α at which Q_n attains its global minimum involves a prohibitive amount of calculation, except in the one-dimensional case. It is also well known that, in general, the K-means algorithm terminates in a local optimum and does not necessarily find the global optimum. The mean of the points must equal to α_{gt}, otherwise Q_n could be decreased by the first replacing α_{gt} by that cluster mean then, if necessary, reassigning some of the y's to new groups. The criterion is, therefore, equivalent to that of minimizing the within group sum of squares.

$$\min_{\widetilde{g}} \frac{1}{T} \sum_{t=1}^{T} \left(\widehat{\alpha}_{\widetilde{g}t} - \alpha_{gt}^0\right)^2 = o_p(1).$$

Now we assume y_i are i.i.d. across individuals and have finite second moments. Define

$$\overline{\alpha} = \arg \min_{\alpha} E \left[\sum_{t=1}^{T} \left(y_{it} - \alpha_{\widehat{g}_i(\alpha)t}\right)^2 \right].$$

Next we show

$$\widehat{\alpha} \xrightarrow{p} \overline{\alpha}$$

as $n \to \infty$ with T fixed. For the purpose of illustration consider $K = 2$ and $T = 1$. Now the problem is to choose optimal centers $\widehat{\alpha}_1$ and $\widehat{\alpha}_2$

to minimize

$$Q_n(\alpha_1, \alpha_2) = \frac{1}{n} \sum_{i=1}^{n} \min\left(|y_i - \alpha_1|^2, |y_i - \alpha_2|^2 \right) \tag{5.3}$$

then allocate each y_i to its nearest center. The optimal centers must lie at the mean of those observations drawn into their clusters. Next we show that $\widehat{\alpha} = (\widehat{\alpha}_1, \widehat{\alpha}_2)'$ converges in probability to $\overline{\alpha} = (\overline{\alpha}_1, \overline{\alpha}_2)'$ as $n \to \infty$, where $\overline{\alpha}$ minimizes

$$Q(\alpha_1, \alpha_2) = E\left[\min\left(|y - \alpha_1|^2, |y - \alpha_2|^2 \right) \right].$$

Clearly, we can use the uniform law of large numbers to show that $Q_n(\alpha_1, \alpha_2)$ converges in probability uniformly to $Q(\alpha_1, \alpha_2)$ as $n \to \infty$. This suggests that $\widehat{\alpha}$ which minimizes $Q_n(\alpha_1, \alpha_2)$ converges in probability to $\overline{\alpha}$ that minimizes $Q(\alpha_1, \alpha_2)$. Assume there exists a unique $\overline{\alpha}$ minimizing $Q(\alpha_1, \alpha_2)$. What happens when this uniqueness condition is violated? We may relax the assumption that $Q(\alpha_1, \alpha_2)$ has a unique minimum, by assuming $Q(\alpha_1, \alpha_2)$ achieves its minimum for each (α_1, α_2) in a region D and argue the distance from the optimal $(\widehat{\alpha}_1, \widehat{\alpha}_2)$ to D converges to zero in probably (or almost surely).[1] Suppose $y_i \overset{\text{i.i.d.}}{\sim} U[0, 1]$, then

$$E\left[\min\left(|y - \alpha_1|^2, |y - \alpha_2|^2 \right) \right] = \int_0^1 \min\left(|y - \alpha_1|^2, |y - \alpha_2|^2 \right) dy.$$

By symmetry we may assume $\alpha_1 \leq \alpha_2$. We can show that

$$Q(\alpha_1, \alpha_2) = \int \left[\left\{ 0 \leq y \leq \frac{1}{2}(\alpha_1 + \alpha_2) \right\} |y - \alpha_1|^2 \right.$$

$$\left. + \left\{ \frac{1}{2}(\alpha_1 + \alpha_2) \leq y \leq 1 \right\} |y - \alpha_2|^2 \right] dy$$

$$= \frac{\alpha_1^3}{3} + \frac{(1 - \alpha_2)^3}{3} + \frac{(\alpha_2 - \alpha_1)^3}{12}.$$

It is easy to show that $Q(\alpha_1, \alpha_2)$ takes a minimum value of $\frac{1}{48}$ at $\overline{\alpha}_1 = \frac{1}{4}$ and $\overline{\alpha}_2 = \frac{3}{4}$. The values of $\widehat{\alpha}$ are found by minimizing $Q_n(\alpha_1, \alpha_2)$. Clearly,

$$Q_n(\overline{\alpha}_1, \overline{\alpha}_2) \overset{p}{\to} Q(\overline{\alpha}_1, \overline{\alpha}_2) = \frac{1}{48}.$$

---

[1]This example is taken from Pollard (1981).

Thus,

$$\limsup Q_n \left(\widehat{\alpha}_1, \widehat{\alpha}_2 \right) \leq \frac{1}{48}$$

because $Q_n \left(\widehat{\alpha}_1, \widehat{\alpha}_2 \right) \leq Q_n \left(\frac{1}{4}, \frac{3}{4} \right)$. Then we can show $\widehat{\alpha} \xrightarrow{p} \overline{\alpha}$ easily. Next we show that

$$\sqrt{n} \left(\widehat{\alpha} - \overline{\alpha} \right) \xrightarrow{d} N \left(0, \Omega \right), \qquad (5.4)$$

where the matrix Ω involves the integrals of the population density over the faces of the optimal clusters. The proof of (5.4) depends on a quadratic approximation

$$Q_n \left(\widehat{\alpha} \right) = Q \left(\overline{\alpha} \right) - \frac{1}{\sqrt{n}} Z_n' \left(\widehat{\alpha} - \overline{\alpha} \right) + \frac{1}{2} \left(\widehat{\alpha} - \overline{\alpha} \right)' \Gamma \left(\widehat{\alpha} - \overline{\alpha} \right)$$

$$+ o_p \left(\frac{1}{\sqrt{n}} r_n \right) + o_p \left(r_n^2 \right), \qquad (5.5)$$

where $r_n = \| \widehat{\alpha} - \overline{\alpha} \|$, Γ is a positive definite matrix and Z_n has an asymptotic $N \left(0, V \right)$. The optimal $\widehat{\alpha}$ that minimizes $Q_n \left(\alpha \right)$ lies close to the vector $\overline{\alpha} + \frac{1}{\sqrt{n}} \Gamma^{-1} Z_n$ that minimizes (5.5) in the sense that $\sqrt{n} \left(\widehat{\alpha} - \overline{\alpha} \right) - \Gamma^{-1} Z_n$ converges to zero in probability.

Again consider $K = 2$ and $T = 1$.[2]

$$m \left(\alpha_1, \alpha_2, y \right) = \min \left(\left| y - \alpha_1 \right|^2, \left| y - \alpha_2 \right|^2 \right).$$

Note

$$\sqrt{n} \left(Q_n \left(\alpha_1, \alpha_2 \right) - Q \left(\alpha_1, \alpha_2 \right) \right)$$

$$= \frac{1}{\sqrt{n}} \sum_{i=1}^{n} \left(m \left(\alpha_1, \alpha_2, y_i \right) - E \left(m \left(\alpha_1, \alpha_2, y_i \right) \right) \right)$$

$$= A_n \left(\alpha_1, \alpha_2 \right).$$

Note that near optimal centers, $\overline{\alpha}_1 = \frac{1}{4}$ and $\overline{\alpha}_2 = \frac{3}{4}$,

$$Q \left(\alpha_1, \alpha_2 \right) = \frac{1}{48} + \frac{3}{8} \left(\alpha_1 - \frac{1}{4} \right)^2 - \frac{1}{4} \left(\alpha_1 - \frac{1}{4} \right) \left(\alpha_2 - \frac{3}{4} \right)$$

$$+ \frac{3}{8} \left(\alpha_2 - \frac{3}{4} \right) + \text{cubic terms}.$$

---

[2] This example is taken from Pollard (1982a, 1984).

Note that $Q\left(\alpha_1, \alpha_2\right)$ has partial derivatives with respect to α_1 and α_2 except at $y = \frac{1}{2}\left(\alpha_1 + \alpha_2\right)$. This suggests .

$$\frac{\partial Q\left(\alpha_1, \alpha_2\right)}{\partial \alpha_1} = -2\left(y - \frac{1}{4}\right)\left\{0 \le y \le \frac{1}{2}\right\}$$

and

$$\frac{\partial Q\left(\alpha_1, \alpha_2\right)}{\partial \alpha_1} = -2\left(y - \frac{3}{4}\right)\left\{\frac{1}{2} \le y \le 1\right\}.$$

Then concentrate on values of $\left(\alpha_1, \alpha_2\right)$ close to the population optimal values $\left(\frac{1}{4}, \frac{3}{4}\right)$

$$\alpha_1 = \frac{1}{4} + \frac{1}{\sqrt{n}}s$$

and

$$\alpha_2 = \frac{3}{4} + \frac{1}{\sqrt{n}}t.$$

Now we take a Taylor expansion of m about $\left(\frac{1}{4}, \frac{3}{4}\right)$

$$A_n\left(\frac{1}{4} + \frac{1}{\sqrt{n}}s, \frac{3}{4} + \frac{1}{\sqrt{n}}t\right) = A_n\left(\frac{1}{4}, \frac{3}{4}\right) + 2\frac{1}{\sqrt{n}}sB_n + 2\frac{1}{\sqrt{n}}tC_n,$$

where

$$B_n = \frac{1}{\sqrt{n}}\sum_{i=1}^{n}\left(y - \frac{1}{4}\right)\left\{0 \le y \le \frac{1}{2}\right\}$$

and

$$C_n = \frac{1}{\sqrt{n}}\sum_{i=1}^{n}\left(y - \frac{3}{4}\right)\left\{\frac{1}{2} \le y \le 1\right\}.$$

Then we get an approximation for $Q_n\left(\alpha_1, \alpha_2\right)$ near the optimal centers

$$Q_n\left(\frac{1}{4} + \frac{1}{\sqrt{n}}s, \frac{3}{4} + \frac{1}{\sqrt{n}}t\right)$$

$$= Q\left(\frac{1}{4} + \frac{1}{\sqrt{n}}s, \frac{3}{4} + \frac{1}{\sqrt{n}}t\right)$$

$$+ \frac{1}{\sqrt{n}}A_n\left(\frac{1}{4}, \frac{3}{4}\right) + 2\frac{1}{n}\left(sB_n + tC_n\right)$$

$$+ \text{ higher order terms}$$

$$= \frac{1}{48} + \frac{1}{n} \left(\frac{3s^2}{8} - \frac{st}{4} + \frac{3t^2}{8} \right)$$

$$+ \frac{1}{\sqrt{n}} A_n \left(\frac{1}{4}, \frac{3}{4} \right) + 2 \frac{1}{n} (sB_n + tC_n) + \text{higher order terms}$$

$$= \frac{1}{48} + \frac{1}{\sqrt{n}} A_n \left(\frac{1}{4}, \frac{3}{4} \right) + \frac{1}{n} (\text{quadratic in } s \text{ and } t) + \text{higher order terms.}$$

To accuracy of the order $\frac{1}{\sqrt{n}}$, the location of the minimum of Q_n can be found by minimizing the quadratic term such that

$$\widehat{\alpha}_1 = \frac{1}{4} + \frac{1}{\sqrt{n}} (\text{linear function of } B_n \text{ and } C_n) + \text{higher order terms}$$

and

$$\widehat{\alpha}_2 = \frac{3}{4} + \frac{1}{\sqrt{n}} (\text{linear function of } B_n \text{ and } C_n) + \text{higher order terms.}$$

The linear functions of B_n and C_n have an asymptotic joint normal distributions, because B_n and C_n have to form a normalized sum of independent random variables. Then optima centers follow a central limit theorem

$$\left(\sqrt{n} \left(\widehat{\alpha}_1 - \frac{1}{4} \right), \sqrt{n} \left(\widehat{\alpha}_1 - \frac{3}{4} \right) \right) \xrightarrow{d} N(0, \Omega),$$

where

$$\Omega = \Gamma^{-1} V \Gamma^{-1},$$

$$\Gamma = \begin{bmatrix} \frac{3}{4} & -\frac{1}{4} \\ -\frac{1}{4} & -\frac{1}{4} \end{bmatrix}$$

and

$$V = \begin{bmatrix} \frac{1}{24} & 0 \\ 0 & \frac{1}{24} \end{bmatrix}.$$

Next we consider the case with large n and large T. Assume $\beta = 0$. Let $\gamma^0 = \{g_1^0, \ldots, g_n^0\}$ denote the population grouping. Let $\gamma = \{g_1, \ldots, g_n\}$ denote any grouping of cross-sectional units into K groups. Note that the dimension of α diverges as T tends to infinity and hence the standard techniques (e.g., Newey and McFadden, 1994) cannot be used to show the asymptotics. Clearly, the grouped fixed model is related to interactive fixed effects (Bai, 2009) with

$$\alpha_{g_i t} = (\alpha_{1t}, \alpha_{2t}, \ldots, \alpha_{Kt}) \times (0, 0, \ldots, 1, \ldots, 0)$$

$$= \sum_{g=1}^{G} 1\{g_i = g\} \alpha_{gt}.$$

Bonhomme and Manresa took the advantage of this connection to establish the consistency of K-means estimator when the dimension α is large. Define

$$\widehat{Q}(\alpha, \gamma) = \frac{1}{nT} \sum_{i=1}^{n} \sum_{t=1}^{T} (y_{it} - \alpha_{g_i t})^2.$$

Note

$$\widehat{Q}(\alpha, \gamma) = \frac{1}{nT} \sum_{i=1}^{n} \sum_{t=1}^{T} (y_{it} - \alpha_{g_i t})^2$$

$$= \frac{1}{nT} \sum_{i=1}^{n} \sum_{t=1}^{T} \left(\varepsilon_{it} + \alpha_{g_i^0 t}^0 - \alpha_{g_i t}\right)^2$$

$$= \frac{1}{nT} \sum_{i=1}^{n} \sum_{t=1}^{T} \varepsilon_{it}^2 + 2\frac{1}{nT} \sum_{i=1}^{n} \sum_{t=1}^{T} \varepsilon_{it} \left(\alpha_{g_i^0 t}^0 - \alpha_{g_i t}\right)$$

$$+ \frac{1}{nT} \sum_{i=1}^{n} \sum_{t=1}^{T} \left(\alpha_{g_i^0 t}^0 - \alpha_{g_i t}\right)^2.$$

We also define

$$\widetilde{Q}(\alpha, \gamma) = \frac{1}{nT} \sum_{i=1}^{n} \sum_{t=1}^{T} \left(y_{it} - \alpha_{g_i^0 t}\right)^2$$

such that

$$\widetilde{Q}(\alpha, \gamma) = \frac{1}{nT} \sum_{i=1}^{n} \sum_{t=1}^{T} \left(\alpha_{g_i^0 t} - \alpha_{g_i t}\right)^2 + \frac{1}{nT} \sum_{i=1}^{n} \sum_{t=1}^{T} \varepsilon_{it}^2.$$

Following Bonhomme and Manresa (2015) we can show

$$\sup_{\alpha, \gamma} \left|\widehat{Q}(\alpha, \gamma) - \widetilde{Q}(\alpha, \gamma)\right| = o_p(1) \tag{5.6}$$

as $(n, T) \to \infty$.

Next we establish that $\widehat{\alpha}$ is consistent for α^0. We consider the following Hausdorff distance d_H:

$$
d_H\left(\alpha^a, \alpha^b\right) = \max\left\{ \max_g \left(\min_{\widetilde{g}} \frac{1}{T} \sum_{t=1}^{T} \left(\alpha^a_{\widetilde{g},t} - \alpha^b_{g,t}\right)^2 \right), \right.
$$

$$
\left. \max_{\widetilde{g}} \left(\min_g \frac{1}{T} \sum_{t=1}^{T} \left(\alpha^a_{\widetilde{g},t} - \alpha^b_{g,t}\right)^2 \right) \right\}.
$$

We can show

$$
d_H\left(\widehat{\alpha}, \alpha^0\right) = o_p\left(1\right).
$$

We note that there exists a permutation σ such that

$$
\frac{1}{T} \sum_{t=1}^{T} \left(\alpha^0_{\sigma(g),t} - \widehat{\alpha}_{g,t}\right)^2 = o_p\left(1\right).
$$

We obtain $\sigma\left(g\right) = g$ by relabeling. Define

$$
N_\eta = \left\{ \alpha : \frac{1}{T} \sum_{t=1}^{T} \left(\alpha^0_{g,t} - \alpha_{g,t}\right)^2 < \eta, \forall g \right\}.
$$

Let

$$
\widehat{g}_i = \arg\min_g \sum_{t=1}^{T} \left(y_{it} - \alpha_{g,t}\right)^2.
$$

We can show that for $\eta > 0$ small enough, we have, for $\delta > 0$,

$$
\sup_\alpha \frac{1}{n} \sum_{i=1}^{n} 1\left\{\widehat{g}_i\left(\alpha\right) \neq g_i^0\right\} = o_p(T^{-\delta}).
$$

Let

$$
\left(\widehat{\alpha}, \widehat{\gamma}\right) = \arg\min_{\alpha,\gamma} \sum_{i=1}^{n} \sum_{t=1}^{T} \left(y_{it} - \alpha_{g_i,t}\right)^2
$$

and

$$
\widetilde{\alpha} = \arg\min_\alpha \sum_{i=1}^{n} \sum_{t=1}^{T} \left(y_{it} - \alpha_{g_i^0,t}\right)^2.
$$

Note that $\tilde{\alpha}$ is the estimator of α when the group membership γ^0 is known. Let

$$n_g = \sum_{i=1}^{n} 1\left\{g_i^0 = g\right\}$$

for all g. We also can show that for all g and t as $(n, T) \to \infty$

$$\tilde{\alpha}_{g,t} - \alpha_{g,t}^0 = O_p\left(\frac{1}{\sqrt{n}}\right) \tag{5.7}$$

if $\frac{n_g}{n} \to \pi$ and for any $\delta > 0$

$$\tilde{\alpha}_{g,t} - \alpha_{g,t}^0 = o_p\left(T^{-\delta}\right). \tag{5.8}$$

Then we can show

$$\hat{\alpha}_{g,t} - \alpha_{g,t}^0 = O_p\left(\frac{1}{\sqrt{n}}\right) \tag{5.9}$$

and

$$\sqrt{n}\left(\hat{\alpha}_{g,t} - \alpha_{g,t}^0\right) \overset{d}{\to} N\left(0, \frac{\omega_{gt}}{\pi_g^2}\right), \tag{5.10}$$

where

$$\omega_{gt} = \lim_{n \to \infty} \frac{1}{n} \sum_{i=1}^{n} \sum_{j=1}^{n} E\left(1\left\{g_i^0 = g_j^0 = g\right\} \varepsilon_{it} \varepsilon_{jt}\right).$$

We can also show

$$\frac{1}{nT} \sum_{i=1}^{n} \sum_{t=1}^{T} \left(\hat{\alpha}_{\hat{g}_i,t} - \alpha_{g_i^0,t}^0\right)^2 = o_p(1). \tag{5.11}$$

Bonhomme, Lamadon and Manresa (2017) study panel data estimators based on a discretization of unobserved heterogeneity when individual heterogeneity is not necessarily discrete in the population. They focus on a two-step grouped fixed effect estimator, where the individual units are classified into groups in a first step using K-means method and the model is estimated in a second step allowing for group-specific heterogeneity. Again we assume $\beta = 0$. Let $f(y_i|\alpha_{i0})$ be the conditional density of y_i conditioning on α_i^0.

In the classification step, one relies on a set of individual-specific moments

$$h_i = \frac{1}{T} \sum_{t=1}^{T} h\left(y_{it}\right)$$

to learn about the unobserved heterogeneity α_i. Classification consists in partitioning individual units into G groups based on the moments. The partition units $\widehat{g}_i$ is obtained by

$$\left(\widehat{h}, \widehat{g}_1, \ldots, \widehat{g}_n\right) = \arg\min_{\widetilde{h}, g_1, \ldots, g_n} \sum_{i=1}^{n} \left\| h_i - \widetilde{h}\left(g_i\right) \right\|^2,$$

where $\{g_i\}$ are partitions of $\{1, \ldots, n\}$ into at most K groups and $\widetilde{h} = \left(\widetilde{h}\left(1\right), \ldots, \widetilde{h}\left(G\right)\right)'$. In the estimation step, one maximizes the log-likelihood function with respect to group-specific effects, where the groups are given by $\widehat{g}_i$ from the first step. Let

$$l_i\left(\alpha_i\right) = \frac{1}{T} \log f\left(y_i | \alpha_i\right)$$

and

$$\widehat{\alpha} = \arg\max_{\alpha} \sum_{i=1}^{n} l_i\left(\alpha_i\left(\widehat{g}_i\right)\right)$$

with

$$\alpha = \left(\alpha\left(1\right)', \ldots, \alpha\left(K\right)'\right)'.$$

Assume there is a Lipschitz continuous function φ such that as $(n, T) \to \infty$

$$\frac{1}{n} \sum_{i=1}^{n} \left\| h_i - \varphi\left(\alpha_i^0\right) \right\|^2 = O_p\left(\frac{1}{T}\right).$$

Let $B_\alpha\left(K\right)$ be the approximation bias of α_i^0

$$B_\alpha\left(K\right) = \min_{\alpha, \{g_i\}} \frac{1}{n} \sum_{i=1}^{n} \left\| \alpha_i^0 - \alpha\left(g_i\right) \right\|^2.$$

Bonhomme *et al.* (2017) provide an upper bound on the rate of convergence of $\widehat{h}\left(\widehat{g}_i\right)$ of $\varphi\left(\alpha_i^0\right)$

$$\frac{1}{n} \sum_{i=1}^{n} \left\| \widehat{h}\left(\widehat{g}_i\right) - \varphi\left(\alpha_i^0\right) \right\|^2 = O_p\left(\frac{1}{T}\right) + O_p\left(B_\alpha\left(K\right)\right). \tag{5.12}$$

5.3.   Conclusion

This chapter reviews the recent developments in homogeneity pursuit in panel models. It focuses on the asymptotics, e.g., consistency and limiting distribution, of K-means-based methods. Other related issues on homogeneity pursuit are taken from the literature and put in exercises. A major challenge in homogeneity pursuit is estimation of the appropriate of groups or clusters. Many existing methods focus on the within-group dispersion, e.g., BIC in Bonhomme and Manresa (2015), resulting from a grouping of the data into K groups.

5.4.   Exercises

Please spell out all the conditions and assumptions you need for the proofs.

(1) (Steinley and Brusco, 2011) Show that the minimum ratio of the within-cluster sum of squares to the corrected total sum of squares for a uniform and a standard normal partitioned into two groups is $\frac{1}{4}$ and $1 - \frac{2}{\pi}$, respectively.

(2) (Mahajan, Nimbhorkar and Varadarajan, 2012) In the K-means clustering problem, we are given a finite set of points S in R^d, an integer $k \geq 1$, and the goal is to find k centers to minimize the sum of the squared Euclidean distance of each point in S to its closest center. Show that K-means clustering is NP-hard even in $d = 2$ dimensions.

(3) Pollard (1981, 1982a,b) has found regularity conditions which assure consistency and asymptotic normality, with a convergence rate of $\sqrt{n}$, of the K-means estimators. One of the regularity conditions is that the Hessian between group sum of squares is nonsingular. Serinko and Babu (1992) consider $K = 2$ and $T = 1$ as in (5.3) and y_i has a double exponential distribution[3]

$$m\left(\alpha_1, \alpha_2, y\right) = \min\left(\left|y - \alpha_1\right|^2, \left|y - \alpha_2\right|^2\right).$$

---

[3]The pdf is

$$f\left(x\right) = \frac{1}{2}\beta^{-1}\exp\left[-\beta\left|x\right|\right]$$

with $\beta > 0$.

Show that

$$n^{1/4} \left(\widehat{\alpha}_j - \alpha_j \right) \xrightarrow{d} a_j \operatorname{sign}(Z) \sqrt{|Z|}$$

$j = 1, 2$, where $Z \sim N(0, 1)$ and a_j are constants.

(4) Qu and Gao (2018) consider a time-invariant group fixed effect model

$$y_{it} = x_{it}\beta + \alpha_{gi} + v_{it},$$

$$x_{it} = \phi z_{it} + \delta \alpha_{gi} + \varepsilon_{it},$$

$i = 1, \ldots, n$; $t = 1, \ldots, T$; $g_i \in \{1, \ldots, K\}$, where $E\left(v_{it} x_{js}\right) = 0$ for $i \neq j$, $t \neq s$. The grouped fixed effect (GFE) estimator of (β, α, γ) is

$$\left(\widehat{\beta}, \widehat{\alpha}, \widehat{\gamma} \right) = \arg \min_{(\theta, \alpha, \gamma)} \sum_{i=1}^{n} \sum_{t=1}^{T} \left(y_{it} - x_{it}\beta - \alpha_{g_i} \right)^2.$$

Now let $P\left(g_i = 1\right) = P\left(g_i = 2\right) = \frac{1}{2}$, $K = 2$ and $T = 1$. Show that

$$\widehat{\beta} \xrightarrow{p} \overline{\beta}$$

with

$$\overline{\beta} = \beta + \frac{a}{b}$$

$$a = \delta \frac{1}{2} \left(\alpha_1^2 + \alpha_1^2 \right) - \frac{1}{2}\delta A^2 - \frac{1}{2}\delta \left[(\alpha_1 + \alpha_2) - A \right]^2 + \frac{2\sigma}{\sqrt{2\pi}} e^{-\frac{(\alpha_1 - \alpha_2)^2}{8\sigma^2}} \delta$$

and

$$b = \phi^2 \sigma_z^2 + \delta^2 \frac{1}{2} \left(\alpha_1^2 + \alpha_2^2 \right) + \sigma_\varepsilon^2 - \frac{\delta^2}{2} A^2 - \frac{\delta^2}{2} \left[(\alpha_1 + \alpha_2) - A \right]^2$$

as $n \to \infty$.

(5) (Bonhomme and Manresa, 2015). We assume that the group-specific effects are time-invariant, $\beta = 0$, and $K = 2$:

$$y_{it} = \alpha_{g_i, t} + \varepsilon_{it},$$

where $\varepsilon_{it} \overset{\text{i.i.d.}}{\sim} N\left(0, \sigma^2\right)$ and $g_i = \{1, 2\}$. Without loss of generality, we assume $\alpha_1 < \alpha_2$. Show that

$$P\left(\widehat{g}_i(\alpha) = 2 | g_i = 1\right) = 1 - \Phi\left(\sqrt{T} \frac{\alpha_2 - \alpha_1}{2\sigma}\right),$$

where $\Phi(\cdot)$ is the cdf of a standard normal. This implies that the group misclassification probability tends to zero at an exponential rate.

(6) Bonhomme and Manresa (2015) consider the following model:

$$y_{it} = x'_{it}\beta^0 + \alpha^0_{g^0_i} + v_{it}$$

with $v_{it} \overset{\text{i.i.d.}}{\sim} N\left(0, \sigma^2\right)$, where the true number of groups is $K^0 = 1$, and where $\alpha^0 = \alpha^0_1$ denotes the true value of α. Let $(\widehat{\beta}, \widehat{\alpha})$ be the GFE estimator of (β^0, α^0) with $K = 2$ groups. Show that as T is fixed and $n \to \infty$

$$\widehat{\beta} \overset{p}{\to} \beta^0$$

and

$$\widehat{\alpha}_g \overset{p}{\to} \alpha^0 \pm \sigma\sqrt{\frac{2}{\pi T}}$$

for $g = 1, 2$.

(7) One of the most pressing questions, in practice is how to determine the number of groups. A popular method for determining the number of groups is the information criteria, such as the Bayesian information criterion (BIC) as in Bonhomme and Manresa (2015)

$$I(K) = \frac{1}{nT} \sum_{i=1}^{n} \sum_{t=1}^{T} \left(y_{it} - \alpha^K_{it}\right)^2 + K h_{nT}$$

and

$$\widehat{K} = \arg \min_{K \in \{1, \ldots, K_{\max}\}} I(K),$$

where $K_{\max}$ is an upper bound. Show that the estimated number of groups $\widehat{K}$ is consistent for K if, as $(n, T) \to \infty$, $h_{nT} \to 0$ with $\min(n, T) h_{nT} \to \infty$.

(8) Prove (5.6).

(9) Prove (5.7)–(5.11).

(10) Prove (5.12).

(11) Let K denote the number of groups and $G = \{g_1, \ldots, g_n\}$ denote the grouped membership such that $g_i = \{1, \ldots, K\}$. Ando and Bai (2016) consider a panel grouped factor model

$$y_{it} = x'_{it}\beta + f_{g_i,t}\lambda_{g_i,i} + \varepsilon_{it},$$

$i = 1, \ldots, n$, $t = 1, \ldots, T$, where x_{it} is a $p \times 1$ vector and $f_{g_i,t}$ is an $r \times 1$ vector of unobservable group-specific factors that affect the units only in group g_i. Here $\lambda_{g_i,i}$ are the factor loadings and ε_{it} is the unit-specific error. Let

$$y_i = (y_{i1}, \ldots, y_{iT})',$$
$$x_i = (x'_{i1}, \ldots, x'_{iT})',$$
$$f_j = (f'_{j,1}, \ldots, f'_{j,T})',$$

and

$$\varepsilon_i = (\varepsilon_{i1}, \ldots, \varepsilon_{iT})'$$

where, for $g_i = j$, $f_{g_i} = f_j$. Let

$$\Lambda_j = (\lambda_{j,1}, \ldots, \lambda_{j,n})$$

be an $r \times n$ factor loading matrix. Define

$$\left(\widehat{\beta}, \widehat{G}, \widehat{f}_1, \ldots, \widehat{f}_S, \widehat{\Lambda}_1, \ldots, \widehat{\Lambda}_S\right)$$

$$= \arg\min \sum_{j=1}^{S} \sum_{i:g_i=j} \left\| y_i - x_i\beta - f_{g_i}\lambda_{g_i,i} \right\|^2 + nT \cdot p_{k,\gamma}\left(|\beta|\right),$$

where $p_{k,\gamma}\left(|\beta|\right)$ is the penalty function. Show that

$$\left\| \widehat{\beta} - \beta^0 \right\| = o_p(1)$$

and for all $\tau > 0$

$$P\left(\sup_{i \in \{1, \ldots, n\}} \left| \widehat{g}_i\left(\widehat{\beta}, \widehat{F}, \widehat{\Lambda}\right) - g_i^0 \right| > 0 \right) = o_p(1) + o\left(\frac{n}{T^\tau} \right)$$

as $(n, T) \to \infty$.

(12) Su, Shi and Phillips (2016) propose a classifier Lasso (C-Lasso) approach to achieve classification and estimation for panel models in which the penalty takes an additive-multiplicative form that forces the parameters to form into different groups. Define

$$Q_{nT}(\beta) = \frac{1}{nT} \sum_{i=1}^{n} \sum_{t=1}^{T} \psi\left(w_{it}; \beta_i, \widehat{\mu}_i(\beta)\right)$$

with

$$\widehat{\mu}_i(\beta) = \arg\min_{\mu_i} \frac{1}{T} \sum_{t=1}^{T} \psi(w_{it}; \beta_i, \mu_i),$$

where $\psi(w_{it}; \beta_i, \mu_i)$ denotes the logarithm of the pseudo-true conditional density function of y_{it} given x_{it}, μ_i are individual effects and β_i is a $p \times 1$ parameter of interest. Assume the true values of β_i, β_i^0, to follow a group pattern

$$\beta_i^0 = \sum_{k=1}^{K_0} \alpha_k^0 1\{i \in G_k^0\}, \tag{5.13}$$

where $\alpha_j^0 \neq \alpha_k^0$ for any $j \neq k$, $\bigcup_{k=1}^{K_0} G_k^0 = \{1, \ldots, n\}$ and $G_k^0 \cap G_j^0 = \varnothing$ for any $j \neq k$. Shi *et al.* propose a classifier Lasso (C-Lasso) estimates, $\widehat{\beta}$ and $\widehat{\alpha}$ to estimate $\beta = (\beta_1, \ldots, \beta_n)$ and $\alpha = (\alpha_1, \ldots, \alpha_k)$ by minimizing the following penalized profile likelihood function:

$$Q_{nT,\lambda}(\beta, \alpha) = Q_{nT}(\beta) + \frac{\lambda}{n} \sum_{i=1}^{n} \prod_{k=1}^{K_0} \|\beta_i - \alpha_i\|,$$

where λ is a tuning parameter. Show that

$$\widehat{\beta}_i - \beta_i^0 = O_p\left(\frac{1}{\sqrt{T}} + \lambda\right)$$

and

$$\frac{1}{n} \sum_{i=1}^{n} \left\|\widehat{\beta}_i - \beta_i^0\right\|^2 = O_p\left(\frac{1}{T}\right).$$

(13) Huang, Jin and Su (2018) consider a panel cointegrated model with latent group structure

$$y_{it} = \mu_i + \beta_{1,i}' x_{1,it} + \beta_{2,i}' x_{2,it} + u_{it}$$

and

$$x_{1,it} = x_{1,it-1} + \varepsilon_{1,it},$$

where μ_i is the unobserved individual fixed effects, $x_{1,it}$ are $I(1)$ and $x_{2,it}$ are $I(0)$ for all i. We allow the true value of $\beta_{1,i}$, $\beta_{1,i}^0$, to follow a grouped pattern

$$\beta_{1,i}^0 = \begin{cases} \alpha_1^0 & \text{if } i \in G_1^0 \\ \vdots & \vdots \\ \alpha_K^0 & \text{if } i \in G_K^0, \end{cases}$$

where $\alpha_j^0 \neq \alpha_k^0$ for any $j \neq k$, $\bigcup_{k=1}^K G_k^0 = \{1, 2, \ldots, n\}$, and $G_k^0 \bigcap G_j^0 = \varnothing$ for any $j \neq k$. Let $\alpha = (\alpha_1, \ldots, \alpha_K)$, $\beta_1 = (\beta_{1,1}, \ldots, \beta_{1,n})$ and $\beta_2 = (\beta_{2,1}, \ldots, \beta_{2,n})$. Here, we assume $\mu_i = 0$ and $\beta_{2,i} = 0$ for all i. Let $\beta_i = \beta_{1,i}$ and $\beta = \beta_1$, and

$$Q_{nT}(\beta) = \frac{1}{nT^2} \sum_{i=1}^n \|y_i - x_{1,i}\beta_i\|^2.$$

Huang *et al.* propose to estimate β and α by minimizing the following C-Lasso-based penalized least squares

$$\left(\widehat{\beta}, \widehat{\alpha}\right) = \arg\min_{\beta,\alpha} Q_{nT,\lambda}^K(\beta, \alpha), \qquad (5.14)$$

where

$$Q_{nT,\lambda}^K(\beta, \alpha) = Q_{nT}(\beta) + \frac{\lambda}{n} \sum_{i=1}^n \prod_{k=1}^K \|\beta_i - \alpha_k\|$$

and $\lambda = \lambda(n, T)$ is a tuning parameter. Show that

$$\left\|\widehat{\beta}_i - \beta_i^0\right\| = O_p\left(\frac{1}{T} + \lambda\right)$$

and

$$\frac{1}{n} \sum_{i=1}^n \left\|\widehat{\beta}_i - \beta_i^0\right\|^2 = O_p\left(\frac{b_T}{T^2}\right),$$

where $b_T = \log\log T$.

(14) Lu and Su (2017) propose a testing procedure to determine the number of groups in panel latent group models. Lu and Su consider the following linear panel regression model:

$$y_{it} = x_{it}'\beta_i^0 + \mu_i + \varepsilon_{it}.$$

Assume n individuals belong to K groups and all individuals in the same group share the same slope coefficients. That is, β_i^0s are homogeneous within each of the K groups but heterogeneous across the K groups as in (5.13). Let $\widehat{\beta}_i$ be the C-Lasso estimator similar to (5.14). Let $\widetilde{y}_{it} = y_{it} - \overline{y}_i$, where $\overline{y}_i = \frac{1}{T} \sum_{t=1}^{T} y_{it}$ and $\widetilde{x}_{it}$ is defined similarly. Let

$$Q_{nT}(\beta) = \frac{1}{nT} \sum_{i=1}^{n} (\widetilde{y}_{it} - \widetilde{x}_{it}\beta_i)^2,$$

$$Q_{nT,\lambda}^{K}(\beta, \alpha) = Q_{nT}(\beta) + \frac{\lambda}{n} \sum_{i=1}^{n} \prod_{k=1}^{K_0} \|\beta_i - \alpha_k\|,$$

and

$$(\widehat{\beta}, \widehat{\alpha}) = \arg\min_{\beta, \alpha} Q_{nT,\lambda}^{K}(\beta, \alpha),$$

where λ is a tuning parameter, $\widehat{\beta} = (\widehat{\beta}_1, \ldots, \widehat{\beta}_n)$ and $\widehat{\alpha} = (\widehat{\alpha}_1, \ldots, \widehat{\alpha}_{K_0})$ be the C-Lasso estimators. Define

$$\widehat{\varepsilon}_{it} = y_{it} - x_{it}'\widehat{\beta}_i - \widehat{\mu}_i$$

with

$$\widehat{\mu}_i = \frac{1}{T} \sum_{t=1}^{T} \left(y_{it} - x_{it}'\widehat{\beta}_i\right)$$

and

$$\widehat{\varepsilon}_{it} = (y_{it} - \overline{y}_{i.}) - (x_{it} - \overline{x}_{i.})'\,\widehat{\beta}_i.$$

Let $\widehat{\varepsilon}_i = (\widehat{\varepsilon}_{i1}, \ldots, \widehat{\varepsilon}_{iT})'$, $x_i = (x_{i1}, \ldots, x_{iT})'$, $M_0 = I_T - \frac{1}{T} i_T i_T'$ and i_T is a $T \times 1$ vector of 1s. Lu and Su propose to use a residual-based Lagrange multiplier (LM) statistic

$$\mathrm{LM}(K_0) = \sum_{i=1}^{n} \widehat{\varepsilon}_i' M_0 x_i \left(x_i' M_0 x_i\right)^{-1} x_i' M_0 \widehat{\varepsilon}_i$$

to test the hypothesis

$$H_0 : K = K_0$$

versus

$$H_1 : K_0 < K \leq K_{\max},$$

where K_0 and $K_{\max}$ are prespecified by researchers. Define

$$J_{nT}(K_0) = \frac{\frac{1}{\sqrt{n}}\mathrm{LM}(K_0) - B_{nT}}{\sqrt{V_{nT}}}$$

with

$$B_{nT} = \frac{1}{\sqrt{n}} \sum_{i=1}^{n} \sum_{t=1}^{T} \varepsilon_{it} h_{i,tt}$$

and

$$V_{nT} = \frac{4}{nT^2} \sum_{i=1}^{n} \sum_{t=1}^{T} E\left[\varepsilon_{it}\right],$$

where $\Omega_i = E(\widehat{\Omega}_i)$ and $\widehat{\Omega}_i = \frac{1}{T} x_i' M_0 x_i$. Show that $J_{nT}(K_0) \overset{d}{\to} N(0,1)$ as $(n, T) \to \infty$.

(15) Let $Q_{i,\tau}$ be the conditional τ-quantile function of y_{it} given x_{it} with the form

$$Q_{i,\tau}\left(y_{it}|x_{it}, \alpha_i(\tau)\right) = x_{it}'\beta(\tau) + \alpha_i(\tau),$$

where $\tau \in (0,1)$ is the quantile index, and individual fixed effects $\alpha_i(\tau)$ taking only K different values, $\alpha_1(\tau), \ldots, \alpha_K(\tau)$. Gu and Volgushev (2019) consider a penalized estimator

$$\left(\widehat{\beta}, \widehat{\alpha}_1, \ldots, \widehat{\alpha}_n\right) = \arg \min_{\beta, \alpha_1, \ldots, \alpha_n} \Theta\left(\beta, \alpha_1, \ldots, \alpha_n\right)$$

with

$$\Theta\left(\beta, \alpha_1, \ldots, \alpha_n\right) = \sum_{i=1}^{n} \sum_{t=1}^{T} \rho_\tau\left(y_{it} - x_{it}'\beta - \alpha_i\right) + \sum_{i \neq j} \lambda_{ij}\left|\alpha_i - \alpha_j\right|,$$

where $\rho_\tau(u) = \{\tau - I(u \leq 0)\}$. Here u is the check function and λ_{ij} are the penalty parameters. Show that

$$\widehat{\beta} - \beta^0 + o_p\left(\|\widehat{\beta} - \beta^0\|\right) = \Gamma_n^{-1}\left[\frac{1}{nT} \sum_{i=1}^{n} \sum_{t=1}^{T} \{\tau - I(u_{it} \leq 0)\}\right]$$

(16) Saggio (2012) considers a nonlinear group fixed effects (NLGFE) estimator

$$y_{it} = 1\left\{x_{it}'\beta^0 + \alpha_{g_i^0} + v_{it} > 0\right\},$$

where β is the common parameter and α_g is the group-specific parameter. Superscript denotes the true parameter values such as g_i^0 denotes the true group membership indicators and $\alpha_{g_i^0}$ the true group effect associated with units that belongs to group g^0. The group membership variables g_i assign each individual $i \in \{1, \ldots, n\}$ into the K groups. Let $\alpha = (\alpha_{g_1}, \ldots, \alpha_{g_n})$ and $\gamma = \{g_1, \ldots, g_n\} \in \Gamma_K$, where Γ_K is the set of all possible groupings of all $\{1, \ldots, n\}$ into K groups. The NLGFE is given by

$$
\left(\widehat{\beta}, \widehat{\alpha}, \gamma\right) = \arg\max_{\beta, \alpha, \gamma} \sum_{i=1}^{n} \sum_{t=1}^{T} y_{it} \log \Phi\left(x_{it}'\beta + \alpha_{g_i}\right)
$$
$$
+ \left(1 - y_{it}\right) \log \left[1 - \Phi\left(x_{it}'\beta + \alpha_{g_i}\right)\right].
$$

Define

$$
\widehat{g}_i\left(\beta, \alpha\right) = \arg\max_{g \in \{1,2,\ldots,G\}} \sum_{i=1}^{n} \sum_{t=1}^{T} y_{it} \log \Phi\left(x_{it}'\beta + \alpha_{g_i}\right)
$$
$$
+ \left(1 - y_{it}\right) \log \left[1 - \Phi\left(x_{it}'\beta + \alpha_{g_i}\right)\right],
$$

which corresponding to the optimal assignment for each i. Then

$$
\widehat{\theta} = \left(\widehat{\beta}, \widehat{\alpha}\right) = \arg\max_{\beta, \alpha} \sum_{i=1}^{n} \sum_{t=1}^{T} y_{it} \log \Phi\left(x_{it}'\beta + \alpha_{\widehat{g}_i(\beta, \alpha)}\right)
$$
$$
+ \left(1 - y_{it}\right) \log \left[1 - \Phi\left(x_{it}'\beta + \alpha_{\widehat{g}_i(\beta, \alpha)}\right)\right].
$$

Let $\widetilde{\theta}$ be the infeasible NLGFE

$$
\widetilde{\theta} = \left(\widetilde{\beta}, \widetilde{\alpha}\right) = \arg\max_{\beta, \alpha} \sum_{i=1}^{n} \sum_{t=1}^{T} y_{it} \log \Phi\left(x_{it}'\beta + \alpha_{g_i^0}\right)
$$
$$
+ \left(1 - y_{it}\right) \log \left[1 - \Phi\left(x_{it}'\beta + \alpha_{g_i^0}\right)\right].
$$

Show that

$$
\sqrt{nT}\left(\widetilde{\theta} - \theta\right) \xrightarrow{d} N\left(0, \Sigma\right)
$$

and

$$
\sqrt{nT}\left(\widehat{\theta} - \theta\right) \xrightarrow{d} N\left(0, \Sigma\right)
$$

as $(n, T) \to \infty$ and $n = \exp(\epsilon\sqrt{T})$ with $\epsilon > 0$, where Σ is a positive definite matrix. Spell out the conditions you need.

(17) Denoted observed data as $\{w_{it}\}$, where $i = 1, \ldots, n$, $t = 1, \ldots, T$. Define

$$Q_{nT}(\beta, \alpha_1, \ldots, \alpha_n) = \frac{1}{nT} \sum_{i=1}^{n} \sum_{t=1}^{T} \varphi(w_{it}, \beta, \alpha_i).$$

Let β be the common parameter, $\{\alpha_i\}$ be individual specific parameters, and $f(w_{it}, \beta, \alpha_i)$ be the density function of w_{it}. Let

$$I_g = \{i : \text{individual } i \text{ belongs to group } g\}$$

$g = 1, \ldots, K$. Bester and Hansen (2016) consider a grouped fixed effect estimator

$$\left(\widehat{\beta}, \{\widehat{\gamma}_g\}\right) = \arg \max_{\left(\theta, \{\gamma_g\}_{g=1}^{K}\right)} \sum_{g=1}^{K} Q_{gT}(\beta, \gamma),$$

where

$$Q_{gT}(\beta, \gamma) = \frac{1}{n_g} \sum_{i \in I_g} \frac{1}{T} \sum_{t=1}^{T} \log f(w_{it}, \beta, \gamma)$$

with $\alpha_i = \gamma_g$ for all $i \in I_g$, where n_g is the number of individuals in group g. Show that

$$\left(\widehat{\beta}, \{\widehat{\gamma}_g\}\right) \xrightarrow{p} \left(\beta^0, \{\alpha_i^0\}\right)$$

and

$$\sqrt{nT}\left(\widehat{\beta} - \beta^0\right) \xrightarrow{d} N\left(0, J^{-}\Omega J^{-1}\right).$$

Let

$$\widehat{\beta}^{FE} = \arg \max_{\beta} \frac{1}{n} \sum_{i=1}^{n} Q_{iT}\left(\beta, \widehat{\alpha}_i(\beta)\right)$$

and

$$\widehat{\alpha}_i(\beta) = \arg \max_{\alpha} Q_{iT}(\beta, \alpha).$$

Show that

$$\sqrt{nT}\left(\widehat{\beta}^{FE} - \beta^0\right) \xrightarrow{d} N\left(cB, J^{-}\Omega J^{-1}\right)$$

as $\frac{n}{T} \to c$, where B is a bias term.

(18) Vogt and Linton (2017) consider a nonparametric panel regression

$$y_{it} = m_i(x_{it}) + u_{it}$$

and

$$u_{it} = \alpha_i + \gamma_t + \varepsilon_{it},$$

where m_i are unknown nonparametric functions and u_{it} denotes the error term. Let $G_1, \ldots, G_K$ be a fixed number of disjoint sets which partition the index set $\{1, \ldots, n\}$, i.e., $G \cup \cdots \cup G_K = \{1, \ldots, n\}$. Suppose for each $k \in \{1, \ldots, K\}$

$$m_i = m_j$$

for all $i, j \in G_k$. Let g_k be the group-specific regression. Vogt and Linton propose a thresholding procedure to estimate the groups $G_1, \ldots, G_K$. Let $S \subseteq \{1, \ldots, n\}$ be some index set and pick an index $i \in S$. Let $G \in \{G_1, \ldots, G_K\}$ be the class to which i belongs and suppose that $G \subseteq S$. We would like to infer which indices in S belong to the group G. Define

$$\Delta_{ij} = \int \{m_i(x) - m_j(x)\}^2 \pi(x) \, dx,$$

$$\widehat{\Delta}_{ij} = \int \{\widehat{m}_i(x) - \widehat{m}_j(x)\}^2 \pi(x) \, dx,$$

$$\widehat{m}_i(x) = \frac{\sum_{t=1}^{T} W_h(x_{it} - x) \widehat{y}_{it}}{\sum_{t=1}^{T} W_h(x_{it} - x)},$$

and

$$\widehat{y}_{it} = y_{it} - \overline{y}_i - \overline{y}_t^{(i)} + \overline{y}^{(i)} \tag{5.15}$$

with

$$\overline{y}_i = \frac{1}{T} \sum_{t=1}^{T} y_{it},$$

$$\overline{y}_t^{(i)} = \frac{1}{n-1} \sum_{j=1, j \neq i}^{n} y_{it},$$

and

$$\overline{y}^{(i)} = \frac{1}{(n-1)T} \sum_{j=1, j \neq i}^{n} \sum_{t=1}^{T} y_{it},$$

where π is some weight function, $W_h(x) = \frac{1}{h}W\left(\frac{x}{h}\right)$, W is a kernel function, and h is the bandwidth. Define the ordered distances as

$$\Delta_{i(1)} \leq \Delta_{i(2)} \leq \cdots \leq \Delta_{i(n_S)}$$

and

$$\widehat{\Delta}_{i[1]} \leq \widehat{\Delta}_{i[2]} \leq \cdots \leq \widehat{\Delta}_{i[n_S]},$$

where $n_S = |S|$, the cardinality of S. Note that $(\cdot)$ and $[\cdot]$ are used to distinguish between the orderings of true and estimated distances. Note that

$$\Delta_{i(j)} \begin{cases} = 0 & \text{for } j \leq p, \\ \geq c & \text{for } j > p, \end{cases}$$

$$\max_{i,j}\left|\widehat{\Delta}_{ij} - \Delta_{ij}\right| = o_p(1),$$

and

$$\widehat{\Delta}_{i[j]} \begin{cases} = 0 & \text{for } j \leq p, \\ \geq c + o_p(1) & \text{for } j > p \end{cases}$$

with some constant $c > 0$. This implies that we can estimate $G = \{(1),\ldots,(p)\}$ by $\widetilde{G} = \{[1],\ldots,[p]\}$ if p were known. Let

$$\widehat{p} = \max\left\{j : \{1,\ldots,n_S\} : \widehat{\Delta}_{i[j]} \leq \tau_{n,T}\right\},$$

where $\tau_{n,T}$ is the threshold parameter such that

$$\max_{j \in G}\widehat{\Delta}_{ij} \leq \tau_{n,T}.$$

Then define $\widehat{G} = \{[1],\ldots,[\widehat{p}]\}$. Define

$$\widehat{g}_k(x) = \frac{1}{|\widehat{G}_k|}\sum_{i \in \widehat{G}_k}\widehat{m}_i(x),$$

where $|\widehat{G}_k|$ denotes the cardinality of the set $\widehat{G}_k$. Show that

$$\widehat{g}_k(x) - g_k(x) = O_p\left(\frac{1}{\sqrt{n_kTh}} + h^2\right)$$

and

$$\sqrt{\widehat{n}_kTh}\left(\widehat{g}_k(x) - g_k(x)\right) \xrightarrow{d} N(B_k, V_k(x))$$

as $n \to \infty$, $\frac{h}{(\widehat{n}_k T)^{-1/5}} \xrightarrow{p} c_k$, for some constant $c_k > 0$, where $\widehat{n}_k = |\widehat{G}_k|$, $n_k = |G_k|$,

$$B_k(x) = \frac{c_k^{5/2}}{2} \int W(\varphi) \varphi^2 d\varphi \lim_{n \to \infty} \left\{ \frac{1}{n_k} \sum_{i \in G_k} \frac{g_k'' f_i(x) + 2g_k'(x) f_i'(x)}{f_i(x)} \right\},$$

and

$$V_k(x) = \int W^2(\varphi) d\varphi \lim_{n \to \infty} \left\{ \frac{1}{n_k} \sum_{i \in G_k} \frac{\sigma_i^2(x)}{f_i(x)} \right\}.$$

(19) Vogt and Linton (2019) propose multiscale estimators of the unknown groups and their unknown number which are free of bandwidth or smoothing parameters. Consider

$$y_{it} = m_i(x_{it}) + u_{it}$$

and

$$u_{it} = \alpha_i + \gamma_t + \varepsilon_{it}.$$

Assume there are K groups, $G_1, \ldots, G_K$, with $\bigcup_{k=1}^{K} G_k = \{1, \ldots, n\}$ such that

$$m_i = m_j$$

for all $i, j \subset G_k$. That is, for each $1 \leq k \leq K_0$,

$$m_i = g_k$$

for all $i \in G_k$ where g_k is the group-specific regression function associated with the class G_k. Define a local linear kernel estimator of m_i

$$\widehat{m}_{i,h}(x) = \frac{\sum_{t=1}^{T} W_{it}(x, h) \widehat{y}_{it}^*}{\sum_{t=1}^{T} W_{it}(x, h)},$$

with the weights $W_{it}(x, h)$ and $\widehat{y}_{it}^*$ is defined in (5.15). Define a multiscale statistic as

$$\widehat{d}_{ij} = \max_{(x,h)} \left\{ \widehat{\psi}_{ij}(x, h) - \lambda(2h) \right\}$$

such that $h_{\min} \leq h \leq h_{\max}$ and $x \in [0, 1]$, where

$$\widehat{\psi}_{ij}(x, h) = \sqrt{Th} \frac{\widehat{m}_{i,h}(x) - \widehat{m}_{j,h}(x)}{\sqrt{\widehat{v}_{ij}(x, h)}},$$

and $\widehat{v}_{ij}(x,h)$ is a scaling factor. Let $S \subseteq \{1,\dots,n\}$ and $S' \subseteq \{1,\dots,n\}$ be two sets of time series. Let

$$\widehat{\Delta}(S,S') = \max_{i\in S, j\in S'} \widehat{d}_{ij}. \tag{5.16}$$

To partition the set of $\{1,\dots,n\}$ into groups, Vogt and Linton suggest to combine the multiscale dissimilarity measure in (5.16) with a hierarchical agglomerative clustering algorithm. Let $\widehat{G}_i^{[0]} = \{i\}$ denote the ith singleton cluster for $1 \leq i \leq n$ and define $\{\widehat{G}_1^{[0]},\dots,\widehat{G}_n^{[0]}\}$ to be the initial partition of $\{1,\dots,n\}$ into clusters. Let $\widehat{G}_1^{[r-1]},\dots,\widehat{G}_{n-(r-1)}^{[r-1]}$ be the $n-(r-1)$ clusters from the previous step. Determine the pair of clusters $\widehat{G}_k^{[r-1]}$ and $\widehat{G}_{k'}^{[r-1]}$ for which

$$\widehat{\Delta}(\widehat{G}_k^{[r-1]},\widehat{G}_{k'}^{[r-1]}) = \min_{1\leq l < l' \leq n-(r-1)} \widehat{\Delta}(\widehat{G}_l^{[r-1]},\widehat{G}_{l'}^{[r-1]})$$

and merge them into a new cluster. Iterating this procedure for $r = 1,\dots,n-1$ yields a tree of nested partitions $\widehat{G}_1^{[r]},\dots,\widehat{G}_{n-r}^{[r]}$. That is, the hierarchical agglomerative clustering algorithm merges the n singleton clusters $\widehat{G}_i^{[0]} = \{i\}$ step by step until we end up with the cluster $\{1,\dots,n\}$. In each step of the algorithm, the closest two clusters are merged, the distance between clusters is measured by $\widehat{\Delta}$. Let

$$\widehat{K} = \min\left\{ K = 1,2,\dots, \max_{1\leq k \leq K} \widehat{\Delta}(\widehat{G}_k^{[n-K]}) \leq \pi_{n,T} \right\},$$

where $\pi_{n,T}$ is a threshold sequence. Show that

$$P\big(\{\widehat{G}_1^{[n-K]},\dots,\widehat{G}_K^{[n-K]}\} = \{G_1,\dots,G_K\}\big) \to 1$$

and

$$P\big(\widehat{K} = K\big) \to 1.$$

(20) Okui and Wang (2019) consider the following panel group structure model:

$$y_{it} = x_{it}'\beta_{g_i,t} + \varepsilon_{it}.$$

Let $G = \{1,\dots,K\}$ be the set of groups where $g_i \in G$ indicates the group membership of unit i. Units in the same group share the same time-varying $\beta_{g,t}$ where $g \in G$. For each group, there are m_g breaks and $\{T_{g,1},\dots,T_{g,m_g}\}$ denotes a set of break dates. Let $\alpha_{g,j}$,

$j = 1, \ldots, m_g$, be the values of coefficients until the jth break date and α_{g,m_g+1} be the value of coefficients in the last period

$$\beta_{g,t} = \alpha_{g,j}$$

if $T_{g,j-1} \leq t \leq T_{g,j}$, where $T_{g,0} = 1$ and $T_{g,m_g+1} = T + 1$. Let $\beta = \left(\beta'_{1,1}, \ldots, \beta'_{1,T}, \beta'_{2,1}, \ldots, \beta'_{K,T}\right)$, $\gamma = \{g_1, \ldots, g_n\}$. Define

$$\left(\widehat{\beta}, \widehat{\gamma}\right) = \arg\min_{\beta,\gamma} \frac{1}{nT} \sum_{i=1}^{n} \sum_{t=1}^{T} \left(y_{it} - x'_{it}\beta_{g_i,t}\right)^2$$

$$+ \lambda \sum_{g \in G} \sum_{t=2}^{T} \dot{w}_{g,t} \left\|\beta_{g,t} - \beta_{g,t-1}\right\|$$

where λ is a tuning parameter and $\dot{w}_{g,t}$ is a data-driven weight defined by

$$\dot{w}_{g,t} = \left\|\dot{\beta}_{g,t} - \dot{\beta}_{g,t-1}\right\|^{-\kappa}$$

with κ being a user specific constant and $\dot{\beta}$ being a preliminary estimate of β. Define

$$\mathring{\beta} = \arg\min_{\beta} \frac{1}{nT} \sum_{i=1}^{n} \sum_{t=1}^{T} \left(y_{it} - x'_{it}\beta_{g_i^0,t}\right)^2 + \lambda \sum_{g \in G} \sum_{t=2}^{T} \dot{w}_{g,t} \left\|\beta_{g,t} - \beta_{g,t-1}\right\|$$

where $\mathring{\beta}$ is the estimator of β when the group memberships γ are known. Denote n_g as the number of units in group g,

$$n_g = \sum_{i=1}^{n} 1\left\{g_i^0 = g\right\}$$

for $g \in G$. Show that for all g and t

$$\widehat{\beta}_{g,t} - \mathring{\beta}_{g,t} = o_p\left(\frac{1}{T^{-\delta}}\right)$$

and

$$\widehat{\beta}_{g,t} - \beta_{g,t}^0 = O_p\left(\frac{1}{\sqrt{n}}\right)$$

for $\delta > 0$ if $\frac{n_b}{n} \to \pi_g$ and $(n, T) \to \infty$ for $0 < \pi_g < 1$.

(21) Let $x_1, \ldots, x_n$ be a random sample from the mixture of exponentials, $(1 - \alpha) Ex(1) + \alpha Ex(\theta)$, where $Ex(\theta)$ denotes the exponential distribution with mean θ. Show that under the homogeneous model where

$\alpha = 0$, the only way to ensure a finite Fisher information is to require $0 < \theta < 2$.

(22) Consider a sample normal mixture model given by $(1 - \alpha) N (0, 1) + \alpha N (\mu, 1)$. Consider the likelihood ratio test for the hypothesis H_0 : $\mu = 0$. Show that the likelihood ratio test statistic goes to infinity in probability as $n \to \infty$.

(23) Let $x_i, \ldots, x_n$ be a random sample of size n from a mixture population with the probability density function (pdf)

$$f (x; \alpha, \theta_1, \theta_2) = (1 - \alpha) N (0, 1) + \alpha N (\theta, 1),$$

where $0 \le \alpha \le 1$ and $|\theta| \le M$. Let R_n be the log-likelihood ratio test statistic for testing $H_0 : \alpha \theta = 0$ versus $H_a : \alpha \theta \ne 0$. Chen and Chen (2001) show that as $n \to \infty$

$$R_n \xrightarrow{d} \left\{ \sup_{|t| \le M} \xi (t) \right\}^2,$$

where $\xi (t)$ is a Gaussian process with zero mean and the covariances

$$\text{Cov}(\xi(s), \xi(t)) = \text{sgn}(st) \frac{e^{st} - 1}{\sqrt{(e^{s^2} - 1)(e^{t^2} - 1)}}.$$

(24) (Bickel and Chernoff, 1993) Suppose that $x_1, \ldots, x_n$ are i.i.d. standard normal random variables. Denote

$$S_n (t) = \frac{1}{\sqrt{n}} \left(e^{tx_i - \frac{t^2}{2}} - 1 \right) e^{-\frac{t^2}{2}}$$

and

$$M_n = \sup_t S_n (t).$$

Show that

$$\lim_{n \to \infty} P\left\{ (\log \log n)^{1/2} \left[M_n - (\log \log n)^{1/2} \right] + \log \left(\sqrt{2\pi} \right) \le x \right\}$$
$$= \exp \left(-e^{-x} \right).$$

(25) (von Luxburg, 2010) Stability is a useful tool for selecting the number of clusters, K. The general rule is to choose K which leads to the most stable clustering results. The clustering C_K of a data set

$S = \{x_1, \ldots, x_n\}$ is a function that assigns labels to all points of S, that is

$$C_K : S \to \{1, \ldots, K\},$$

where K is the number of clusters. Define the instability of a clustering algorithm as the expected distance between two clusterings $C_K(S_n), C_K(S_n')$ on different data sets S_n, S_n' of size n:

$$\text{Instab}(K, n) = E\big(d\big(C_K(S_n), C_K(S_n')\big)\big),$$

where $d(C, C')$ is a distance between clustering C and C'. Define

$$\widehat{\text{Instab}}(K, n) = \frac{1}{b_{\max}^2} \sum_{b,b'=1}^{b_{\max}} d(C_b, C_{b'})$$

and

$$\widehat{K} = \arg\min_k \widehat{\text{Instab}}(K, n).$$

Let

$$Q_n(c_1, \ldots, c_K) = \frac{1}{n} \sum_{i=1}^{n} \min_k \|x_i - c_k\|^2$$

and

$$Q = E\left[\min_k \|x - c_k\|^2 \right]$$

$$= \int \min_k \|x - c_k\|^2 \, dP,$$

where P is the underlying probability distribution of x. Show that if Q has a unique global minimum, then the K-means algorithm is stable as $n \to \infty$,

$$\lim_{n\to\infty} \text{Instab}(K, n) = 0$$

and if Q has several global minima, then the K-means algorithm is unstable as $n \to \infty$,

$$\lim_{n\to\infty} \text{Instab}(K, n) > 0.$$

(26) (*Continued*) Assume that the underlying distribution P is a mixture of two well-separated Gaussian. Denote the means of the Gaussian by μ_1 and μ_2.

(a) Assume that we run the K-means algorithm with $K = 2$ and we use an initialization scheme that places on initial center in each of the true clusters. Show that the K-means algorithm is stable. That is, it terminates in a solution with one center close to μ_1 and one center close to μ_2.

(b) Assume that we run the K-means algorithm with $K = 3$ and we use an initialization scheme that places at least one of the initial centers in each of the true clusters. Show that the K-means algorithm is unstable in the sense that with probability close to 0.5 it terminates in a solution that considers the first Gaussian as cluster, but splits the second Gaussian into two clusters; and with probability close to 0.5, it does it the other way round.

Bibliography

Ahn, S. C., Lee, Y. H., and Schmidt, P. (2013), Panel Data Models with Multiple Time-varying Individual Effects, *Journal of Econometrics*, 174, 1–14.

Alvarez, J., and Arellano, M. (2003), The Time Series and Cross-Section Asymptotics of Dynamic Panel Data Estimators, *Econometrica*, 71, 1121–1159.

Anderson, T. W. (2003), *An Introduction to Multivariate Statistical Analysis*, Wiley.

Ando, T., and Bai, J. (2016), Panel Data Models with Grouped Factor Structure Under Unknown Group Membership, *Journal of Applied Econometrics*, 31, 163–191.

Andrews, D. W. K. (2005), Cross-Section Regression with Common Shocks, *Econometrica*, 73, 1551–1585.

Anselin, L. (1988), *Spatial Econometrics: Methods and Models*. Kluwer Academic Publishers, Dordrecht.

Anselin, L., and Bera, A. K. (1998), Spatial Dependence in Linear Regression Models with an Introduction to Spatial Econometrics, In: Ullah, A. and Giles, D. E. A. (Eds.), *Handbook of Applied Economic Statistics*, Marcel Dekker, New York.

Arellano, M. (1987), Computing Robust Standard Errors for Within-groups Estimators, *Oxford Bulletin of Economics and Statistics*, 49, 431–434.

Arellano, M., and Bond, S. (1991), Some Tests of Specification for Panel Data: Monte Carlo Evidence and an Application of Employment Equations, *Review of Economics Studies*, 58, 277–297.

Bai, J. (1994), Estimation of Structural Change Based on Wald-Type Statistics, Working paper 94-6, Economics Department, MIT.

Bai, J. (1997a), Estimation of a Change Point in Multiple Regression Models, *Review of Economics and Statistics*, 79, 551–563.

Bai, J. (1997b), Estimating Multiple Breaks One at a Time, *Econometric Theory*, 13, 315–352.

Bai, J. (2000), Vector Autoregressive Models with Structural Change in Regression Coefficients and in Variance–Covariance Matrix, *Annals of Economics and Finance*, 1, 303–339.

Bai, J. (2009), Panel Data Models With Interactive Fixed Effects, *Econometrica*, 77, 1229–1279.

Bai, J. (2010), Common Breaks in Means and Variances for Panel Data, *Journal of Econometrics*, 157, 78–92.

Bai, J. (2013), Likelihood Approach to Dynamic Panel Models with Interactive Effects, MPRA Paper No. 50267.

Bai, J., and Carrion-i-Silvestre, J. L. (2009), Structural Changes, Common Stochastic Trends, and Unit Roots in Panel Data, *Review of Economic Studies*, 76, 471–501.

Bai, J., Han, X., and Shi, Y. (2019), Estimation and Inference of Change Points in High-Dimensional Factor Models, *Journal of Econometrics*, forthcoming.

Bai, J., and Li, K. (2012), Statistical Analysis of Factor Models of High Dimension. *Annals of Statistics*, 40, 436–465.

Bai, J., and Li, K. (2014), Theory and Methods of Panel Data Models with Interactive Effects, *Annals of Statistics*, 42, 142–170.

Bai, J., and Liao, Y. (2013), Statistical Inference Using Large Estimated Covariances for Panel Data and Factor Models, Working paper.

Bai, J., and Liao, Y. (2016), Efficient Estimation of Approximate Factor Models Via Penalized Maximum Likelihood, *Journal of Econometrics*, 191, 1–18.

Bai, J., Lumsdaine, R., and Stock, J. (1998), Testing For and Dating Common Breaks in Multivariate Time Series, *Review of Economic Studies*, 65, 395–432.

Bai, J., and Ng, S. (2002), Determining the Number of Factors in Approximate Factor Models, *Econometrica*, 70, 191–221.

Bai, J., and Perron, P. (1998), Estimating and Testing Linear Models with Multiple Structural Changes, *Econometrica*, 66, 47–79.

Bai, J., and Perron, P. (2003), Computation and Analysis of Multiple Structural Change Models, *Journal of Applied Econometrics*, 18, 1–22.

Bai, Z. D. (1999), Methodologies in Spectral Analysis of Large Dimensional Random Matrices, A Review, *Statistica Sinica*, 9, 611–677.

Bai, Z. D., and Silverstein, J. (2006), *Spectral Analysis of Large Dimensional Random Matrices*, Science Press, Beijing.

Baltagi, B. H. (2008), *Econometric Analysis of Panel Data*, John Wiley & Sons, Chichester.

Baltagi, B. H., Feng, Q., and Kao, C. (2011), Testing for Sphericity in a Fixed Effects Panel Data Model, *Econometrics Journal*, 14, 25–47.

Baltagi, B. H., Feng, Q., and Kao, C. (2012), A Lagrange Multiplier Test for Cross-sectional Dependence in a Fixed Effects Panel Data Model, *Journal of Econometrics*, 170, 164–177.

Baltagi, B. H., Feng, Q., and Kao, C. (2016), Estimation of Heterogeneous Panels with Structural Breaks, *Journal of Econometrics*, 191, 176–195.

Baltagi, B. H., Feng, Q., and Kao, C. (2019), Structural Changes in Heterogeneous Panels with Endogenous Regressors, *Journal of Applied Econometrics*, 34, 883–892.

Baltagi, B. H., Kao, C., and L. Liu (2017), Estimation and Identification of Change Points in Panel Models with Nonstationary or Stationary Regressors and Error Term, *Econometric Review*, 36, 85–102.

Baltagi, B. H., Kao, C., and Wang, F. (2017), Identification and Estimation of a Large Factor Model with Structural Instability, *Journal of Econometrics*, 197, 87–100.

Baltagi, B. H., and Pirotte, A. (2010), Panel Data Inference Under Spatial Dependence, *Economic Modelling*, 27, 1368–1381.

Baltagi, B. H., Song, S. H., and Koh, W. (2003), Testing Panel Data Regression Models with Spatial Error Correlation, *Journal of Econometrics*, 117, 123–150.

Baltagi, B. H., Song, S. H., and Kwon, J. (2009), Testing for Heteroskedasticity and Spatial Correlation in a Random Effects Panel Data Model, *Computational Statistics & Data Analysis*, 53, 2897–2922.

Banerjee, A., and Carrion-i-Silvestre, J. L. (2011), Testing for Panel Cointegration Using Common Correlated Effects Estimators, Department of Economics Discussion Paper 11-16, University of Birmingham.

Banerjee, A., Marcellino, M., and Masten, I. (2008), Forecasting Macroeconomic Variables Using Diffusion Indexes in Short Samples with Structural Change, CEPR Discussion Papers 6706.

Barigozzi, M., and Cho. H. (2019), Consistent Estimation of High-dimensional Factor Models When the Factor Number is Over-estimated, Working paper.

Bester, C. A., Conley, T. G., and Hansen, C. B. (2009), Inference with Dependent Data Using Cluster Covariance Estimators, Working paper, University of Chicago, Graduate School of Business, Chicago, IL.

Bester, C. A., and Hansen, C. B. (2916), Grouped Effects Estimators in Fixed Effects Models, *Journal of Econometrics*, 190, 197–208.

Bhattacharjee, M., Banerjee, M., and Michailidis, G. (2017), Common Change Point Estimation in Panel Data from the Least Squares and Maximum Likelihood Viewpoints, working paper.

Bickel, A., and Chernoff, H. (1993), Asymptotic Distribution of the Likelihood Ratio Statistic in Prototypical Non Regular Problem, In: Ghosh, J. K. et al. (Eds.), *Statistics and Probability*, Wiley Eastern Limited, New Delhi, pp. 83–96.

Birke, M., and Dette, H. (2005), A Note on Testing the Covariance Matrix for Large Dimension, *Statistics and Probability Letters*, 74, 281–289.

Boneva, L., and Linton, O. (2017), A Discrete-choice Model for Large Heterogeneous Panels with Interactive Fixed Effects with an Application to the Determinants of Corporate Bond Issuance, *Journal of Applied Econometrics*, 32, 1226–1243.

Bonhomme, S., Lamadon, T., and Manresa, E. (2017), Discretizing Unobserved Heterogeneity, Working paper.

Bonhomme, S., and Manresa, E. (2015), Grouped Patterns of Heterogeneity in Panel Data, *Econometrica*, 83, 1147–1187.

Breitung, J., and Eickmeier, S. (2011), Testing for Structural Breaks in Dynamic Factor Models, *Journal of Econometrics*, 163, 71–84.

Breusch, T., and Pagan, A. (1980), The Lagrange Multiplier Test and Its Application to Model Specification in Econometrics, *Review of Economic Studies*, 47, 239–254.

Bun, M. J. G., and Carree, M. A. (2005), Bias-Corrected Estimation in Dynamic Panel Data Models, *Journal of Business and Economic Statistics*, 23, 200–210.

Calderon, C., Moral-Benito, E., and Serven, L. (2015), Is Infrastructure Capital Productive? A Dynamic Heterogeneous Approach, *Journal of Applied Econometrics*, 30, 177–198.

Chen, H., and Chen, J. (2001), Large Sample Distribution of the Likelihood Ratio Test for Normal Mixtures, *Statistics & Probability Letters*, 52, 125–133.

Chen, H., and Jiang, T. (2018), A Study of Two High-Dimensional Likelihood Ratio Tests Under Alternative Hypotheses, *Random Matrices: Theory and Applications*, 7, [1750016].

Chen, J., Gao, J., and Li, D. (2012), A New Diagnostic Test for Cross-sectional Uncorrelatedness in Nonparametric Panel Data Model, *Econometric Theory*, 28, 1144–1163.

Chen, L., Dolado, J., and Gonzalo, J. (2014), Detecting Big Structural Breaks in Large Factor Models, *Journal of Econometrics*, 180, 30–48.

Chen, S. X., Zhang, L. X., and Zhong, P. S. (2010), Tests for High-Dimensional Covariance Matrices, *Journal of the American Statistical Association*, 105, 810–819.

Chirinko, R. S., and Wilson, D. J. (2017), Tax Competition Among U.S. States: Racing to the Bottom or Riding on a Seesaw? *Journal of Public Economics*, 155, 147–163.

Chong, T. (1995), Partial Parameter Consistency in a Misspecified Structural Change Model, *Economics Letters*, 49, 351–357.

Chudik A., and Pesaran M. H. (2015), Common Correlated Effects Estimation of Heterogeneous Dynamic Panel Data Models with Weakly Exogenous regressors, *Journal of Econometrics*, 188, 393–420.

Chudik, A., Pesaran, M. H., and Tosetti, E. (2011), Weak and Strong Cross-Section Dependence and Estimation of Large Panels, *Econometrics Journal*, 14, 45–90.

Conley, T. G. (1999), GMM Estimation with Cross Sectional Dependence, *Journal of Econometrics*, 92, 1–45.

Conley, T. G., and Molinari, F. (2007), Spatial Correlation Robust Inference with Errors in Location or Distance, *Journal of Econometrics*, 140, 76–96.

De Wachter, S., and Tzavalis, E. (2012), Detection of Structural Breaks in Linear Dynamic Panel Data Models, *Computational Statistics & Data Analysis*, 56, 3020–3034.

Demetrescu, M., and Homm, U. (2016), Directed Tests of no Cross-sectional Correlation in Large-N Panel Data Models, *Journal of Applied Econometrics*, 31, 4–31.

Doz, C., Giannone, D., and Reichlin, L. (2012), A Quasi-maximum Likelihood Approach for Large Approximate Dynamic Factors Models, *Review of Economics and Statistics*, 94, 1014–1024.

Eberhardt, M., Helmers, C., and H. Strauss, H. (2013), Do Spillovers Matter When Estimating Private Returns to R&D? *Review of Economics and Statistics*, 95, 436–448.

Eberhardt, M., and Presbitero, A. (2015), Public Debt and Growth: Heterogeneity and Non-linearity, *Journal of International Economics*, 97, 45–58.

Fan, J., Liao, Y., and Liu, H. (2016), An Overview of the Estimation of Large Covariance and Precision Matrices, *Journal of Econometrics*, 19, 1–32.

Fan, J., Liao, Y., and Yao, J. (2015), Power Enhancement In High-Dimensional Cross-Sectional Tests, *Econometrica*, 83, 1497–1541.

Feng, Q. (2020), Common Factors and Common Breaks in Panels: An Empirical Investigation, *Economics Letters*, 187, 108897.

Feng, Q., Kao, C., and Lazarova, S. (2009), Estimation of Change Points in Panels, Working Paper, Syracuse University.

Feng, Q., and Wu, G. L. (2018), On the Reverse Causality Between Output and Infrastructure: the Case of China, *Economic Modelling*, 74, 97–104.

Fleisher, B., Li, H., and Zhao, M. Q. (2010), Human Capital, Economic Growth, and Regional Inequality in China, *Journal of Development Economics*, 92, 215–231.

Frees, E. W. (1995), Assessing Cross-Sectional Correlation in Panel Data, *Journal of Econometrics*, 69, 393–414.

Geman, S. (1980), A Limit Theorem for the Norm of Random Matrices, *Annals of Probability*, 8, 252–261.

Gobillon, L., and Magnac, T. (2016), Regional Policy Evaluation: Interactive Fixed Effects and Synthetic Controls, *Review of Economics and Statistics*, 98, 535–551.

Gomez, M. (2015), REGIFE: Stata Module to Estimate Linear Models with Interactive Fixed Effect. Statistical Software Components.

Gramlich, E. (1994), Infrastructure Investment: A Review Essay. *Journal of Economic Literature*, 32, 1176–1196.

Gu, J., and Volgushev, S. (2018), Panel Data Quantile Regression with Grouped Fixed Effects, Working paper.

Hahn, J., and Kuersteiner, G. (2002), Asymptotically Unbiased Inference for a Dynamic Panel Data Model with Fixed Effects, *Econometrica*, 70, 1639–1657.

Hall, A.R., Han, S., and Boldea, O. (2012), Inference Regarding Multiple Structural Changes in Linear Models with Endogenous Regressors, *Journal of Econometrics*, 170, 281–302.

Halunga, A., Orme, C. D., and Yamagata, T. (2017), A Heteroskedasticity Robust Breusch-Pagan Test for Contemporaneous Correlation in Dynamic Panel Data Models, *Journal of Econometrics*, 198, 209–230.

Hansen, C. B. (2007), Asymptotic Properties of a Robust Variance Matrix Estimator for Panel Data when T is Large, *Journal of Econometrics*, 141, 597–620.

Hayakawa, K. (2009), A Simple Efficient Instrumental Variable Estimator for Panel AR(p) Models When Both N and T are Large, *Econometric Theory*, 25, 873–890.

Horn, R., and Johnson, C. (1985), *Matrix Analysis*, Cambridge University Press.

Horváth, L., and Hušková, M. (2012), Change-Point Detection in Panel Data, *Journal of Time Series Analysis*, 33, 631–648.

Hsiao, C. (2018), Panel Models with Interactive Effects, *Journal of Econometrics*, 206, 645–673.

Hsiao, C., Pesaran, M. H., and Pick, A. (2012), Diagnostic Tests of Cross-section Independence for Limited Dependent Variable Panel Data Models, *Oxford Bulletin of Economics and Statistics*, 74, 253–277.

Hsu, C.-C., and Lin, C.-C. (2012), Change-Point Estimation for Nonstationary Panel Data, Working Paper, National Central University.

Huang, W., Jin, S., and Su, L. (2018), Identifying Latent Grouped Patterns in Cointegrated Panels, Working paper.

Huang, Y. (2009), The Political Economy of Financial Reform: Are Abiad and Mody Right? *Journal of Applied Econometrics*, 24, 1207–1213.

Im, K. S., Ahn, S. C., Schmidt, P., and Wooldridge, J. M. (1999), Efficient Estimation of Panel Data Models with Strictly Exogenous Explanatory Variables, *Journal of Econometrics*, 93, 177–201.

Jiang, T. (2004), The Asymptotic Distributions of the Largest Entries of Sample Correlation Matrices, *Annals of Applied Probability*, 14, 865–880.

Jiang, T., and Yang, F. (2013), Central Limit Theorems for Classical Likelihood Ratio Tests for High-Dimensional Normal Distributions, *Annals of Statistics*, 41, 2029–2074.

John, S. (1971), Some Optimal Multivariate Test, *Biometrika*, 58, 123–127.

John, S. (1972), The Distribution of a Statistic Used for Testing Sphericity of Normal Distributions, *Biometrika*, 59, 169–173.

Johnstone, I. (2001), On the Distribution of the Largest Principal Component, *Annals of Statistics*, 29, 295–327.

Juhl, T. (2011), A Direct Test for Cross-Sectional Correlation in Panel Data Models, Working Paper, University of Kansas.

Kao, C. (1999), Spurious Regression and Residual-Based Tests for Cointegration in Panel Data, *Journal of Econometrics*, 90, 1–44.

Kao, C., and Oh, J. (2017), On the Over-Detection Probability of the Number of Factors, Working Paper.

Kao, C., Trapani, L., and Urga, U. (2018), Testing for Instability in Covariance Structures, *Bernoulli*, 24, 740–771.

Kapetanios, G. (2004), On Testing for Diagonality of Large Dimensional Covariance Matrices, Working Paper, Queen Mary, University of London.

Kapetanios, G., Pesaran, M. H., and Yamagata, T. (2011), Panels with Nonstationary Multifactor Error Structures, *Journal of Econometrics*, 160, 326–348.

Kapoor, M., Kelejian, H., and Prucha, I. (2007), Panel Data Models with Spatially Correlated Error Components, *Journal of Econometrics*, 140, 97–130.

Kelejian, H., and Prucha, I. (1999), A Generalized Moments Estimator for the Autoregressive Parameter in a Spatial Model, *International Economic Review*, 40, 509–533.

Kelejian, H., and Prucha, I. (2007), HAC Estimation in a Spatial Framework, *Journal of Econometrics*, 140, 131–154.

Kim, D. (2011), Estimating a Common Deterministic Time Trend Break in Large Panels with Cross Sectional Dependence, *Journal of Econometrics*, 164, 310–330.

Kim, D. (2014), Common Local Breaks in Time Trends for Large Panels, *Econometrics Journal*, 17, 301–337.

Kim, D., and T. Oka (2014), Divorce Law Reforms and Divorce Rates in the U.S.: An Interactive Fixed Effects Approach, *Journal of Applied Econometrics*, 29(2), 231–245.

Kiviet, J. F. (1995), On Bias, Inconsistency, and Efficiency of Various Estimators in Dynamic Panel Models, *Journal of Econometrics*, 68, 53–78.

Ledoit, O., and Wolf, M. (2002), Some Hypothesis Tests for the Covariance Matrix When the Dimension is Large Compared to the Sample Size, *Annals of Statistics*, 30, 1081–1102.

Ledoit, O., and Wolf, M. (2004), A Well-conditioned Estimator for Large-Dimensional Covariance Matrices, *Journal of Multivariate Analysis*, 88, 365–411.

Lee, L. (2002), Consistency and Efficiency of Least Squares Estimation for Mixed Regressive, Spatial Autoregressive Models, *Econometric Theory*, 18, 252–277.

Lee, L. (2007), GMM and 2SLS Estimation of Mixed Regressive, Spatial Autoregressive Models, *Journal of Econometrics*, 137, 489–514.

Lee, L., and Yu, J. (2010), Estimation of Spatial Autoregressive Panel Data Models with Fixed Effects, *Journal of Econometrics*, 154, 165–185.

Li, D., Chen, J., and Gao, J. (2011), Nonparametric Time-Varying Coefficient Panel Data Models with Fixed Effects, *Econometrics Journal* 14, 387–408.

Li, D., Qian, J., and Su, L. (2016), Panel Data Models with Interactive Fixed Effects and Multiple Structural Breaks, *Journal of the American Statistical Association*, 111, 1804–1819.

Li, P., Cui, G., and Lu, L. (2019), Efficient Estimation of Heterogeneous Coefficients in Panel Data Models with Common Shocks, *Journal of Econometrics*, forthcoming.

Liao, W., and Wang, P. (2012), Structural Breaks in Panel Data Models: a Common Distribution Method, HKUST Working Paper.

Long, J. S., and Ervin, H. (2000), Using Heteroskedasticity Consistent Standard Errors in the Linear Regression Model, *The American Statistician*, 54, 217–224.

Lu, X., and Su, L. (2017), Determining the Number of Groups in Latent Panel Structures with an Application to Income Democracy, *Quantitative Economics*, 8, 729–760.

MacKinnon, J. G., and White, H. (1985), Some Heteroskedasticity Consistent Covariance Matrix Estimators with Improved Finite Sample Properties, *Journal of Econometrics*, 29, 53–57.

Mahajan, M., Nimbhorkar, P., and Varadarajan, K. (2012), The Planar k-means Problem is NP-hard, *Theoretical Computer Science*, 442, 13–21.

Mao, G. (2016), Testing for Error Cross-Sectional Independence Using Pairwise Augmented Regressions, *Econometrics Journal*, 19, 237–260.

Massacci, D. (2017), Least Squares Estimation of Large Dimensional Threshold Factor Models, *Journal of Econometrics*, 197, 101–129.

Moon H. R., and Weidner M. (2017), Dynamic Linear Regression Models with Interactive Fixed Effects, *Econometric Theory*, 33, 158–195.

Moscone, F., and Tosetti, E. (2009), A Review and Comparison of Tests of Cross-Section Independence in Panels, *Journal of Economic Surveys*, 23, 528–561.

Newey, W., and McFadden, D. (1994), Large Sample Estimation and Hypothesis Testing. In: Engle III, R. F., and McFadden, D. L. (Eds.), *Handbook of Econometrics*, Vol. 4. North-Holland, Amsterdam.

Newey, W., and West, K. (1987), A Simple, Positive Semi-definite, Heteroskedasticity and Autocorrelation Consistent Covariance Matrix, *Econometrica*, 55, 703–708.

Ng, S. (2006), Testing Cross-Section Correlation in Panel Data Using Spacings, *Journal of Business and Economic Statistics*, 24, 12–23.

Nickell, S. (1981), Biases in Dynamic Models with Fixed Effects, *Econometrica*, 49, 1417–1425.

Oka, T., and Perron, P. (2018), Testing for Common Breaks in a Multiple Equations System, *Journal of Econometrics*, 204, 66–85.

Okui, R., and Wang, W. (2019), Heterogeneous Structural Breaks in Panel Data Models, Working paper.

Pauwels, L., Chan, F., and Mancini-Griffoli, T. (2012), Testing for Structural Change in Heterogeneous Panels with an Application to the Euro's Trade Effect, *Journal of Time Series Econometrics*, 4, doi:10.1515/1941-1928.1141.

Pesaran, M. H. (2004), General Diagnostic Test for Cross Section Dependence in Panels, Working Paper, University of Cambridge.

Pesaran, M. H. (2006), Estimation and Inference in Large Heterogeneous Panels with Multifactor Error Structure, *Econometrica*, 74, 967–1012.

Pesaran, M. H. (2015), Testing Weak Cross-Sectional Dependence in Large Panels, *Econometric Reviews*, 34, 1089–117.

Pesaran, M. H., and Smith, R. (1995), Estimating Long-run Relationships from Dynamic Heterogeneous Panels, *Journal of Econometrics*, 68, 79–113.

Pesaran, M. H., and Timmermann, A. (2002), Market Timing and Return Prediction Under Model Instability, *Journal of Empirical Finance*, 9, 495–510.

Pesaran, M. H., and Tosetti, E. (2011), Large Panels with Common Factors and Spatial Correlation, *Journal of Econometrics*, 161, 182–202.

Pesaran, M. H., Ullah, A., and Yamagata, T. (2008), A Bias-Adjusted LM Test of Error Cross Section Independence, *Econometrics Journal*, 11, 105–127.

Pesaran, M. H., and Yamagata, T. (2008), Testing Slope Homogeneity in Large Panels, *Journal of Econometrics*, 142, 50–93.

Perron, P., and Yamamoto, Y. (2015), Using OLS to Estimate and Test for Multiple Structural Changes in Models with Endogenous Regressors, *Journal of Applied Econometrics*, 30, 119–144.

Pestova, B., and Pesta, M. (2017), Change Point Estimation in Panel Data without Boundary, *Risk*, 5, 7.

Phillips, P. C. B., and Moon, H. R. (1999), Linear Regression Limit Theory for Nonstationary Panel Data, *Econometrica*, 67, 1057–1111.

Phillips, P. C. B., and Sul, D. (2007), Bias in Dynamic Panel Estimation with Fixed Effects, Incidental Trends and Cross Section Dependence, *Journal of Econometrics*, 137, 162–188.

Pollard, D. (1981), Strong Consistency of k-Means Clustering, *Annals of Statistics*, 9, 135–140.

Pollard, D. (1982a), A Central Limit Theorem for k-Means Clustering, *Annals of Probability*, 10, 919–926.

Pollard, D. (1982b), Quantization and the Method of k-Means, *IEEE Transactions on Information Theory*, IT-28, 199–205.

Pollard, D. (1984), *Convergence of Stochastic Processes*, Springer-Verlag, New York.

Qian, J., and L. Su (2016), Shrinkage Estimation of Common Breaks in Panel Data Models via Adaptive Group Fused Lasso, *Journal of Econometrics*, 191, 86–109.

Qu, H., and Gao, W. (2019), A Two-Stage Estimation for Panel Data Models with Grouped Fixed Effects, *Communication in Statistics — Simulation and Computation*, 48, 2539–2551.

Qu, Z., and Perron, P. (2007), Estimating and Testing Structural Changes in Multivariate Regressions, *Econometrica*, 75, 459–503.

Robertson, D., and Sarafidis, V. (2015), IV Estimation of Panels with Factor Residuals, *Journal of Econometrics*, 185, 526–541.

Roy, N. (2002), Is Adaptive Estimation Useful for Panel Models with Heteroskedasticity in the Individual Specific Error Component? Some Monte Carlo Evidence, *Econometric Reviews*, 21, 189–203.

Saggio, R. (2012), Discrete Unobserved Heterogeneity in Discrete Choice Panel Data Models, Working paper.

Sarafidis, V., Yamagata, T., and Robertson, D. (2009), A Test of Cross Section Dependence for a Linear Dynamic Panel Model with Regressors, *Journal of Econometrics*, 148, 149–161.

Schott, J. (2005), Testing for Complete Independence in High Dimensions, *Biometrika*, 92, 951–956.

Serinko, R., and Basu, G. J. (1992), Weak Limit Theorems for Univarite k-Mean Clustering under a Nonregular Condition, *Journal of Multivariate Analysis*, 41, 273–296.

Song, M. (2012), Asymptotic Theory for Dynamic Heterogeneous Panels with Cross-Sectional Dependence and Its Application, Working Paper, Columbia University.

Srivastava, M. S. (2005), Some Test Concerning the Covariance Matrix in High Dimensional Data, *Journal of Japanese Statistical Society*, 35, 251–272.

Steinley, D., and Brusco, M. (2011), Choosing the Number of Clusters in k-Means Clustering, *Psychological Methods*, 16, 285–297.

Stock J., and Watson, M. W. (2002), Forecasting Using Principal Components from a Large Number of Predictors, *Journal of the American Statistical Association*, 97, 1167–1179.

Stock, J. H., and Watson, M. W. (2008), Heteroskedasticity-Robust Standard Errors for Fixed Effects Panel Data Regression, *Econometrica*, 76, 155–174.

Stock J., and Watson, M. W. (2009), Forecasting in Dynamic Factor Models Subject to Structural Instability, In: Shephard, N. and Castle, J. (Eds.), *The Methodology and Practice of Econometrics: A Festschrift in Honor of D.F. Hendry*. Oxford University Press, pp. 1–57.

Su, L., Shi, Z., and Phillips, P. C. B. (2016), Identifying Latent Structures in Panel Data, *Econometrica*, 84, 2215–2264.

Su, L., and Zhang, Y. (2011), Testing Cross-Sectional Independence in Nonparametric Panel Data Models, Working Paper, Singapore Management University.

Temple, J., and Van de Sijpe, N. (2017), Foreign Aid and Domestic Absorption, *Journal of International Economics*, 108, 431–443.

Totty, E. (2017), The Effect of Minimum Wages on Employment: A Factor Model Approach, *Economic Inquiry*, 55, 1712–1737.

Vogt, M., and Linton, O. (2017), Classification of Non-Parametric Regression Functions in Longitudinal Data Models, *Journal of Royal Statistical Society, Series B*, 79, 5–27.

Vogt, M., and Linton, O. (2019), Multiscale Clustering on Nonparametric Regression Curves, Working paper.

von Luxburg, U. (2010), Clustering Stability: An Overview, *Foundations and Trends in Machine Learning*, 2, 235–274.

Westerlund, J. (2019), Common Breaks in Means for Cross-correlated Fixed-T Panel Data, *Journal of Time Series Analysis*, 40, 248–255.

Westerlund, J., and Urbain, J. (2013), On the Estimation and Inference in Factor-augmented Panel Regressions with Correlated Loadings, *Economics Letters*, 119, 247–250.

Index

Printed in the United States
By Bookmasters